A Sort of Homecoming

A Sort of Homecoming

Essays Honoring the Academic and Community Work of Brian Walsh

EDITED BY

Marcia Boniferro,
Amanda Jagt, AND
Andrew Stephens-Rennie

☙PICKWICK *Publications* • Eugene, Oregon

A SORT OF HOMECOMING
Essays Honoring the Academic and Community Work of Brian Walsh

Copyright © 2020 Wipf and Stock Publishers. All rights reserved. Except for brief quotations in critical publications or reviews, no part of this book may be reproduced in any manner without prior written permission from the publisher. Write: Permis-sions, Wipf and Stock Publishers, 199 W. 8th Ave., Suite 3, Eugene, OR 97401.

Pickwick Publications
An Imprint of Wipf and Stock Publishers
199 W. 8th Ave., Suite 3
Eugene, OR 97401

www.wipfandstock.com
PAPERBACK ISBN: 978-1-5326-8355-8
HARDCOVER ISBN: 978-1-5326-8356-5
EBOOK ISBN: 978-1-5326-8357-2

Cataloguing-in-Publication data:

Names: Boniferro, Marcia, editor. | Jagt, Amanda, editor. | Stephens-Rennie, Andrew, editor.

Title: A sort of homecoming : essays honoring the academic and community work of Brian Walsh / edited by Marcia Boniferro, Amanda Jagt, and Andrew Stephens-Rennie.

Description: Eugene, OR: Pickwick Publications, 2020. | Includes bibliographi-cal references.

Identifiers: ISBN 978-1-5326-8355-8 (paperback). | ISBN 978-1-5326-8356-5 (hardcover). | ISBN 978-1-5326-8357-2 (ebook).

Subjects: LCSH: Walsh, Brian, 1953-. | Theology. | Christian life. | Bible. O.T.—Criticism, interpretation, etc. | Bible. N.T.—Criticism, interpretation, etc. | Communities.| Homelessness—Religious aspects—Christianity.

Classification: BT10 S61 2020 (print). | BT10 (ebook).

Scripture quotations labeled NRSV are from New Revised Standard Version Bible, copyright © 1989 National Council of the Churches of Christ in the United States of America. Used by permission. All rights reserved worldwide. http://nrsvbibles.org/

Scripture quotations labeled NIV are taken from the Holy Bible, New International Version®, NIV®. Copyright © 1973, 1978, 1984, 2011 by Biblica, Inc.™ Used by permission of Zondervan. All rights reserved worldwide. www.zondervan.com The "NIV" and "New International Version" are trademarks registered in the United States Patent and Trademark Office by Biblica, Inc.™

Scripture quotations labeled RSV are from Revised Standard Version of the Bible, copyright © 1946, 1952, and 1971 National Council of the Churches of Christ in the United States of America. Used by permission. All rights reserved worldwide. http://nrsvbibles.org/

Scripture quotations labeled NASB are taken from the New American Standard Bible® (NASB), Copyright © 1960, 1962, 1963, 1968, 1971, 1972, 1973,1975, 1977, 1995 by The Lockman Foundation. Used by permission. www.Lockman.org

Scripture texts labeled NAB are from the *New American Bible, revised edition* © 2010, 1991, 1986, 1970 Confraternity of Christian Doctrine, Washington, DC and are used by permission of the copyright owner. All Rights Reserved. No part of the New American Bible may be reproduced in any form without permission in writing from the copyright owner.

The essay "Searching For Home, Discovering Peace" by Jamie Howison includes a quote from Gord Johnson, "Our souls find rest in God alone." Copyright © 2018 by Gord Johnson, unpublished lyrics. Printed by permission of Gord Johnson.

The essays "Iris and Nereus Here and Now" by Greg Paul and "Hospitality as Hermeneutic and Way of Life" by Rachel Tulloch include quotes from Red Rain, "City of Refuge." Copyright © 2006 by Red Rain, self-published compact disc. Printed by permission of Greg Paul.

The essay "The Reconciling Power of Public Art In a Broken Home" by Adrienne Dengerink Chaplin and Jonathan Chaplin includes images by the Bogside Artists, "The Petrol Bomber" and "Photo of Artists with the Petrol Bomber." Copyright © 1994, 2017. Printed by permission of Kevin Hasson.

The essay "Places That Shape Us: The Long Way Home" by Deborah C. Bowen includes photographs by John P. Bowen. Copyright © 2019, unpublished. Printed by permission of John P. Bowen.

Manufactured in the U.S.A.   12/20/19

for Brian J. Walsh
our pastor, mentor, brother, friend

Contents

Preface | xi
—Andrew Stephens-Rennie

Acknowledgments | xvii
Abbreviations | xix
List of Contributors | xxiii
About the Editors | xxv

1 Jesus as the Face of God | 1
   —Hendrik Hart

2 Places That Shape Us: The Long Way Home | 14
   —Deborah C. Bowen

3 Heaven as Home in Christian Hope | 23
   —Andrew T. Lincoln

4 Searching For Home, Discovering Peace | 38
   —Jamie Howison

5 Reflections on Interfaith Work and City-Building: Past, Present, and Future | 46
   —Joe Mihevc

6 Jewelry in the Apocalypse | 63
   —Grant LeMarquand

7   Welcome Home~~less~~: One Village Idiot's Journey of Discovering the Meaning of Home | 82
    —Alan Graham

8   Voices from the Ragged Edge: The Gritty Spirituality of the Lament Psalms | 90
    —J. Richard Middleton

9   Iris and Nereus Here and Now | 109
    —Greg Paul

10 Hospitality as Hermeneutic and Way of Life | 115
    —Rachel Tulloch

11 Springtime in Cape Town: The Sacramental, Prophetic Imagination of Desmond Tutu | 127
    —Stephen Martin

12 The Wit(h)ness of Suffering Love | 143
    —James Olthuis

13 The Reconciling Power of Public Art In a Broken Home | 159
    —Adrienne Dengerink Chaplin and Jonathan Chaplin

14 Of Tents and Temples: A Sermon for the Wine Before Breakfast Community—1 Corinthians 3 | 179
    —Beth Carlson-Malena

15 Revillaging the City: How One Congregation Transformed Its Charitable Food Ministry to an Agent of Shalom | 185
    —Andrew Stephens-Rennie

16 Setting Another Place at the Table | 193
    —Matt Bonzo

17 Reconciling the World? Theology and Exegesis in 2 Corinthians 5 | 203
    —N. T. Wright

18 Holiness and Homemaking: The Christian Doctrine of Creation Performed | 218
—Steven Bouma-Prediger

19 Animism Reconsidered: Coming Home in a More-Than-Human World | 232
—Rodney Clapp

20 Home Is Where the Wild Rice Is | 244
—Sylvia C. Keesmaat

Afterword | 260
—Martyn Joseph

Preface

—— Andrew Stephens-Rennie ——

Nearly thirty years ago, in *Subversive Christianity*, Brian Walsh wrote:

> I feel, and I suspect that most of us feel, a gap in our lives: a gap between our worldview and our way of life. Or to put this in more biblical terms, most of us sense a gap between our conscious commitment to Jesus Christ and the way we live it in our lives.[1]

Brian has spent the intervening years inviting members of the Christian household to close the gap between what we profess to believe and the lives we lead. As a writer, a teacher, a pastor, and a friend, Brian has never shied away from taking a stand on the most pressing issues of our time. In the ministry entrusted to him, Brian has taken stands against the tyranny of climate change, colonialism, misogyny, exploitative economics, and all aspects of our multifaceted homelessness. This posture has been marked by his faithfully imaginative wrestling with Scripture. In recent years, he has worked to create brave, loving spaces—places of home—for those suffering from post-evangelical traumatic stress, for those whose lives are lived close to the street, and for members of the LGBTQ+ community whom Jesus continues to call beloved and to call into his body.

All of this because a sixteen-year-old suburban kid couldn't shake Jesus' call, and was, against all the odds, "saved."[2]

It seems to me that these early experiences of God's holistic salvation have been the guiding light for one whose ministry reveals a vocational impulse to home-making on the margins. As one who received a wide

---

1. Walsh, *Subversive Christianity*, 28.
2. Keesmaat and Walsh, *Romans Disarmed*, 366.

welcome in Christian community, a community still saving him from "a life of meaninglessness" and "a life without a father who loved him,"[3] Brian has taken the fuel of suffering and lament and built a fire, inviting us to gather around.

This encompasses my own experience of welcome as I stumbled bleary-eyed, caffeine-starved, and theologically-disoriented into Brian's subterranean office in the catacombs beneath the University of Toronto's Wycliffe College. It was in that office that I was introduced to the image of the suffering servant, an image that seems to have guided Brian's own pastoral response to those of us who have, and who do, find ourselves battered and bruised by the weight of the world:

> Here is my servant, whom I uphold,
>   my chosen, in whom my soul delights;
> I have put my spirit upon him;
>   he will bring forth justice to the nations.
> He will not cry or lift up his voice,
>   or make it heard in the street;
>   a bruised reed he will not break,
>   and a dimly burning wick he will not quench;
>   he will faithfully bring forth justice.
> He will not grow faint or be crushed
>   until he has established justice in the earth;
>   and the coastlands wait for his teaching. (Isaiah 42:1–4)[4]

This was a teaching I didn't know I was waiting for. I first showed up to Wine Before Breakfast[5] done with church, yet profoundly knowing that Jesus wasn't yet done with me. Stumbling through the halls of Wycliffe College one Tuesday morning, I showed up to find a community that—it became clear—had space for my cold and broken hallelujahs. This gave me hope that I might once again be able to be a Christian.

I came to know Brian over the years, although it took nearly six months for him to stop calling me by another name. In the end, it was the road trip to Michigan with Brian and my supposed doppelgänger, David Krause, that

---

3. Keesmaat and Walsh, *Romans Disarmed*, 366.

4. All Scripture references are from the NRSV.

5. Wine Before Breakfast is a worshipping community which is part of the Christian Reformed Campus Ministry at the University of Toronto, where Brian has worked as the full-time campus minister for the last twenty-five years. The first gathering, which took place in September 2001, was a service of lament in light of the events of 9/11. Wine Before Breakfast continues to be a eucharistic community of embodied hope drawing together students, university faculty, people doing front-line street ministry, and many others into a weekly gathering at 7.22 am each Tuesday morning.

finally convinced Brian we should each be allowed our respective identities. Hurtling down the freeway, we swapped stories, talked politics, and, by the end of the trip, we had also introduced Brian to a breadth of music beyond the Cockburn canon.

What stands out from that journey was Brian's invitation into his own life and the ways in which he wrestled with putting his understanding of good news into practice. It became clear that, to Brian, a disembodied faith was no faith at all. Not satisfied to talk about a so-called subversive Christianity from the comfort and safety of a subterranean classroom, this transforming vision had to mean something on the streets. Out there, those following in the way of Jesus had to be prepared and equipped to make a subversive home, grounded in fidelity to God, land, and neighbor, in the shadow of whatever empire was ruling the day.

In the spring of 2019, Brian visited me and my family at our home in the cohousing community we helped to envision and build in the city colonially known as Vancouver, British Columbia. Walking streets superimposed on lands never ceded to colonial governments, we found ourselves reflecting on Robin Wall Kimmerer's holistic vision shared in *Braiding Sweetgrass*. Of course he loved it. This is a book weaving together scientific wisdom, sacred story, and the challenges of modern-day existence. Rereading a well-thumbed passage days later, I felt deep resonances with Brian's own project:

> After all these generations since Columbus, some of the wisest of Native elders still puzzle over the people who came to our shores. They look at the toll on the land and say, "The problem with these new people is that they don't have both feet on the shore. One is still on the boat. They don't seem to know whether they're staying or not."[6]

What then, is home? Where is it? And what does it mean to make this—or any place—our home? In the face of climate catastrophe and economic collapse; in the face of ever-increasing income inequality; in the face of polarization and fear, how do we make home? Part of the answer, of course, is to put down roots. Or, as Jeremiah suggests to the exiles in Babylon, we need to build houses, plant gardens, and love everyone.[7] We need to do so in ways that dismantle the dominant extractive paradigms that keep us enslaved. Kimmerer goes on to suggest, "this same observation is heard from some contemporary scholars who see in the social

---

6. Kimmerer, *Braiding Sweetgrass*, 207.
7. See Jer 29:4–10.

pathologies and relentlessly materialist culture the fruit of homelessness, a rootless past."[8] Exactly.

What Brian seeks to do, and has been doing for decades, is to help nurture these roots, helping us to root more deeply in the Jesus he first encountered in the gospels. To some, he comes off as a radical (which is, I'm sure, all right by him). And yet, in a time of rootlessness, what we need (what I need!) are deeper roots and mutual connectivity. As a way of tending that ecosystem, Brian keeps pointing us back towards the biblical witness, helping to connect us to the life-giving stories of Christian faith. Where these stories have been misused and abused, he offers new and liberating interpretations. But not on his own—often with a co-author and always in conversation with real people in the real world. This is how the empires of all times will be disarmed.

We are not city trees, disconnected and autonomous, doing what we can on our own. In so many ways, Brian's life and work remind us that we are trees of the forest connected by an intricate, generous, and mutually responsive, mycelial layer.[9] This, for Brian, is ultimately how the gospel is lived: in ways as interdependent and diverse as the dawning of a creation dream.

This volume, in honor of Brian Walsh, takes us on a journey into diverse terrain. Not only does it bear witness to the expanse of his work, but more importantly, to the breadth and depth of relationships forged in co-laboring for the gospel. Such co-laboring does not, of course, mean that we always agree! Contributors are students and colleagues; academics and practitioners; pastors, prophets, and poets. What we hold in common is our friendship with Brian, and a desire to honor the ways in which our lives have become intertwined as an interdependent ecosystem in which Brian plays a vital part. As you will read in these pages, this volume is, in itself, a sort of homecoming. It is the sort of homecoming that comes with a potluck feast to which each contributor has brought their best to share. I have heard Brian say, more times than I can count, that "much depends on dinner." Well, my friends, the table is set. Come, let us feast.

Vancouver Cohousing
Feast of the Ascension
2019

---

8. Kimmerer, *Braiding Sweetgrass*, 207.
9. Walsh et al. "Trees," 154.

Bibliography

Keesmaat, Sylvia C., and Brian Walsh. *Romans Disarmed: Resisting Empire, Demanding Justice*. Grand Rapids: Baker, 2019.

Kimmerer, Robin Wall. *Braiding Sweetgrass: Indigenous Wisdom, Scientific Knowledge, and the Teachings of Plants*. Minneapolis: Milkweed, 2013.

Walsh, Brian J. *Subversive Christianity: Imagining God in a Dangerous Time*. Seattle: Alta Vista, 1994.

Walsh, Brian J., et al. "Trees, Forestry, and the Responsiveness of Creation." *Cross Currents* 44/2 (Summer 1994) 149–63.

Acknowledgments

It is with great warmth and gratitude that we thank all the contributors to this book who shared their time and energy to produce such creative and interesting pieces. Particular thanks go to Sylvia Keesmaat for her ongoing support and advice. The Innovation Fund of Resonate of the Christian Reformed Church provided financial assistance for several facets of this project for which we are deeply grateful. We also thank Pickwick Publications and Wipf & Stock for taking on this volume and for the editorial guidance of Matthew Wimer. Lastly, we say a special thank-you to Brian for his great faithfulness and zest over many years of ministry, academic, and community work. As Brian retires from his position as Christian Reformed Campus Minister after twenty-four years, we pray God's blessing upon him. Brian, may you continue to share the hopeful, joyful, mysterious, life-changing, liberating, good news of Jesus Christ for many years to come.

Marcia Boniferro
Amanda Jagt
Andrew Stephens-Rennie

Abbreviations

General

BCE / BC	before Common Era / Before Christ
CE / AD	Common Era / *Anno Domini*
cf.	*confer*, compare
ed.	edition, edited by, editor
e.g.	*exempli gratia*, for example
et al.	*et alia*, and others
i.e.	*id est*, that is
trans.	translated by, translation, translator
v(v).	verse(s)
vol(s).	volume(s)

Modern Scripture Versions

NAB	New American Bible
NASB	New American Standard Bible
NIV	New International Version
NRSV	New Revised Standard Version
RSV	Revised Standard Version

Old Testament

Gen	Genesis
Exod	Exodus
Lev	Leviticus

Deut	Deuteronomy
Josh	Joshua
Judg	Judges
Ruth	Ruth
1–2 Sam	1–2 Samuel
1–2 Kgs	1–2 Kings
1–2 Chr	1–2 Chronicles
Ezra	Ezra
Neh	Nehemiah
Esther	Esther
Job	Job
Ps / Pss	Psalm / Psalms
Prov	Proverbs
Eccl (or Qoh)	Ecclesiasties
Song	Song of Songs
Isa	Isaiah
Jer	Jeremiah
Lam	Lamentations
Ezek	Ezekiel
Dan	Daniel
Hos	Hosea
Joel	Joel
Amos	Amos
Obad	Obadiah
Jonah	Jonah
Mic	Micah
Nah	Nahum
Hab	Habakkuk
Zeph	Zephaniah
Hag	Haggai
Zech	Zechariah
Mal	Malachi

New Testament

Matt	Matthew
Mark	Mark
Luke	Luke
John	John
Acts	Acts
Rom	Romans
1–2 Cor	1–2 Corinthians
Gal	Galatians
Eph	Ephesians
Phil	Philippians
Col	Colossians
1–2 Thess	1–2 Thessalonians
1–2 Tim	1–2 Timothy
Titus	Titus
Phlm	Philemon
Heb	Hebrews
Jas	James
1–2 Pet	1–2 Peter
1–2–3 John	1–3 John
Jude	Jude
Rev	Revelation

Pseudepigrapha

Enoch	Enoch

Contributors

Matt Bonzo is Professor of Philosophy at Cornerstone University in Grand Rapids, Michigan.

Steven Bouma-Prediger is the Leonard and Marjorie Maas Professor of Reformed Theology at Hope College in Holland, Michigan.

Deborah C. Bowen is Professor Emerita of English at Redeemer University College in Ancaster, Ontario.

Beth Carlson-Malena is the Pastor of Open Way Community Church in Vancouver, British Columbia.

Jonathan Chaplin is a Member of the Divinity Faculty at the University of Cambridge, England.

Rodney Clapp is an Editor at Cascade Books in Eugene, Oregon.

Adrienne Dengerink Chaplin is a Visiting Research Fellow at King's College London, England.

Alan Graham is the CEO and Founder of Mobile Loaves & Fishes in Austin, Texas.

Hendrik Hart is a Retired Senior Member at the Institute for Christian Studies in Toronto, Ontario.

Jamie Howison is the priest-missioner of saint benedict's table in Winnipeg, Manitoba.

CONTRIBUTORS

Martyn Joseph is a Musician and Activist from Cardiff, Wales.

Sylvia C. Keesmaat is Adjunct Professor of Biblical Studies at Trinity College and Wycliffe College and Biblical Scholar in Residence at St. James Anglican Church in Fenelon Falls, Ontario. She is married to Brian J. Walsh.

Grant LeMarquand is Professor of Mission and Professor Emeritus of Biblical Studies at the Trinity School for Ministry in Ambridge, Pennsylvania.

Andrew T. Lincoln is Emeritus Professor of New Testament at the University of Gloucestershire in Cheltenham, England.

Stephen Martin is Associate Professor of Theology at The King's University in Edmonton, Alberta.

J. Richard Middleton is Professor of Biblical Worldview and Exegesis, Northeastern Seminary at Roberts Wesleyan College in Rochester, New York.

Joe Mihevc is Visiting Professor at York University, a former Toronto City Councilor, and a Community Advocate in Toronto, Ontario.

James H. Olthuis is Emeritus Professor of Philosophical Theology at the Institute for Christian Studies in Toronto, and a Counselor at Christian Counselling Services in Toronto, Ontario.

Greg Paul is an Author and Pastor at Sanctuary Ministries in Toronto, Ontario.

Andrew Stephens-Rennie is Director of Ministry Innovation at Christ Church Cathedral in Vancouver, British Columbia.

Rachel Tulloch is a ThD candidate at the University of Toronto in Toronto, Ontario.

N. T. Wright is Research Professor of New Testament and Early Christianity at the University of St. Andrews, Scotland.

About the Editors

Marcia Boniferro is a Chaplain with the Christian Reformed Campus Ministry at the University of Toronto, serving alongside Brian J. Walsh in leadership of the Wine Before Breakfast worshipping community. Marcia focuses on pastoral care within the community while also leading worship, discussions, silent retreats, and women's gatherings. With a background in restorative justice and integrating high-risk people into communities, Marcia aims to help people engage deeply, safely, and meaningfully with the world, their faith, and each other.

Amanda Jagt is a writer and member of the Wine Before Breakfast community, where she served for three years as Emerging Leader alongside Brian J. Walsh and Marcia Boniferro, and where she continues to thoughtfully and creatively craft prayer litanies. Through her gifts of writing, editing, and administration, Amanda contributes to the spiritual formation, essential pruning, and Spirit-led growth of Christian communities throughout the city of Toronto.

Andrew Stephens-Rennie is a writer, preacher, and church planter serving as the Director of Ministry Innovation at Christ Church Anglican Cathedral in Vancouver, British Columbia. His work focuses on helping individuals and congregations to deepen their ministries and to better tell the story of what God is doing in their midst. With Brian J. Walsh, Andrew is co-founder and contributing editor at www.empireremixed.com, a blog exploring the intersection of faith, culture, and justice.

1

Jesus as the Face of God

Hendrik Hart

Readings of rich texts with long histories of interpretation almost naturally yield a large number of different results. Offering readings of Scripture's rich texts has been a significant dimension of Brian Walsh's ministry, and he and I first engaged in such explorations nearly half a century ago in a class at the Institute for Christian Studies in Toronto, offered as an orientation for the work done there. Fittingly, this is a reading in the Gospel of John, for which Brian and I ever since that class have maintained a profound love. And it is a reading focused on the prologue to the Gospel, read as key to all that follows, offering the good news that in Jesus, God has come home. Home is a theme that features prominently in Brian's ministry.

1. First Reading: The Prologue

I propose to read the end of the prologue to John's Gospel as its climax: "No one has ever seen God; the only Son, who is in the bosom of the Father, has made him known" (John 1:18).[1] Traditionally that ending has often been read as being about Jesus as God. It is then taken, together with other texts in John, to proclaim Jesus' divinity. A slightly different reading, however, could offer a somewhat different meaning, in which this text may not intend to be about Jesus as God, but more about God as (in) Jesus. As I read it the text tells me, besides the many other things it may also be saying, that the God who was never seen (known) becomes visible (known) in Jesus who was God's intimate. God is God in Jesus. "Seeing" is a many layered word in

1. All biblical quotations are from the NIV except for John 1:18, which is from the NRSV.

John. Here it can be read as a way of knowing: Moses in Exodus didn't see/know God in all fullness; that glorious fullness first became visible/known in Jesus. Or, more broadly: God was not fully known until Jesus became God's incarnate presence.

This reading of who God is connects the end of the prologue with its opening. "In the beginning was the Word" (John 1:1) and "In the beginning God created the heavens and the earth" (Gen 1:1) are here related to tell a fuller story. The Maker of heaven and earth is now specifically made known as the Word who became flesh in Jesus. It is no surprise that John starts the prologue of the Gospel of Jesus with the creation as its setting. He thereby provides a familiar orientation for his Jewish readers, who knew God the Creator as their help in danger. The Maker of heaven and earth was Israel's Redeemer and the Redeemer was the Maker of heaven and earth. When pilgrims went up to Jerusalem to celebrate their arch deliverance from Egypt, they sang songs of ascent as they went. Three of these songs praise their Creator as their help in all danger (Pss 121; 124; 134). Creator and helper are one as sides of a coin.

Israel's confession and experience of God as the Maker of heaven and earth and therefore as helper has profound significance and is not confined to the psalms. The Creator God as helper appears throughout the Old and New Testaments, as well as in how the Apostles and Nicene Creeds name God. John Calvin was so powerfully gripped by this confession that he ordered worship in the churches to open with: "Our help is in the name of the Lord who made heaven and earth" (Ps 124:8). This opening of worship services was still used when I was younger.

John's story of creation at the opening of the prologue tells us that from the very beginning the Maker of heaven and earth was our helper in the Word that became flesh. So startling was this proclamation that when Israel's helper came to his own in that Word made flesh, he was no longer recognizable. The incarnation, intended to fully reveal God as helper, began in alienation as John tells it. The God who came home found nobody home, a far cry from the vision of God finding a home among people in the beginning of Revelation 21, and far removed also from Jesus alluding to his father's home, in John 14, as God dwelling in us. How can we understand this non-recognition?

In this reading, John unveils the disconnection between the reception of the Word of origin and of the Word incarnate as a clash between different understandings of Exod 34:6–7: "And he passed in front of Moses, proclaiming, 'The Lord, the Lord, the compassionate and gracious God, slow to anger, abounding in love and faithfulness, maintaining love to thousands, and forgiving wickedness, rebellion and sin. Yet he does not leave the guilty unpunished; he punishes the children and their children for the sin of the parents to the third and fourth generation.'"

This brief but highly significant passage is sometimes referred to as Israel's grounding creed. References to it appear throughout the Bible, e.g., in the Torah, the Psalms, and several minor prophets. The context is God's self-revelation to Moses after the shocking event of Israel's worship of the golden calf. This glorious self-revelation was a response to Moses' request to see God's glory. God grants this request in part: Moses will see God's goodness in full, but not God's face (Exod 33:17–23). The self-revelation, however, besides proclaiming all God's goodness in full glory, emphatically also includes God's intent to punish the guilty for as long as four generations.

The Christian church best knows the message of that last sentence from the ten commandments. Wherever the law was read in church, people heard that God is a jealous God who punishes iniquity (Deut 5:9). However, that is followed by: "but showing love to a thousand generations of those who love me and keep my commandments" (Deut 5:10). From the time that I was able to understand this, it engaged me: do the compassionate God and the jealous God go together? Some of Israel's minor prophets addressed this question as well: they struggled with Israel's confession of an all-forgiving God who was also a punishing God in God's revelation to Moses. Among the Old Testament's minor prophets we find differences in their interpretation of Exod 34:6–7 on precisely this point. Generally speaking, when these prophets quote or refer to vv. 6 and 7, some focus on 6–7a and intentionally ignore 7b, while others do the very opposite.[2] So, usually they refer either to God's boundless goodness or to God's punishment, but not both. John, as a Jew, would have been familiar with this, and I read the prologue as his addressing of this difference. John joins the prophets who stress God's boundless love. God as known in Jesus (v. 18) is God the Creator-helper (vv. 1–4) who is fully revealed in Jesus as fullness of grace. John, perhaps unique in this respect among New Testament authors, knows no boundaries to God's grace.

In the prologue vv. 14–18, in my reading, John tells us that what Moses asked for but didn't get became fully real in Jesus:

> The Word became flesh and made his dwelling among us. We have seen his glory, the glory of the one and only Son, who came

---

2. See Jonah 1 and 4:1–2 for an interesting example. The text implies that Jonah did not want to go to Nineveh because he suspected that although he was told to preach its destruction, God would save the city. His apparent hope was that if he preached against the city, God would in fact destroy it. Yet, his suspicion that God would be a God of love and forgiveness (Exod vv. 6–7a) is fulfilled, and his hope for God's punishment (v. 7b) is dashed and he becomes angry as a result.

from the Father, full of grace and truth (John testified concerning him. He cried out, saying, "This is the one I spoke about when I said, 'He who comes after me has surpassed me because he was before me.'") Out of his fullness we have all received grace in place of grace already given. For the law was given through Moses; grace and truth came through Jesus Christ. No one has ever seen God; the only Son, who is in the bosom of the Father, he has made him known.

So, I read John's good news of the incarnation as intertwined with Exod 34:6–7a and intentionally leaving out 7b. He proclaims the incarnation as God's coming home to creation in Jesus as the all-forgiving God made flesh. God in Jesus, as John tells it, fulfills the boundless love of Exod 34:6–7a and passes over 7b. The prologue's end in vs 18, so read, specifically intends to identify God not as the jealous God of the ten commandments, but as the forgiving God made known in Jesus. But this identification would be a stumbling block to all who continue to worship and serve a God who forgives and also punishes. They, then as now, do not welcome God to come home in Jesus in this manner. In short, John's prologue to his Gospel proclaims that God, the Maker of heaven and earth, fully becomes manifest as Israel's and the world's helper in Jesus the son. With revealing allusions to Exod 34:6–7a in the context of Exod 33:12—34:9, John preaches a gospel of full forgiveness: God is the faithfully loving and reliable one: *hesed* and *emeth*, usually translated as *grace* and *truth*, though *grace* and *faithful love* come closer to the original meanings. So, the close of the prologue announces that Jesus has made God known as the God full of grace and truth, the God of Exod 34:6–7a, the Maker of heaven and earth visible as helper in full glory. Jesus is the face of God; we, unlike Moses, can now come close enough to see God's glory. The face of God is now visible in Jesus. So far no one had seen God, not even Moses. But at the end of the prologue we get to know that in Jesus God's glory has become visible as the glory of the son.

In the ministry of Moses, God gave us the law. The law demands punishment when transgressed. In the ministry of Jesus, God gives us the fullness of glory in what Exod 34:6–7a calls God's *hesed* and *emeth*. Transgression now meets with forgiveness. In my reading, John's language here makes the fullest sense in the context of the Exodus passage. For John, the differences among the minor prophets have been resolved in Jesus. God has come to dwell among us in a triumph of grace. But this is not experienced by all. The God who is our help in full glory can remain unrecognized. In John God seemed to be coming home to closed doors.

2. Evidence: The Stories

One way in which John works out his vision of God going unrecognized in Jesus is by way of a "conversation" between Moses and Jesus, law and grace, which is a theme throughout this Gospel. To help make this clear I consider briefly five of the Gospel's stories through the lens of its prologue. Though all five are rich in meaning on multiple levels, my focus is primarily on their echoes of the prologue. For each I will first present John's story, then follow it with my comments; keep in mind that none of these stories necessarily reflects every dimension of the prologue.

The Wedding in Cana

> On the third day there was a marriage at Cana in Galilee, and the mother of Jesus was there; Jesus also was invited to the marriage, with his disciples. When the wine gave out, the mother of Jesus said to him, "They have no wine." And Jesus said to her, "O woman, what have you to do with me? My hour has not yet come." His mother said to the servants, "Do whatever he tells you." Now six stone jars were standing there, for the Jewish rites of purification, each holding twenty or thirty gallons. Jesus said to them, "Fill the jars with water." And they filled them up to the brim. He said to them, "Now draw some out, and take it to the steward of the feast." So they took it. When the steward of the feast tasted the water now become wine, and did not know where it came from (though the servants who had drawn the water knew), the steward of the feast called the bridegroom and said to him, "Every man serves the good wine first; and when men have drunk freely, then the poor wine; but you have kept the good wine until now." This, the first of his signs, Jesus did at Cana in Galilee, and manifested his glory; and his disciples believed in him. (John 2:1–11)

The prologue is recognizable here in Jesus as the creating Word and in the glory this reveals. John refers to the changing of water into wine as the first miracle and as the miracle that gave the disciples faith because they saw Jesus' glory. The word translated as "first" does not really capture the full meaning for it does not so much refer to the beginning of a sequence in which this is the first. Rather, the word can better be translated as "proto," so that this is the "proto" miracle, the miracle of miracles, the mother of all miracles, the miracle that was in the beginning, the miracle of a new creation. Jesus acts as the Word of creation, truly the Creator-helper, who makes things new and provides new wine. The vessels of cleansing from the time of Moses now become vessels of celebration because the Word makes all things new. The disciples recognized their Creator-helper in this act because they experienced the divine glory in it.

Healing at Bethza'tha

After this there was a feast of the Jews, and Jesus went up to Jerusalem.

Now there is in Jerusalem by the Sheep Gate a pool, in Hebrew called Bethza'tha, which has five porticoes. In these lay a multitude of invalids, blind, lame, paralyzed. One man was there, who had been ill for thirty-eight years. When Jesus saw him and knew that he had been lying there a long time, he said to him, "Do you want to be healed?" The sick man answered him, "Sir, I have no man to put me into the pool when the water is troubled, and while I am going another steps down before me." Jesus said to him, "Rise, take up your pallet, and walk." And at once the man was healed, and he took up his pallet and walked.

Now that day was the sabbath. So the Jews said to the man who was cured, "It is the sabbath, it is not lawful for you to carry your pallet." But he answered them, "The man who healed me said to me, 'Take up your pallet, and walk.'" They asked him, "Who is the man who said to you, 'Take up your pallet, and walk'?" Now the man who had been healed did not know who it was, for Jesus had withdrawn, as there was a crowd in the place. Afterward, Jesus found him in the temple, and said to him, "See, you are well! Sin no more, that nothing worse befall you." The man went away and told the Jews that it was Jesus who had healed him. And this was why the Jews persecuted Jesus, because he did this on the sabbath. But Jesus answered them, "My Father is working still, and I am working." This was why the Jews sought all the more to kill him, because he not only broke the sabbath but also called God his own Father, making himself equal with God. (John 5:1–18)

In this literary masterpiece John narrates the prologue's distinction between the law of Moses, distorted by the lawyers, and the grace of Jesus. The helper-God who heals is sadly misread by the ministers of the law. The story presents a step-by-step demonstration of the light coming into the world but being resisted yet not overcome by the darkness. John has Jesus going to a feast, but the lawyers specify it was a sabbath with its rules. The healed man identifies Jesus as the man who healed him, the lawyers identify him as the man who issues illegal orders. Jesus says he is doing God's work, the lawyers called him a sabbath-breaker.

Was the healed man a sinner? Jesus tells him, as he does the woman in the next story, to sin no more. The sinner has not only been healed but walks in the grace of his healer who is doing God's work. The only suggestion of punishment comes from the lawyers. They seek to kill Jesus in keeping with the law of Moses as they uphold it. They do not recognize Jesus as the incarnation of the Creator-helper.

The Woman Caught in Adultery

> They went each to his own house, but Jesus went to the Mount of Olives. Early in the morning he came again to the temple; all the people came to him, and he sat down and taught them. The scribes and the Pharisees brought a woman who had been caught in adultery, and placing her in the midst they said to him, "Teacher, this woman has been caught in the act of adultery. Now in the law Moses commanded us to stone such. What do you say about her?" This they said to test him, that they might have some charge to bring against him. Jesus bent down and wrote with his finger on the ground. And as they continued to ask him, he stood up and said to them, "Let him who is without sin among you be the first to throw a stone at her." And once more he bent down and wrote with his finger on the ground. But when they heard it, they went away, one by one, beginning with the eldest, and Jesus was left alone with the woman standing before him. Jesus looked up and said to her, "Woman, where are they? Has no one condemned you?" She said, "No one, Lord." And Jesus said, "Neither do I condemn you; go, and do not sin again." (John 7:53—8:11)

This story is not found in any of the ancient manuscripts. How did it get into the canon? It was likely a well-known story in the early church and it seems fitting that a copier of manuscripts, knowing how basic stories were to John, wrote it down as a powerful manifestation of glory in grace. The ministers of the law are not in a position to condemn if it turns out they themselves have transgressed. Jesus also does not condemn and writes in the sand with his finger. The law of Moses had been written with God's finger; Jesus writing with his finger may suggest he is writing his new commandment, to love one another. In that way, as John says at the end of the prologue, he lets us know God in doing the work of God.

The difference between teachers of the law and the incarnation of God's grace is even stronger here than in the preceding story. The lawyers present a strong case calling for punishment spelled out in the law. But by the grace of God Jesus shows they are not qualified to punish the guilty, being guilty themselves. And he himself has not come to condemn, not even to condemn a demonstrably guilty lawbreaker. He invites the woman to confess she has not been condemned. His grace shone gloriously.

The Risen Jesus Appears to the Disciples

Events in the preceding three stories came before the resurrection. As could be expected, stories after the resurrection are even clearer about the meaning of Jesus as the gracious forgiver of sins. I read John's post-resurrection stories as ways of making known the meaning of life after the resurrection. I will explore this reading in two of those stories.

The Outpouring of the Spirit

The first story is John's version of the outpouring of the Spirit. The recipients are people gathered behind closed doors in fear.

> On the evening of that day, the first day of the week, the doors being shut where the disciples were, for fear of the Jews, Jesus came and stood among them and said to them, "Peace be with you." When he had said this, he showed them his hands and his side. Then the disciples were glad when they saw the Lord. Jesus said to them again, "Peace be with you. As the Father has sent me, even so I send you." And when he had said this, he breathed on them, and said to them, "Receive the Holy Spirit. If you forgive the sins of any, they are forgiven; if you retain the sins of any, they are retained." (John 20:19–23)

Just as Jesus received God's calling in the beginning of the Gospel when the Spirit descended on him, John's Pentecost is also about receiving God's calling: the calling to forgive through the taking away of sin. The language for his commission of forgiving is the same as that in Exodus 34. He passes this on to the disciples and says: "Receive the Holy Spirit. If you forgive anyone's sins, their sins are forgiven; if you do not forgive them, they are not forgiven." A traditional reading of John here is that by receiving the Spirit the disciples are empowered not to forgive. Might this be read differently? It seems foreign to this Gospel to understand resurrection, even in part, as authority to leave people in their sin. That could possibly be Moses as read by the authorities. Can it be the Jesus of John? In re-reading the passage and using as analogy giving bread to the hungry, it can read: if you feed them they will no longer hunger and if you don't feed them they will continue in their hunger. The second part emphasizes the horror of not feeding the hungry, as a rhetorical way of saying: so by all means feed them. I take it John can be read this way: if you do not forgive you leave people in their sin [so you must forgive]. The resurrected Jesus incarnates grace, for as the prologue states, "grace and truth came through [him]" (John 1:17), and Jesus' followers are commissioned to be ministers of grace.

Jesus' Conversation with Peter

The second story is the remarkable conversation Jesus has with Peter at the end of the Gospel.

> When they had finished eating, Jesus said to Simon Peter, "Simon son of John, do you love me more than these?" "Yes, Lord," he said, "you know that I love you." Jesus said, "Feed my lambs." Again Jesus said, "Simon son of John, do you love me?" He answered, "Yes, Lord, you know that I love you." Jesus said, "Take care of my sheep." The third time he said to him, "Simon son of John, do you love me?" Peter was hurt because Jesus asked him the third time, "Do you love me?" He said, "Lord, you know all things; you know that I love you." Jesus said, "Feed my sheep. Very truly I tell you, when you were younger you dressed yourself and went where you wanted; but when you are old you will stretch out your hands, and someone else will dress you and lead you where you do not want to go." Jesus said this to indicate the kind of death by which Peter would glorify God. Then he said to him, "Follow me!" (John 21:15–19)

This story has, like the others, multiple layers of meaning. I will limit myself to one: Jesus does not explicitly address Peter's denial, and Peter does not say he is sorry. It is there in the background, but out of focus. Instead Jesus three times commissions Peter and calls him to be a leading follower in ministry to other followers. The central issue for Jesus is whether Peter loves him. So Jesus asks Peter three times about his love. Peter responds reluctantly and each time he responds he is less generous in his love. Jesus in his questions makes room for Peter's hesitance. (The Greek text shows these subtleties of language better than the translation.) But in whatever language, Peter's embarrassment and Jesus' affirmation are clear. And clearly as well, repentance is not at issue. Peter had denied Jesus, Jesus appoints him as leader of his followers.

Following Exodus as it surfaces in John's prologue, I read this story as John showing us the unqualified fullness of God's glory incarnate in Jesus: full of forgiveness, to the point of demonstrating the opposite of Exod 34:7b. He holds the guilty guiltless. The grace of Jesus transforms the grace of the law of Moses. It is grace in its very fullness. So writes John in the prologue: "From [Jesus'] fullness we have all received, grace upon grace. The law indeed was given through Moses; grace and truth came through Jesus Christ" (John 1:16–17). Moses pleaded with God. Jesus loves to the end. Followers of the Shepherd of Psalm 23:6 will experience that God pursues us with nothing but goodness and mercy, with grace upon grace. When God is our shepherd, goodness and love will follow us all the days of our life, and we will with Jesus be the home of God forever.

The fullness of grace made known in Jesus is a gift to Peter. But the gift comes at a price. In following the resurrected Jesus and called to be an agent of forgiveness, his work will lead him to where he did not choose to go. As Paul says in Romans 8, to inherit Jesus' glory, we must suffer with him.

3. Second Reading: God's Cosmic Love

With hindsight it could probably be said that the message of the fourth Gospel in the light of the prologue's interplay with Exod 34:6–7 could in large measure also be discerned without knowing, or needing to know, about the Exodus connection. The emphasis on love in 1 John provides a similar outlook. Chapter 4:17–18 proclaims that those who walk in the way of love have no need to fear God's punishment. And that same text sees followers being in the world as Jesus was, embodying the love of God. Thus the Johannine community underwrites John's Gospel, becoming a home for God in the world. But Exodus 34 is not visible. I will show this with a second, shorter reading of early parts of the Gospel that, with one exception, were also in the first reading. This time I will tie the readings together by interspersing them with fragments from Psalm 121 and John 3:16, which will bring a note of celebration to the love of God as helper of the world.

"For God so loved the world . . ." (John 3:16). Especially in its abbreviated form this may be the best-known verse in the Bible. It is also perhaps the most ill-treated verse when no attention is paid to God's sending Jesus "into the world, not to condemn the world, but that the world might be saved through him" (John 3:17). In the short space of vv. 16–17, "world" occurs four times, just as it does in vv. 9–10 of the prologue. The incarnation is a cosmic event in its redemptive intent. Israel's helper is aptly identified as the Maker of heaven and earth, who came on the scene as helper from the very beginning, when Adam was alone and needed help (Gen 2:18–23).

Psalm 121, with its moving language for God as helper, deliverer, rescuer, and savior, does have a direct relation to the exodus. For the great celebration of the end of their slavery, Passover, Israel's primal event of deliverance, pilgrims going up to Jerusalem sang songs of ascent, climbing Mount Zion while singing. Psalm 121, one of these fifteen songs of ascent, celebrates God as helper:

> I lift up my eyes to the hills—
> from where will my help come?
> My help comes from the Lord,
> who made heaven and earth. (vv. 1–2)

As Creator, God is helper. For God so loved the world. During their Lenten pilgrimage to Jerusalem, Jesus and his disciples would sing these words. Their God so loved the world—God, Maker of heaven and earth. God Almighty.

It was an arch confession for Israel to sing: "Our help comes from the Lord, who made heaven and earth." This God protects from all danger, whether we are coming or going, by day or by night:

> The sun shall not strike you by day,
> nor the moon by night . . .
> The Lord will keep
> your going out and your coming in . . . (Ps 121:6, 8)

God Almighty, Maker of all that is made, so loved the world. And nothing was made that wasn't made by the Word that was in the beginning, the Word that became flesh.

Understandably, John begins his Gospel of redeeming love with the Word of God through whom all things were made, the Creator-helper of the Old Testament so familiar to Jewish readers. He tells good news starting with God Almighty, Creator of heaven and earth, our helper. For God so loved the world, the world that God had made and had called good.

But something went wrong: "He was in the world, and the world came into being through him; yet the world did not know him. He came to what was his own, and his own people did not accept him" (John 1:10–11).

Is John writing about the Jews? Not really. Recognizing God's presence is not a Jewish but a human problem. When we read this today we need to hear its echo in the beginning of Romans: God is visible in all of creation, but human foolishness makes us blind (Rom 1:19–22). So when love for the world makes God come home in human flesh, that looks like a problem.

Is the problem gone today? Suppose someone you know became pregnant and became convinced her baby would be Immanu-el, God-with-us? Surely that would be a problem for us. But then why wouldn't Jesus be unbelievable as well? He came from Nazareth, son of carpenter Joseph and his wife Mary. Why would anyone recognize the Maker of heaven and earth in a wood worker's child? Is that how God helps? Whether we're coming or going, by day or by night?

John now tells a story of a wedding without wine. A wedding with a problem. Who can help? God's creation is for celebration, for a wedding with wine. In Cana there is only water, six huge vats for washing off the world's misery, six vats for ritual cleansing. Then the Word, through whom all things were made, present in the flesh (for God so loved the world), brings God's help to these vats. Soon the party can go on: there is wine. And the carpenter's son is recognizable. Now the disciples behold the Word-of-God come-in-the-flesh, their helper who deserves their trust, the way you trust God, whether you're coming or going, by day or by night. For God so loved the world: the wedding goes on; there's wine.

And John tells another story, the story about Nicodemus that leads to 3:16. Nicodemus came to see Jesus by night. Why not? If in Jesus God is our helper coming and going by day and by night, why not come by night?

"Now there was a Pharisee named Nicodemus, a leader of the Jews. He came to Jesus by night and said to him, 'Rabbi, we know that you are a teacher who has come from God; for no one can do these signs that you do apart from the presence of God'" (John 3:1–2).

Nicodemus didn't quite know whether he was coming or going. Surely Jesus had a powerful connection to God. But his father was Joseph and he came from Nazareth. Better not make a fool of yourself. Go talk to him when no one else can see your coming or going, talk to the light in the darkness. Maybe this way it's safe to make up your mind about God coming home in the flesh. But if God so loved the world, why come to the light at night? Well, maybe because in the night we need to see light.

Jesus has a conversation with Nicodemus: "'Very truly, I tell you, no one can see the kingdom of God without being born from above.' . . . Nicodemus said to him, 'How can these things be?' Jesus answered him, 'Are you a teacher of Israel, and yet you do not understand these things?'" (John 2:3, 9–10) Do you not understand God is love? Do you not remember Moses and the serpent? Let me tell you, "just as Moses lifted up the serpent in the wilderness, so must the Son of Man be lifted up, that whoever believes in him may have eternal life" (John 2:4–5).

Nicodemus knew about lifting up your eyes. When looking for help, lift up your eyes to the hills. When a snake has bitten you in the desert, lift up your eyes to the man of God who lifts high the very snake that bit you. So now he must trust what God is doing in that man and he will be healed. Trust now, says Jesus, your helper-made-flesh who is lifted up on a cross. You will be given your life as surely as the water was made into wine. A savior has come to the world, recognizable by his birth in a manger, a sign for humble shepherds. He humbled himself on a cross, that all who lift up their eyes may live, generation upon generation. Jesus, the face of God, the fullness of God's glory, the fulfillment of the boundless love of Exod 34:6–7a, God's homecoming to creation.

John explains: for God so loved the world! That's the bottom line, the heart of the matter. God loves with a cosmic love. And his love is to save and not to condemn. Our entry into every mystery is the love of God. God creates in love, God redeems in love. And, as John tells the story of Jesus washing the disciples' feet, Jesus says there is no love greater than laying down your life. That's love divine all loves excelling. God's cosmic love is worthy of our life.

In John's telling the incarnation is at once an invitation. God is now with us, home with us. Those who would be followers, who wish to have their feet washed, will trust Jesus' invitation to image the God who loves the world. Followers are invited to lay down our lives, to wash feet, to live as vessels in which Jesus changed the water of misery into wine of joy. Followers are invited to drink his cup. "As he is, so are we in this world" (1 John 4:17).

The invitation to embody God's love in Christ is the gateway to the presence of God's redeeming love in the world. "Ubi caritas et amor, Deus ibi est" (1 John 4:12). He will be in this world when and where followers of the son are in the world. God invites followers to be the Eve of God's Adam, the bride of Christ, Jesus' helper. Without a body of Christ, God's love in Christ remains invisible in our world. Followers are, says Paul, "ambassadors for Christ, since God is making his appeal through us . . ." (2 Cor 5:20). Jesus' followers are invited to love as God loves, to give themselves in love as Jesus loved, to accept the commission to be ministers of grace. Followers, like Jesus, will be filled with God's fullness. They will be home to God.

Those whose love mirrors God's love in Christ will love like the Samaritan, love like the thief on the cross. God's redeeming love will be visible in their love. Christ, the second Adam, will have a helper, his body, his Eve, his bride. And God will have a home—in us.

2

Places That Shape Us

The Long Way Home[1]

——— Deborah C. Bowen ———

"The story begins with a homemaking God
who creates a world for inhabitation.

This God is a primordial homemaker,
and creation is a home for all creatures."[2]

—Steven Bouma-Prediger and Brian Walsh

* * *

---

1. An earlier version of this piece appeared in *EarthLines: The Culture of Nature*, 47–49 and was reprinted online as "The Long Way Home" in *Topology Magazine*. I am grateful to these publications for permission to reprint in this volume.

2. Bouma-Prediger and Walsh, *Beyond Homelessness*, 14.

All photographs by John P. Bowen,
contributing to this volume with great pleasure.

When I first immigrated from England to southern Ontario, I felt as if I'd moved from a human-sized land to a land that needed me to wear seven-league boots. I needed boots that would leap over the wide spaces on the map where nothing happened. No ancient villages, each with a church, a pub, a village green, a post-office and a general store. No twisty country lanes winding like the threads of spiderwebs up and down the landscape, giving the walker or cyclist or horse-rider or driver a dozen different options of ways to get from here to there. No pretty pub gardens where one could sit with a glass of cold beer and order a ploughman's lunch. No footpaths, with their stiles and gates and tracings of the earth's cultivated contours. And no one here even knew what a bridle-path was. There was just mile upon mile of wild, scrubby, rocky land. Why did it have to take four-plus hours to drive from Ottawa to Toronto? Couldn't we just take a pair of scissors and cut a piece of that wildness out of the map? What was all that land *for*? As early Spanish explorers are reputed to have declared when arriving on the East coast, "Aca nada—nothing here."

> *I sit in a Tim Horton's between Kingston and Toronto, drinking almost-hot decaffeinated coffee from a paper cup. I watch the traffic careen by. The land is flat, the view nondescript. Possibly Lake Ontario would offer a beautiful vista, if it weren't for a four-lane highway between me and the water. Plus the gas station and the truck stop and the Eezee Stay restrooms. I am grateful for the restrooms. I am grateful for the coffee, and yes, will roll up the rim for a prize of more of it. Remember this.*

My first acquaintances in Ontario were politely dismissive when I asked if they thought there was such a thing as mental geography. A way of understanding the landscape determined by the geography of one's childhood, perhaps, or of summer vacations. My childhood countryside was populated by high hedges, narrow winding country roads, uneven green fields with five-barred gates, flighty horses, stolid ponies and the occasional donkey, phlegmatic dairy cattle, and the ubiquitous invitation of damp, grassy footpaths. In our summer vacations at or near the sea (usually the English Channel, which the French, we children learned with astonishment, wrongly called La Manche), the countryside would change to springy heath grass, drystone walls demarcating small irregular fields, steep coastal paths, prickly yellow gorse, tiny bright blue harebells, the high, faerie song of skylarks, and everywhere the white blobs of grazing sheep. In either case this was a human-sized countryside, its byways and passages and even its contours created by farmers over centuries past. It was a humanitarian countryside of stiles and streams and stopping-places, where strangers would commonly greet one another with a wave of the hand, and where it would not be unusual to meet up again serendipitously at a lunchtime pub. It was a countryside meant to be explored, meant to be walked, meant to be enjoyed.

> *I am six or seven. We are walking a coastal path right at the edge of the cliff along the South Downs in southern England; the wind is quite strong and I must be careful. Today I am collecting pink flowers for my scrapbook; yesterday it was yellow flowers; tomorrow, blue. So far today I have five different species of pink flower,*

> *I think, though possibly two of them are campions at different stages. I see a promising glint of pink to my right, and step off the track, around a tussock of wiry grass. At my feet a small flurry, and a little brown bird rises vertically up into the sky, singing and singing in its ascent till it's so high I can no longer see it. Skylark. In appearance unimpressive, even dowdy, but its song, to distract wildly from its nest on the ground, is sheer enchantment. Even my childhood self recognizes this glory.*

My first experiences of Ontarian countryside, by contrast, were stark reminders of my inadequacy and the inhospitable nature of both the environment and, unless you knew them already, the people who had put in the physical hard work to stake out their claims to it. Where were the footpaths? I seemed to spend many summer vacations slipping on the shale of the soft shoulder along the highway, or walking a long forested trail to be met by a "Private: No Entry" sign at the other end. The lines were straight, the natives not particularly friendly. There were few birds, and their songs seemed raucous or tuneless. The land seemed dull, the houses flimsy. The lakefronts were owned by people who didn't want to share them with casual hikers. Pubs were nonexistent, or a shabby, makeshift poor relation to the family-friendly places I'd grown up with. Even the famed cottage-country lakes seemed cold and muddy, requiring me to wade through weed to get to the open water. I missed the bracing salt of the ocean, the way the tide every day cleaned away the detritus of the day before, the high gulls and the soothing susurrus of the waves pulling at the shore.

> *It is high summer. We are staying at a friend's rustic cabin on an island in Lake Nipissing. I am kneeling on a flat rock, washing dishes in the lake. Someone calls for me to come back to the cabin; I am anxious not to leave the dishes to float off into the water. My friend laughs at me: those dishes are not going anywhere, she reassures me; they'll still be there when you get back. So wired I am to the ocean's tidal imperiousness.*

I think the change in my mental geography began with those lakes. Gradually I learned to appreciate their permissiveness. That birch-trees could stand calmly right at the water's edge, and grasses could settle and flourish. That loons could build nests there which the following year they might find still intact, still livable, unless a rash of motor-boats and jet-skiers had veered thoughtlessly close. That the gold-dust in the water of one summer would be still gold-dust the following year, and the red lichen between the planks of the mooring dock would persist in its antediluvian presence, even if the dock itself were a little more crooked, a little nearer to the water, after the winter ice. I learned that a teaspoon dropped carelessly from a dock one summer would still be there the following summer, awaiting a diver with patience and clear goggles. I learned the eerie, haunting cry of the loon over the evening water, and the spate of falling stars each August. After a few years, when we had saved up for a trip to the south coast of England with the kids, they found the water bone-cold and sticky, the seaweed slimy, and the jellyfish unnerving; the shingle was painful on their feet and they longed to return to the smooth rocks and the clean, cool water of Ontario lakes.

> *It is Canada Day, and we are with a group of campers in Muskoka. Someone has put together a bunch of fireworks for a display from the diving platform. The air is damp; the fireworks take off fitfully. We feign enthusiasm for the kids' sake. Suddenly, a wild flash to our left, and we all gasp as the whole night sky fills with green and white and lemon and blue sheets and scarves of dancing light. The Northern Lights, so immensely more dramatic than our paltry human display. We laugh. It's a moment of cosmic irony.*

The rocks of the Canadian Shield were my other teacher. They lay bared to the sun and the rain and the snow like the well-tuned limbs of a gigantic, benign overlord. They gave me their warmth and their assuredness. They allowed us to scramble around on them, but not to chart them with permanent footpaths; they expected our respect. Gradually I came to love the sense of being in touch with the hard, massive body of the land, which over the course of every year survived with impunity temperatures from -40 to +40 Celsius. In the same way I came to honor the plants and animals and peoples that over the millennia had adjusted to survival through such extremes of heat and cold. And slowly I came to realize that, in the very places where I had at first seen nothing, those living beings for whom these strange spaces were home composed a text of extraordinary complexity and diversity. An Indigenous person's reading of that "empty" eastern Ontario landscape would be as intricate in detail as any ordnance-survey map in England. Here was another language barrier to overcome.

And look now, there's the landmark of our favorite old maple tree again, still budding, still twistily leaning over the cold rush of this northern river, despite all that the elements can throw at her. Every year she is there, a little wilder, a little more battered. Grand old dame: she is crooked and gnarled, but elegantly clothed in every season.

Sure, I still miss the places that first shaped me. When I go back to England now, there is a sense of knownness, a sense of physical comfort with the ground under my feet, that I suspect will never quite be replicated in Canada. But at the same time that English landscape feels small, it feels crowded, as if there's no room to stretch out your arms. The hedgerows lean in towards the middle of the little country roads, the leaves meet and blend overhead, and the tunnels they create are something from a Lilliputian world. I tread the footpaths with care; when I'm driving I breathe in to make space for the oncoming car to pass next to me. I notice the litter in the village hedgerows and the damp walls inside the pub. People out with dogs habitually fail to pick up their dogs' poop; people riding horses expect everyone to get out of their way, flattening themselves against the prickly hedges.

I am eleven. It is a Saturday morning in late spring, and I am on a solitary walking adventure. Honor demands that I never return home by the same route. I cross the field at the back of our house, meander around the copse, climb through the fence and over the

> *five-barred gate; I skirt along the side of a field of cows, aiming to find an unaccustomed route to the old hamlet two miles away across the meadows. In the next field, today, there are several tall horses, skittish and wild-eyed; possibly their owners race these horses, or show them—at any rate, they are temperamentally very different from the sturdy ponies some of my friends like to ride on Sunday afternoons. I breathe deeply and hasten past; now the only way out is over a barbed-wire fence. I climb it hurriedly, catch my leg in the descent, and tear a two-inch half-moon on my right calf. I stanch the blood and bind it up with an old handkerchief. I don't go home the short way. The scar on my calf will be with me for the rest of my life.*

And yes, Ontario has its share of goose poop along the shores of its lakes; the water at those cottages must be boiled or chlorinated for domestic use, because the lakes are shared with ducks and deer and beaver as well as motor-boats and jet-skis. But it's clear to me that my mental geography has shifted. In our lakeside city my son and his family live in a little century-old house with a central gable, and the summer sun shines hot on their backyard full of tomato plants and squashes and raspberry canes. In a country town a forty-five-minute drive away, my daughter and her husband keep heritage chickens at the end of their long thin leafy yard; every day there are three or four eggs, different colors from pale blue to speckled brown. She and her little boy can cross the road to walk by an old river and feed the ducks, and cycle through the covered bridge to get to the summer ice-cream parlor on the water. Each morning when I walk the Bruce Trail behind our house, I am blessed by the quiet trees and the ancient rocks. Walkers, joggers and cyclists mostly nod good morning as they pass. A cardinal swoops brilliantly past; a monarch flutters on the goldenrod. This province has shaped me to its own contours now; I have come the long way home.

* * *

"More than merely where we reside, ecologically understood, home is our habitat, and as such, it includes our non-human neighbors. Home roots us in the sights, smells, and sounds of a particular piece of earth."[3]

"Home is a matter of knowing our place and knowing that our place will be respected, a place where we experience both identity and security."[4]

—STEVEN BOUMA-PREDIGER AND BRIAN WALSH

* * *

3. Bouma-Prediger and Walsh, *Beyond Homelessness*, 66.
4. Bouma-Prediger and Walsh, *Beyond Homelessness*, 124.

Bibiliography

Bouma-Prediger, Steven, and Brian J. Walsh. *Beyond Homelessness: Christian Faith in a Culture of Displacement*. Grand Rapids: Eerdmans, 2008.

Bowen, Deborah. "The Long Way Home." *Topology Magazine*, July 2016. http://www.topologymagazine.org/essay/the-long-way-home.

———. "Places that Shape Us: The Long Way Home." *EarthLines: The Culture of Nature* 6 (August 2013) 47–49.

3

Heaven as Home in Christian Hope

Andrew T. Lincoln

"This world is not my home, I'm just a passing through . . .
If heaven's not my home, then, Lord, what will I do?"

It is safe to say that these lyrics from the well-known gospel song are not among Brian Walsh's favorites.[1] He is not alone in his disapproval. In the trend to downplay or decry the traditional Christian notion of going to heaven when one dies these lyrics are frequently excoriated. Within Christian circles the trend has received impetus from N. T. Wright's emphasis on "life after life after death."[2] Some now want to banish heaven from discourse about the Christian's hope and home altogether. Walsh's friend and former co-author, Richard Middleton, produced the book, *A New Heaven and a New Earth: Reclaiming Biblical Eschatology*, in which he suggested Wright's proposals had not gone far enough, because Wright unnecessarily concedes that Second Temple Judaism and the New Testament assumed an intermediate state as a future destiny of the people of God. Instead Middleton concludes, "for reasons exegetical, theological, and ethical, I have come to repent of using the term 'heaven' to describe the future God has in store for the faithful. It is my hope that readers of this book would, after thoughtful consideration, join me in this repentance."[3] Walsh has been an

---

1. See Bouma-Prediger and Walsh, *Beyond Homelessness*, 185n63, where, in an explicit contrast to these lyrics, we are told that "the earth is and always will be our home."

2. Many of his writings are relevant to this topic, but Wright, *Surprised by Hope*, esp. 160–64, provides a convenient summary discussion of resurrection as life after life after death, including his view that talk of going to heaven is distorting and misleading.

3. Middleton, *A New Heaven*, 236n53, 237.

enthusiastic participant in this trend.[4] If Middleton thinks Wright has not gone far enough, Walsh, in a paper commending Middleton's book, declares that Middleton has not gone far enough! Middleton could have specified more concretely the habits of discourse and practice that must now be abandoned and so Walsh provides some suggestions.[5] This essay will suggest that this whole trend of marginalizing an afterlife in heaven has itself gone too far and in particular that there should be no problem with thinking about heaven as in some sense home.[6]

Joining the discussion at this point is not where one would choose to start in any adequate treatment of the role of heaven in Christian eschatology. The latter would require a broader conversation about how such an eschatology employs biblical resources. This is particularly pressing since the perspectives of the biblical writers are so dependent on ancient cosmologies that we can no longer accept. This applies as much to talk of earth as to that of heaven. Our view of the nature of the earth and its place in the cosmos is so different from that of the ancients that we cannot assume that, in ditching talk of heaven, we can simply reclaim their notion of a renewed earth and mean the same thing.[7] Just as theological anthropology interacts with contemporary thinking about the human, so Christian eschatology needs to be in conversation with recent scientific discussion about the nature and future of the cosmos, including changing notions of space and time.[8] When biblical materials are part of that conversation, employment of the sort of demythologizing that affirms the truth of myth is inevitable. That does not, however, appear to be a concern for the proponents of the recent trend who are content to speak of a biblical eschatology that can be reclaimed. But, even within this narrower framework, the notion of a biblical eschatology would need probing. Is there only one coherent canonical story about the future of God's purposes or is there room for recognizing significant diversity in the

---

4. This attempt to push back against the trend is offered as part of the celebration of Brian's life and ministry with deep gratitude for all I have learned from him, for his and Sylvia's hospitality in their home, and for their friendship. It is offered in the belief that expressing disagreement can be the highest form of respect for a friend and colleague and that, if the stimulating discussions I frequently had with Brian in his basement office at Wycliffe College are any guide, he will not be short of suitably robust comebacks!

5. Walsh, "Repenting of Heaven."

6. For the sake of full disclosure, I should declare my own interest as someone whose PhD was published as *Paradise Now and Not Yet: Studies in the Role of the Heavenly Dimension in Paul's Thought with Special Reference to His Eschatology*.

7. For a good recent reminder of this, see Parry, *The Biblical Cosmos*.

8. See, e.g., Polkinghorne and Welker, eds., *The End of the World and the Ends of God: Science and Theology on Eschatology*; Russell, "Cosmology and Eschatology"; Imfeld and Losch, eds., *Our Common Cosmos*.

ways biblical writers envisage the end-times? Is not any so-called biblical eschatology already a theological construal of disparate materials? Should not one be thinking instead of a Christian eschatology that is accountable to those materials but critically and imaginatively relates them to settings quite different from those of the biblical writings? But this is not the place for the broader hermeneutical and theological discussion. Instead, while assuming some form of retrieval for Christian eschatology, this essay simply attempts to show that, on its own terms, the account of the biblical resources and their implications by proponents of the trend is deficient. And, given this volume's theme, its focus is on talk of heaven as home and why this need not and should not be abandoned.

We should clarify at the outset what is and is not being argued. There is no debate about whether a dominant notion in the biblical sources, and one that has sometimes been neglected, is that of a future hope of a new heaven and new earth, and that one way of depicting this is in terms of God making God's home on a transformed earth, as in Revelation 21. What is at issue is whether this version of believers' ultimate hope is incompatible with also expecting to be with Christ in heaven after death. Or, if not incompatible, does it require that the latter be marginalized to the extent that it should not be thought of in terms of home, a depiction of the future hope only applicable to the consummation of salvation in the new creation? "Heaven is not my home," declares the recent rhetoric.[9] One can sympathize with this as an overreaction to both skeptical jibes about "pie in the sky when you die" and a version of Christianity that has been so concerned with the salvation of individual souls that it has disparaged present earthly existence and had little concern for the cultural, social and ecological implications of the lordship of Christ over all of life. But what is at issue includes whether the belief in going to heaven when one dies, set in the context of Christian eschatology as a whole, necessarily has these undesirable consequences;[10] whether abuse of such a belief requires that it be dismissed rather than corrected; and whether abandoning any notion of going to heaven is not itself a distortion of Christian eschatology with its own set of potentially negative side effects.

My use of the terms "heaven" and "home" will attempt to recognize their fluidity. Broadly speaking, in the biblical writings the terms translated as "heaven" or "the heavens" have three main referents. The reference can be simply to the sky in contrast to the ground, the upper celestial part of visible

9. See also, e.g., Marshall, *Heaven Is Not My Home*; Wright, "Heaven Is Not Our Home."

10. There is no reason, for instance, that the initiatives on actual homelessness that in part led to the book and have also been inspired by its discussion need be affected at all by the inclusion of heaven in one's eschatology.

created reality in contrast to the earthly part below. In other uses, however, the sky was thought to point beyond itself to another level of created reality, so that heaven could be thought of as the invisible realm of angels and spirits. Just as the earthly realm could be seen as invaded by evil, so could this realm, and so one finds talk of war in heaven between good and evil spiritual powers. In Hebrew, the phrase "heaven and earth" became a way of denoting the cosmos as a whole, where the "heaven" aspect would include both the sky and the spirit realm beyond as the upper part of created reality. Of course, this part of created reality was also thought to point beyond itself to its transcendent Creator and so heaven was held to be God's place or just God's presence itself. So, for example, in Matthew's Gospel the Lord's Prayer addresses "Our Father in heaven" but also by use of metonymy—substituting a closely associated notion for the actual referent—the kingdom of heaven becomes another way of talking about the kingdom of God.[11] To complicate matters further, just as heaven can refer to both aspects of created reality, the sky and the invisible realm beyond it, so sometimes heaven is used to refer to a combination of the second and third meanings—both the invisible spiritual realm and the divine abode to which it points. Despite the totally different cosmology of present-day science, heaven still sometimes functions as a symbol of transcendence and the way the notion of transcendence is used can have similarities to what we have seen of heaven's usage. Transcendence can refer to what lies beyond the material within a secular immanent framework but can also refer to that which is totally beyond that framework, a framework that, as Christians would insist, is itself dependent on that more ultimate reality.

A key observation here is that the fluidity in the function of talk of heaven is not insignificant. We can empathize with Marilynne Robinson's character, Rev. John Ames, when he muses, "This morning I have been trying to think about heaven, but without much success. I don't know why I should expect to have any idea of heaven. I could never have imagined this world if I hadn't spent almost eight decades walking around in it."[12] Discourse about transcendence and eschatology is inevitably inadequate and at its best involves recognition that we need metaphor, imagination, and images that are open-ended and point beyond themselves. Retaining talk of heaven should be an insistent reminder of the limits of what has been revealed about the future and of our earth-bound conceptuality. Hope requires imagination and a vision that goes beyond the normal.[13] Poetry frequently provides that imagina-

---

11. All scripture references are from the NRSV.
12. Robinson, *Gilead*, 77.
13. A point well made in Bouma-Prediger and Walsh, *Beyond Homelessness*, 315–17.

tive vision. If poetry is "a sort of homecoming,"[14] then singing of heaven may be precisely what is needed to fuel a vision that goes beyond the normal and earth-bound. Even in the vision of a new creation, it is important to retain the notion of a beyond, of a new heaven, so that this vision is not simply reduced to a renewed or transformed earth and becomes geocentric. Heaven in the imaginary helps to ensure that God, participation in the life of God, and seeing God in the beatific vision remain central in any hope for the consummation of God's purposes for humanity.

To clarify talk of home one need do little more than build on the phenomenology of home in the fine discussion by Bouma-Prediger and Walsh.[15] When home is used as a metaphor, it stands for everything that makes home more than house or habitat. What turn the latter into home are the relationships, memories, and stories we associate with them or attribute to them. So, ideally, home stands for somewhere to abide or dwell. It's where we belong, supplying affiliation and identity. Home provides orientation, giving a sense of order and direction. It's a locus of hospitality and community. It's where we find rest and safety. It's where we are recognized and accepted for who we are, where we are loved and able to love. The only qualification that needs to be made is to the authors' depiction of home as a place of permanence. In the light of their insistence on the new creation as humans' permanent home, earthly homes in their literal and metaphorical variety are in any case going to be temporary in comparison. Clearly, regular shifting of place is unlikely to be helpful to a sense of home but the experience of moving home is a common one and it is not the same as moving house. Perhaps stability, that which can provide an anchor for daily living, is a better way of depicting the characteristic being sought. Even mobile homes need not be thought of simply as a symptom of the desire for freedom from the responsibilities of particular places and communal traditions,[16] but, within a society that for better or worse is mobile, as still furnishing some of the essentials of what is meant by home. Interestingly, outside the Rock and Roll Hall of Fame in Cleveland, Ohio, stands J. C. Unit One, the bus of Johnny Cash that he considered his home away from home. "I have a home that takes me anywhere I need to go, that cradles me and comforts me . . ." said the Man

---

14. The U2 song, of course, took its inspiration from Paul Celan's *The Meridian* speech. In it Celan can talk of art in terms of "flight to Paradise" and of the poem's participation in the mysterious encounter with the Other, possibly the Wholly Other, as "a kind of homecoming" (39) cf. Celan and Glenn, "The Meridian," 29–40. The title of the speech is intriguing; one sense of meridian being the axis of heaven as the celestial dome and thus the site of possible opening to what is beyond.

15. Bouma-Prediger and Walsh, *Beyond Homelessness*, 56–66.

16. Bouma-Prediger and Walsh, *Beyond Homelessness*, 258–59.

In Black, "When I make it off another plane through another airport, the sight of that big black MCI waiting by the curb sends waves of relief through me—Aah!—safety, familiarity, solitude. Peace at last."[17] One does not need to have only one permanent, fixed place to have a home. Throughout a life a number of sites, and sometimes more than one at a time, may function in this way so that, paradoxically, any sense of permanence may be a temporary phenomenon. It will already be clear where this observation is heading. Even if one wishes to say that the new heavens and new earth are believers' ultimate home, that should not, of course, be thought to rule out describing a prior or intermediate state in heaven as also home.

A key chapter in *Beyond Homelessness* sets out the authors' spirituality of sojourning.[18] Its positive insights are prefaced by the following denunciation:

> . . . a God who is understood as living high above this temporal realm in a heavenly home to which he invites forgiven sinners is not a God of creational homemaking. If we embrace a theology rooted in neo-Platonism and with a stark dualism between earth and heaven, temporality and eternity, finite and infinite, body and soul, grace and nature, then homecoming can never be in this world . . . Homecoming in such a theology is always somewhere else. Indeed, if home is identified as living eternally with God in a heavenly realm divorced from finite, temporal, bodily, and creational life, then socioeconomic, ecological, and cultural homemaking is irrelevant.[19]

If this theology accurately describes the beliefs of some North American Christians, it is a caricature of any traditional belief in an intermediate state providing a homecoming as part of Christian eschatology. Such eschatology is rooted in a theology in which the high God of heaven is at the same time the God who is immanent in creation. Indeed, it is because God is the radically transcendent source of all being that this God is able to make a home within creation without that being thought to be in competition with being in heaven in one of its meanings. The authors themselves make this point well in their discussion of interrelationality within the triune God and between divine transcendence and immanence.[20] But distinction within intimate relationship, without either confusion or divorce, is precisely the judgment that needs to be made also about earth and heaven, body and

---

17. See "JC Unit One" (website listed in bibliography).
18. Bouma-Prediger and Walsh, *Beyond Homelessness*, 271–304.
19. Bouma-Prediger and Walsh, *Beyond Homelessness*, 274.
20. Bouma-Prediger and Walsh, *Beyond Homelessness*, 280–84.

soul, and the other categories listed above. The dualities they involve are already part of the biblical materials, whether or not these interacted with or were influenced by Platonism! Further, there is absolutely no reason why going to heaven when you die as a way of describing part of Christian hope should entail giving up on one's present responsibilities in what the above quotation designates as "this world." There is, of course, a sense in which what it deems to be a damaging consequence—"homecoming can never be in this world"—is in fact the case. Even if one's eschatology is limited to a new creation, homecoming will not be in *this* world but in one that has been completely transformed.

There is an ambivalence about this world being home that runs throughout the book's spirituality of sojourning. Early on we are told that Christian faith is "not a faith about passing through this world, but a faith that declares this world—this blue green planet so battered and bruised, yet lovely—as our home."[21] Well, yes and no. This world was meant to be our home but there is a major strand of biblical material that indicates that it is not the place it was meant to be and is now the locus of "this age" or "this world," the sphere that is dominated by evil and from which humans need to be rescued by God in Christ. For Paul "this age" was a period in which the created cosmos of heaven and earth had become tainted by death, dearth, and disease and, as a spatio-temporal complex, it was synonymous with "this world" (cf., e.g., 1 Cor 1:20; 2:6; 3:18, 19). Because of this world's present alienation from its Creator, it can at best provide only a temporary home. At times the book appears to acknowledge this, though there is a tendency to treat the earth as neutral habitat and to downplay the intimate systemic relation of humans and the rest of created life. But the discussion of ecological homelessness states, "We feel homeless . . . alienated from our only home."[22] The explanation offered for this state of affairs is that we are becoming homeless. However, there is a real sense in which we are born into a world that is already no longer home. Is the exhortation "to live as redemptive homemakers in this world of ecological homelessness"[23] a recognition that this is indeed the case? The danger of underestimating the effects of alienation from the Creator has the accompanying danger of underestimating the radicality of the redemption required. If we know from

---

21. Bouma-Prediger and Walsh, *Beyond Homelessness*, xii.

22. Bouma-Prediger and Walsh, *Beyond Homelessness*, 186. Ironically, this echoes the lyrics "I can't feel at home in this world anymore" from "This world is not my home." Elsewhere, 291, it is recognized that humans at present "are alienated from the earth," but it is as if the alienation had not affected the whole of created reality, including earth, and only humanity is in need of redemption.

23. Bouma-Prediger and Walsh, *Beyond Homelessness*, 224.

Paul anything about the bodies that will be part of believers' home in the age to come, it is precisely that they will not be earthly. The earthly characterizes the descendants of the first man in this age, but it is the heavenly that characterizes the risen Christ as the last man and those who will share his resurrection life (1 Cor 15:47–49).[24]

What is surprising about the recent trend dismissing heaven as home in order to emphasize resurrected bodies on a renewed earth is the lack of attention to the significance of resurrection for Christ himself. Not only does Paul insist that the resurrected Christ has become heavenly but also the conviction runs throughout the New Testament that the resurrection entailed Christ's exaltation, whether that was thought of as one complex or separated out into two separate events, as in Luke's account of the ascension in Acts. To the question "where is the resurrected Christ now located?" the response of his early followers, supported by an appeal to Ps 110:1, would have been that he was in heaven at the right hand of God. And given that it was believed that the risen Christ retained a transformed creaturely body with its inherent social dimension, heaven would here have been thought of in terms of an overlapping of the second and third uses described earlier, a combination of the loci of the transcendent God and of glorified creatures. Whatever the mysteries of this conception, the main point here is that any attempt to provide an account of earth and heaven in the biblical materials and its implications for eschatology and present Christian existence needs to take seriously the vertical dimensions of Christology. The related convictions that believers participated in the events of Christ's death and resurrection, that they had a relationship with the exalted Christ through the Spirit, that it made sense to talk of its intimacy as being in or with him, all meant that heaven as Christ's present location was significant not just for him but also for them. In so far as salvation is thought of in terms of a cosmic drama, it could be said that its center of gravity had shifted from earth to heaven. Indeed, heaven could take on for Christ-followers many of what we have seen to be defining characteristics of home as a metaphor. Heaven became a locus of family associations, of orientation for living, of a belonging that provides identity, of stability, safety and rest.

It is worth providing a few examples. Heaven is home in terms of family relationships. For Matthew, Jesus' disciples are children of God as their heavenly Father (cf., e.g., 5:45, 48; 6:9, 14; 23:9); in John 20:17 the risen Jesus tells the disciples, "I am ascending to my Father and your Father;" and for Ephesians this is the Father from whom every family in heaven and on earth

---

24. See Lincoln, *Paradise*, 45–54.

derives its name (3:14, 15).[25] Hebrews urges its readers to fix their thoughts on Christ as the Son exalted to heaven, who thereby pioneered the way to glory for his brothers and sisters who now share in this heavenly calling (2:10–13; 3:1). They will become part of the heavenly Jerusalem, constituting "the assembly of the firstborn who are enrolled in heaven" (12:23) as those who share the inheritance of the One who is the firstborn par excellence (1:6). Maternal associations are also appropriate. In Galatians Paul can tell his readers that the Jerusalem above, the heavenly Jerusalem, "is free and is our mother" (4:25, 26). In the face of allegations that he was in fact dependent on the mother church in Jerusalem with its Torah-centered approach and that he should fall back into line with its practices, Paul's allegory claims that the present Jerusalem is in fact in bondage. As his citation of Isa 54:1 indicates, he takes up hope for a new Jerusalem at the center of the age to come and, as in some apocalypses and Hebrews, holds that the Jerusalem to come already exists in heaven. Because of Christ's presence in heaven, it can stand for the eschatological benefits that believers share ahead of time. Here, as mother, it is the symbol of the source of life and liberation for the true people of God, both Jews and Gentiles who are "born according to the Spirit" (4:29). The heavenly realm has all the connotations of the family home.

If home also represents that which gives orientation and direction to our lives, then because Christ has been exalted to heaven, heaven has that function for his followers. In a passage in Philippians where he talks of believers' ultimate hope in terms of Christ coming from heaven "to transform the body of our humiliation so that it may be conformed to the body of his glory," Paul also strikingly states, "our citizenship is in heaven" (3:20). The term *politeuma*, translated as "citizenship," is more accurately, but more awkwardly, rendered as "commonwealth," "state," or "constitutive government."[26] Octavian had conferred the Roman form of constitutional government on Philippi in 42 B.C.E. and its administration reflected that of Rome. Paul calls for his Philippian readers to see heaven rather than Rome as the state governing them. Because this is Christ's locus, his rule and its values are to provide their orientation and be reflected in their aspirations and living.[27] That is also one of the roles heaven plays in Colossians and Ephesians. Because resurrection life is also heavenly life and because believers have been raised with Christ, the audience of Colossians can be exhorted to seek and to set their minds on the things above where Christ is, seated at the right

25. All biblical quotations are taken from the NRSV.

26. See Lincoln, *Paradise*, 97–101 for fuller discussion and justification.

27. See also Bockmuehl, "Did St. Paul Go to Heaven When He Died?," 221: "The image really does seem to concern where believers ultimately belong and have their identity ('Heaven is Home,' indeed), not what they have left behind for good."

hand of God. Indeed, their relationship to Christ in heaven is such that he can be described as their life. They take their identity from him, though that is at present hidden with him and in the life of God in the invisible heavenly realm until Christ's final appearance (3:1–4). Not only is Christian existence here inseparable from the heavenly dimension but it is also explicitly contrasted with a concern for earthly things. Again, far from earth being seen as home, it is the primary setting of a fallen creation, of this present evil age. And far from this heavenly-mindedness with its focus on a transcendent realm leading to a disregard for ordinary life, it is expected to work itself out not only in love, peace, wisdom, and worship but also in the whole of life, including husband-wife, parent-child and master-slave relationships (3:5–4:1). "The heavenlies" in Ephesians are the equivalent of the things above or the heavenly realm and are where the exalted Christ is located at God's right hand in a position of superiority in relation to any other cosmic forces (1:20, 21). Because of their union with Christ, it can even be said of believers that they have been seated in the heavenlies, thus sharing not only his exalted life but also his position of decisive victory over all other powers (2:6). Heaven, then, is a key feature in providing the locus of the identity and orientation to life for which home is a metaphor.

Central to Hebrews is the depiction of Christ as the exalted Son and High Priest in heaven (8:1) and what follows for those who confess this. One consequence is that they now have through his presence a sure and steadfast anchor for living and hoping (6:17–20). A distinguishing feature of this letter's eschatology is this characterization of heaven as a realm of permanence because of Christ's once for all saving achievement. In its spirituality of sojourning, those who share the faith of the patriarchs acknowledge that they are "strangers and foreigners on the earth" who "are seeking a homeland . . . a better country, that is, a heavenly one," in which "God has prepared a city for them" (11:13–16). This future city is the heavenly Jerusalem, to which, as previously noted, believers already have access though Jesus as mediator (12:22–24). Heaven here is both a present and future homeland.[28]

If the response so far is a willingness to concede that in the New Testament heaven may function for present Christian existence in a way analogous to home but to insist that this is all pre-mortem and so has no real bearing on whether believers go to heaven at death, then this would be to miss the point. It would run against the whole of what has been said about believers' relationship to their Lord in heaven, if that relationship simply came to an end at death. Their inseparable union with Christ in heaven will remain until its manifestation at the eschaton (Col 3:3, 4). Whether it is in

---

28. On the eschatology of Hebrews, see Lincoln, *Hebrews*, 92–105.

Paul or John, there is an insistence that nothing, especially death, is able to separate believers from Christ and from the life, the eternal life of the age to come, in which they already participate through him (cf., e.g., Rom 6:23; 8:34–39; 14:7–9; 1 Cor 3:21–23; John 6:58; 10:28; 11:25, 26).

If heaven continues to be the locus of the exalted Christ until the eschaton, it also continues to be home for deceased believers who are united to him. This is, of course, spelled out explicitly in Paul's discussion in 2 Cor 5:1–10. Earlier, in 1 Corinthians 15, the apostle reckons with the possibility that at the eschaton he might be among those still alive and thus experience resurrection as the transformation involved in this perishable body putting on immortality (15:51–55), But here, in the light of his recent experiences of deadly peril (1:8–10), he appears to have taken far more seriously the possibility of his own death before the parousia. He remains convinced that if this body, the earthly tent, is destroyed in death, then believers will have a resurrection body, the eternal heavenly house or dwelling. Mixing metaphors of building and clothing, he longs simply to have the heavenly dwelling put on as further clothing rather than having to undergo a period of being unclothed or naked (5:1–4). Yet Paul remains confident. Living by faith rather than sight, he knows that even if death reduces him to the nakedness of being without a body, the relationship with Christ holds and he will be with him. He employs the verbs for being at home (*endēmein*) and being away from home (*ekdēmein*) to depict this situation—"while we are at home in the body we are away from the Lord . . . and we would rather be away from the body and at home with the Lord" (5:6–8). Death before the end-time resurrection will involve being at home with Christ in heaven. Fear of finding anthropological dualism or Platonism in Paul has prevented some writers from seeing what is going on here and led to fanciful and implausible alternative readings.[29] If, as some claim, belief in going to heaven at death is Platonic, then Platonism had already penetrated the thinking of other Second Temple Jewish writings to which early followers of Christ were heirs. So, for example, 1 Enoch 39:3, 4 talk of the dwelling-places of the holy and the resting-places of the righteous in heaven while in 1 Enoch 71:14–16 the seer ascends to heaven where the peace of the world to come is proclaimed to him and he sees the Son of man, with whom the dwelling-places and inheritance of the righteous will be and from whom they will never be separated. In 1 Enoch 103:34 the spirits of the righteous dead are said to have a lot that is abundantly better than the lot of the living. This is similar to the way in which Paul reiterates his perspective on life after death

---

29. E.g., Middleton, *A New Heaven*, 227–37, who rules out the most obvious interpretation of this passage and those that follow below on the basis of what he has already determined is "the biblical worldview."

in Phil 1:20-23 where, not knowing whether he will survive imprisonment, he weighs the benefits of staying alive to continue his mission over against those of dying. He is clear about his personal preference. Though remaining in the flesh is more necessary for his churches, his desire is to depart and to be with Christ. Dying, therefore, is seen as "gain" and "far better." To be with Christ in heaven will produce a fuller enjoyment of that relationship than can be experienced in this life. This view of heaven as home, because it means being with the One to whom one belongs, is, it should be noted, perfectly compatible with the expectation, expressed a little later in 3:20,21, of Christ coming from heaven to transform believers' bodies.

The Gospel of John also combines both perspectives. Alongside the expectation of an end-time resurrection (5:28, 29; 11:25, 26), Jesus assures his disciples that after his departure he will prepare a place for them, since in his Father's house, where he will be, there are many dwelling places (14:2, 3). Talk of dwelling places in heaven, viewed as God's house, is again reminiscent of the imagery of 1 Enoch. The term employed here is *monē*, abode, a cognate of the characteristically Johannine verb *menein*, to abide. Notions of a temporary stopping place have to be read into the term from elsewhere. The same term is used later in the passage for God and Christ taking up their dwelling place (NRSV "home") in believers (14:23). Since this takes place through the Spirit, who will be with them for ever (14:16), any connotations of impermanence are far from the usage of dwelling place in this part of the farewell discourse. What is intriguing is that Jesus goes on to say that he will come again to take his followers to be with him in the place prepared for them. This appears to have originally been a reference to the parousia, the consequence of which will be going to be with Christ in heaven. The evangelist has no problems about passing on this tradition as an aspect of Christian hope.

While the aim of the parable of the rich man and Lazarus in Luke 16:19-31 is not to teach about the circumstances of the afterlife, the parable does depend for its plausibility and effectiveness on a general belief in conscious existence in a post-mortem state, where the bosom of Abraham represents the place of consolation for the departed righteous in heaven. Luke endorses a version of such belief more directly in 23:39-43, where he has Jesus say to one of the criminals crucified with him, "Truly I tell you, today you will be with me in Paradise." In the writings of second temple Judaism, Paradise is typically seen as Eden restored, an ideal home, and located in heaven. Paul in 2 Cor 12:4 places it in the third heaven, as do Apocalypse of Moses 37:5 and 2 Enoch 8:1. So Luke clearly conveys the expectation of being with Christ in heaven immediately upon death. In Revelation 6:9-10 the seer has a vision of the souls of the martyrs who are in heaven and consciously awaiting the end-time judgment and in 7:9–17 sees a great multitude in heaven worshipping before the throne of God and the Lamb. Worship in heaven in the afterlife is also important in Hebrews. In 12:18–24 the writer contrasts the old and new covenants by comparing what happened at Sinai to believers' access now to Mount Zion and the heavenly Jerusalem. In addition to God, the judge of all, and Jesus, the mediator of a new covenant, those whom believers are now able to approach in the heavenly city include myriads of angels in festal gathering. They also meet the assembly of the firstborn who are enrolled in heaven, that is, as noted earlier, believers in Christ who have died, and the spirits of the righteous made perfect, that is, most likely, the figures of faith from Israel's history, of whom it is said that "they would not, apart from us, be made perfect" (11:40). New covenant worship brings believers into the heavenly realm where Christ is and therefore also into the presence of those who have gone before, the spirits of their ancestors in the faith.

This highlights a further reason why heaven remained important as part of Christian hope. It helped to explain the relation between living and deceased believers. Early followers of Christ saw themselves as integral to a corporate group, members of the body of Christ, as Paul put it. But what happened to that relationship once some of them died? This was an issue that arose from the start of the Christian movement, and which Paul addresses as a legitimate concern in 1 Thess 4:13–18, "We do not want you to be uninformed, brothers and sisters, about those who have died, so that you may not grieve as others do who have no hope." His response is primarily to link present and past believers together in the imminent scenario of Christ's coming to raise the dead. Expecting still to be alive himself, he says that those who are alive will not experience that coming and its transformation separately from the already dead. Indeed, the latter will be raised from the dead first and then meet up together with the living to accompany Christ on his coming to earth. But once this scenario did not occur within the early generations of believers, it was not of much comfort to suggest that the only contact with dead loved ones would come at the resurrection at the end of history, whenever that might be. A more appropriate pastoral response was required in order to provide assurance that death need not sever the links between believers. A basis for that different response is found already in the passage from Hebrews 12 just discussed which suggests not only a reunion of the faithful in heaven but also a mutuality of relationship in the new covenant community between those on earth and those already in heaven, as the former have access to the latter in the context of worship. This is, of course, the perspective that developed into the creedal confession—"I believe . . . in the communion of saints."[30]

Early Christians' main expectation for the future was a return of Christ that would usher in new heavens and earth (Rev 21:1) or, expressed differently, reconcile or sum up all things in heaven and on earth in Christ (Col 1:20; Eph 1:10). It should be clear by now that they also held that, because they were in a relationship to Christ in heaven, when they died that relationship would continue with him where he was until the completion of God's purposes. It should hardly be surprising that this latter perspective on the future would become increasingly important in the Christian tradition once it was recognized that the coming of the new heavens and earth and the reception of heavenly bodies had not occurred as soon as expected. Increasingly these had to be seen as a hope for a more distant future. So, when those who are dying talk of "going home" and have in view the hope of going to heaven to be with Christ, this may well need to be supplemented in a full Christian eschatology by further perspectives but should not be caricatured and labelled as a Platonic or Gnostic deviation. The increased focus, after the first century, on death as enabling a heavenly homecoming is not so much a development to be lamented but one for which to be thankful. Of course, for present-day Christians it raises contested issues about what it is to be human, the relationship of matter and consciousness, and the possibility of continued existence in some disembodied form. But there are similar issues for those who stress belief in a future resurrection of the body. There has to be some element of continuity between the deceased person and any future embodiment for the new form of life to be identifiable as that particular person. Any so-called holistic eschatology has to come to terms with some element of anthropological duality.

Repentance brings joy in heaven, but we should not want to join Middleton or Walsh in repenting of the use of the term "heaven" itself to describe the future God has in store for the faithful. "No more songs about going to heaven," declares Walsh.[31] There goes not only *This World Is Not My Home* but also *Amazing Grace* and its now forbidden lyrics—"I shall possess, within the veil (the phrase echoes Hebrews' language for heaven), A life of joy and peace."[32] That would be a loss, not least because its other

---

30. For an excellent discussion of the communion of the saints in the biblical writings and in its later development, cf. Esler, *New Testament Theology*, esp. 191–212.

31. See n5 above.

32. Middleton, *A New Heaven*, 27–30, had already decried a variety of hymns, including objecting to Newton's original last stanza of *Amazing Grace* because of its words "The earth will soon dissolve like snow, The sun forbear to shine," perfectly appropriate "biblical" metaphorical language for the discontinuity entailed by the notion of a new

lines—"'Tis grace hath brought me safe thus far, and grace will lead me home"—are a fitting articulation of Christian hope. If the notion of heaven evokes all that God has in store beyond our ability to imagine, grace will lead us home, this essay suggests, not just to resurrection bodies in the new creation but also to being with Christ after death and to participation in the life of the triune God.

Bibliography

Bockmuehl, Markus. "Did St. Paul Go to Heaven When He Died?" In *Jesus, Paul and the People of God: A Theological Dialogue with N. T. Wright*, edited by Nicholas Perrin and Richard B. Hays, 211–31. London: SPCK, 2011.

Bouma-Prediger, Steven, and Brian J. Walsh. *Beyond Homelessness: Christian Faith in a Culture of Displacement*. Grand Rapids: Eerdmans, 2008.

Celan, Paul, and Jerry Glenn. "The Meridian." *Chicago Review* 29.3 (1978) 29–40.

Esler, Philip F. *New Testament Theology: Communion and Community*. Minneapolis: Fortress, 2005.

Imfeld, Zoë Lehmann, and Andreas Losch, eds., *Our Common Cosmos. Exploring the Future of Theology, Human Culture and Space Sciences*. London: T&T Clark, 2018.

"JC Unit One: On the Road In Johnny Cash's Custom Tour Bus." *Opposite Lock*. January 9, 2014. https://oppositelock.kinja.com/jc-unit-one-on-the-road-in-johnny-cashs-custom-tour-b-1498195896.

Lincoln, Andrew T. *Hebrews: A Guide*. London: T. & T. Clark, 2006.

Lincoln, Andrew T. *Paradise Now and Not Yet: Studies in the Role of the Heavenly Dimension in Paul's Thought with Special Reference to His Eschatology*. SNTSMS 43. Cambridge: Cambridge University Press, 1981.

Marshall, Paul, with Lela Gilbert. *Heaven Is not My Home: Learning to Live in God's Creation*. Nashville: Word, 1998.

Middleton, J. Richard. *A New Heaven and a New Earth: Reclaiming Biblical Eschatology*. Grand Rapids: Baker Academic, 2014.

Parry, Robin A. *The Biblical Cosmos: A Pilgrim's Guide to the Weird and Wonderful World of the Bible*. Eugene, OR.: Cascade Books, 2014.

Polkinghorne, John, and Michael Welker, eds., *The End of the World and the Ends of God: Science and Theology on Eschatology*. Harrisburg, PA: Trinity, 2000.

Robinson, Marilynne. *Gilead*. London: Virago, 2005.

Russell, Robert J. "Cosmology and Eschatology." In *The Oxford Handbook of Eschatology*, edited by Jerry L. Walls, 563–80. Oxford: Oxford University Press, 2008.

Walsh, Brian J. "Repenting of Heaven." *Empire Remixed*. June 14, 2015. http://empireremixed.com/2015/06/04/repenting-of-heaven.

Wright, N. T. "Heaven Is not Our Home." *Christianity Today*, March 24, 2008.

———. *Surprised by Hope*. London: SPCK, 2007.

---

creation.

4

Searching For Home, Discovering Peace

Jamie Howison

Our souls find rest in God alone

We pine, we strive, we run, we roam

And 'neath the stray the deeper tone

Our inmost longing to find home

Come home, come home, come home[1]

—Gord Johnson

We called it home for eighteen years. Built in the early 1900s, it was a three-storey house that the previous owner had gone to great lengths to restore, to the extent of having it lifted so that a new concrete basement could be poured. A century-old house with a ten-year-old high and dry basement was a real find, made all the more attractive by the fact that the previous owner's working principle had been not renovation or modernization, but restoration. All of the character was fully intact, yet the plumbing, electrical, and insulation had all been attended to. Sold.

We continued to follow that same principle of restoration over the years, adding a wood stove and a screened back porch, then redoing the

---

1. Johnson, "Our Souls Find Rest in God Alone." Used with permission.

kitchen and bathroom. The wood siding was scraped and painted, the heavily treed yard landscaped and planted with shade-tolerant perennials. The aging windows were all replaced, but with ones manufactured by a company that specialized in products that suited older homes. We'd tell one another that we weren't going to move from that house until all of those stairs became a problem; not quite "they'll have to carry me out feet first," but awfully close. Often as I'd begin to make my way up the staircase I would place my hand on the heavy old wooden banister, feel its smoothness against my palm, and say aloud to no one in particular, "This is our *home*."

And then the disruption came, unexpected and deeply disorienting, and I began a slow year-long process of letting go of that home and sorting out the question of where next. I became a very familiar face at the local Salvation Army thrift store over those months. Bit by bit I cleared things out of the basement, which, like so many basements, was filled with things that really shouldn't have been kept. The third floor study had a hundred and fifty linear feet of built-in bookshelves, and knowing I'd not again have anything like that in a new place, I spent a week culling my library, setting out five hundred volumes to sell in a book sale I advertized at the church and on social media. Pieces of furniture, some of the artwork, the extra set of dishes we'd rarely ever used, the eight-foot Christmas tree, the ancient Singer sewing machine passed to us by a grandmother, and countless other things all had to go, for I knew that wherever I landed it would never have the space for so many things. At first it was all a bit overwhelming and even heartbreaking, but then it began to feel liberating to so freely release so much. When I heard that a young woman from the church was setting herself up in her own place for the first time, I offered to give her a couch. A friend had always been quite taken by a painting that hung in the hallway, so one day when he was visiting I just took it off the wall and gave it to him. At my little book sale I took real delight in picking out books that I thought each person might like, and letting them have them for the princely sum of a dollar or two. At the end of that afternoon there were still about a hundred and fifty books remaining, which another friend loaded into his van and took off to donate to the Children's Hospital Book Market. Twice have I gone looking for a book, only to realize that it was one of the ones I'd let go. That's only two books out of five hundred, which told me I'd been long overdue in coming to hold my library a bit more lightly.

I'd arranged for professional cleaners to come the day after the movers had done their work, to spend four hours doing the sort of deep cleaning that removes all of the finger marks from all of the walls and leaves the floors, kitchen cupboards, and bathroom tile gleaming. I wanted the new owners to be able to walk into the house and see it as a clean, blank slate that they could then begin to make into their own home. Once the cleaners were finished, I did one last walk through the whole house, from that third floor study right down to the high and dry basement. In each room I stopped, aware of how things echoed in emptiness, remembering all the life that had been lived in each space. I paused at the back door, and without really even thinking I dropped to my knees and kissed the hardwood floor. I locked the back door for the last time, and went out into the yard and wept.

* * *

I am deeply drawn to ritual, which is why I so naturally dropped to my knees that day. Deep within myself I had just *known* that I needed to do something to mark that moment, and so I did. My ritual sensibility is a good part of why I have found myself so very at home in Anglicanism, and why, in the context of my ministry at saint benedict's table, I have done so many home blessings over the years. Sometimes those were for people moving into a newly purchased house or condominium, but often as not they've been for someone who is renting a new place or someone who is making some sort of a significant transition in the place they've called home for some time. I've done home blessings for people entering that stage called "empty nesting," for a woman who had lost her husband and was needing to sort out what it meant to live on her own, and for someone who had just finished a complete remodeling of the house she'd owned for close to twenty years and wanted to celebrate a new beginning. I always encourage people to invite friends and family, and we tailor it according to what makes most sense for each particular occasion. Often we celebrate a simple communion as part of the blessing, though only if most of the people who are invited will feel fully able to participate. Sometimes there is a dinner and sometimes wine and appetizers, but one way or the other there is always food and drink to share. At various times I've been accompanied by a musician to get us all singing, anointed a front door lintel with chrism, splashed water all around, lit entire spaces with nothing but candles, and even swung an antique incense thurible.

I always emphasize that a home is blessed by the life that is lived in it, but that it is also significant to create a ritual and sacramental pause in which prayers of blessing and celebratory hospitality are shared with some of the people who most matter in our lives. For years now I've been using a liturgy that includes elements adapted from a form developed by the Iona community, which has everyone gather in a circle in the living area, with one person standing on the outside as the symbolic stranger. Holding a candle, that person speaks words drawn from Rev 3:20: "I stand at the door and knock. If anyone hears my voice and opens the door I will come into that house."[2] This is followed by an exchange between me and the householders, which calls them to commit to having hearts open to those who come; open to seeing that in welcoming the guest in a spirit of biblical hospitality, they are in fact welcoming Christ.

Jesus, of course, was the one who famously said, "Foxes have holes, and birds of the air have nests; but the Son of Man has nowhere to lay his head," (Luke 9:58) which, when you think about it, means that he had voluntarily rendered himself homeless for the sake of the rest of us. All the more reason, then, to follow that famous Benedictine teaching, "All guests who present themselves are to be welcomed as Christ, for he himself will say: *I was a stranger and you welcomed me*,"[3] because if not us, then who? Besides, as I was rebuilding and reshaping my life and trying to find for myself a new home, I discovered something quite deeply true about extending hospitality.

* * *

The energy it requires to slowly release a place you have long called home is one thing; the energy needed to find somewhere that could be a new home quite another. After looking at the listings online I knew that I needed help, so I contacted the realtor with whom we had worked eighteen years earlier, and who, before that, had worked with my parents and with my brother and his family. His approach to his work is about more than sales, the housing market, and the potential resale value of a purchase. No, he is interested in helping people find homes, and in the case of the house my parents bought and lived in for many years, he had helped them see past all of the decorating, design, and landscaping missteps the previous owner had made, to glimpse what was potentially there for them. Had they gone to view the property on their own, they would have hardly stepped past the front entranceway. In reality it turned out to be the best sort of place for them, an open, bright, and almost elegant sort of home.

When we met together I explained to him that I wanted to live in a condominium, centrally located so that I could walk or bike most of the places I needed to go, but with at least some character. I listed the three neighborhoods I thought were most promising, and over the next month he sent weekly listings that I might consider. Though I was not quite yet in a position to make any offers, he began to take me to see various properties, as much so he could get a better sense of what I was after. Of the first four

2. Scripture quotations are from the NRSV.
3. Fry, *Rule*, 73.

we saw only one had any appeal, and only marginally so. One of the other three was in a brand new building, and its ceilings were low, its hallways narrow, and the natural light marginal at best. Not a chance. "I wouldn't let you purchase something this new anyway," he'd said. "The condominium board is unproven, the quality of construction still impossible to determine. But this does give me a better sense of what you aren't looking for."

Then one day about six weeks later, my eye was caught by one of the listings that had landed in my email inbox. Even in the photographs you could see that the place was filled with natural light, thanks to its large windows. And are those built-in bookshelves? It was located in a former factory building in Winnipeg's historic Exchange district, which also promised character. I called him, and the next day he picked me up to go and take a look.

As soon we walked in the door I began to think, "This is it." The entranceway opened into the kitchen, which itself opened into a large living and dining room, with a wall of windows facing out into the Western prairie sky. Those windows ran just over sixteen feet across, and seven feet from bottom to top. Framed by exposed brick on each side, the effect of all that light was to open the whole space into the city sky. And then there were those bookcases, from hardwood floor to high ceiling, filling the entire dining area wall. Made of heavy timbers and stained a deep, rich brown, they all but filled before my eyes with my books. "This is it," I said. "Well, lets look closer, to see what the potential problems might be. Then I'll need to look at the condominium documents and reserve fund, to make sure it is all in order." "Okay," I replied, "but unless you find something seriously wrong, this is the one."

It was—and is—the one. Aside from a bit of painting and patching, it was what the realtors call "move-in ready," yet on the day that I actually moved in I found myself strangely conflicted. The carpet we'd bought ten years earlier on a backpacking journey in Turkey was laid out on the floor, looking as if it had always been meant for this place. As the furniture from the house was arranged, I had the same response. It suits, it fits, it reflects me, and it is good and right. At the same time there were all of the boxes of books on the floor, artwork leaning against the walls, a bed to be reassembled, and all too many other boxes full of everything from files to winter clothing to records and CDs. After everyone had left I sat and looked at what still needed to be done, and began to wonder at all that I had lost. I finished making up the bed for the night, set up my stereo so that I could at least have some music for company, dug out towels for the bathroom, and then picked up a book, my laptop, and a bottle of wine, and drove back to the house. The cleaners weren't going to be there until the next day, after which one of my daughters was going to come with a truck to pick up the furniture from the back porch, so I went and sat out on that porch for the last time, sipping my wine, clearing off email, reading my book, and pretending I still belonged there.

The next morning when I awoke back in the condo, I had these funny few moments of disconnect, almost like, "Who put all of my stuff in this hotel room?" Wandering from the bedroom out into the living area, the sight of all those unpacked boxes just made me sigh. The day my realtor had shown me the place I had been able to *see* my books on those shelves, but now? Just boxes that needed to be unpacked. That evening my daughter and her husband came by to help me hang the art, including a large canvas he had painted for me the previous summer. That helped. Then two days later my other daughter came to help with those books, and as I stood on the ladder she handed them up to me in little bundles, all organized by category and author. That helped even more. When I got out of bed on the fourth morning, I was greeted by an organized library in a space filled with art and light and color, and I knew that this really was going to be home.

Yet there was one other discovery to be made, which ties back to that Benedictine teaching on hospitality. I discovered that each time someone came by for a visit to see my new place, it would feel even more deeply like home. I organized a house blessing with a circle of friends, which we ended by praying the service of Compline together, with smoke from that thurible filling the room to the point that I began to wonder about the sensitivity of the smoke detector. I began to invite different friends to come by for a meal or appetizers and a drink, and each time the extension of that simple hospitality did a good and deep kind of work on my soul.

I began to expand my practice of hospitality, adding, "To extend hospitality in my home on a regular basis" to the rule of life that I'd framed for myself the previous winter while on retreat. That expansion meant that I'd not just open my door to my family and closest friends, but to others as well. A particularly happy discovery was that my dining room table fits comfortably in this home of mine, and with both leaves in place it can easily seat eight guests. I began gathering my church's adult baptism and confirmation group in my home, always over a meal that I've prepared, which is something I really enjoy doing. I soon began hosting our community's monthly Artist Network meetings, at which anyone from the church who is involved in an arts practice is welcome to come for encouragement, friendship, and the sharing of our work. I've hosted a few gatherings of what we've affectionately dubbed the "Wise Elders"; basically a group of seven or eight men from the church who have an annual weekend away at a cottage where we barbeque, drink beer, nap, read, and in long rambling conversations attempt to solve all of the puzzles of our various lives. On the occasions when we decide to gather in the city for an evening, I'm quick to offer to host, and mildly disappointed when someone beats me to it. I've currently got a plan in the works for some "listening evenings," in which I will invite interested people to come for a bit of food and drink, and then sit together and listen to some carefully selected music. The first one might well be the original cast recording of *Jesus Christ Superstar* (on vinyl, no less . . .), which I'd schedule for the coming season of Lent, offering some sort of Lent-friendly appetizers. Who will show up for that? Well, that's the adventure, isn't it?

None of those gatherings are exactly what you'd call "radical hospitality," and as I look back at the words of Frederick Buechner in his book *The Longing for Home*, I find myself at least challenged, if not more than a little humbled. In an essay from the book called "The News of the Day," part of what Buechner emphasizes is how important it is that we not settle ourselves into indifferent silos when it comes to the longings and needs of the world. As he brings his essay to a close, he offers these words:

> To be homeless the way people like you and me are apt to be homeless is to have homes all over the place but not to be really at home in any of them. To be really at home is to be really at peace, and our lives are so intricately interwoven that there can be no real peace for any of us until there is real peace for all of us. That is the truth that underlies not just the news of the world but the news of every one of our own days.[4]

Reflecting on the work and commitments of Brian Walsh, I can all but hear him say, "alleluia brother!" And I know that it is true, that there really can be no deep or real or lasting peace for any of us until there is real peace for all of us, which is finally an eschatological hope and proclamation. God is not yet finished with us and our world—thank God, because just look at what we have done—but in the meantime those of us who really believe that we've not been abandoned to our own devices need to keep opening our doors and opening our hearts. And when we do land well in a place that feels like home, may that never become a silo in which we hide from the longings and hurts and hungers of our neighbors, but instead may it become a resting place that gives us enough peace to muster the courage to get up and do it again.

* * *

And finally a note to Brian, for the next time something brings you to Winnipeg. I don't have a spare bedroom anymore, so it will be different from

---

4. Buechner, *Longing*, 140.

the last time you stayed with me. But I do have a hide-a-bed in the living room, and the last guest who slept there tells me it is a good one. Just give me enough notice to get out the sheets and perhaps get something good simmering on the stove.

Bibliography

Buechner, Frederick. *The Longing for Home: Recollections and Reflections.* San Francisco: HarperSanFrancisco, 1996.
Fry, Timothy, ed. *The Rule of St. Benedict in English.* Collegeville, MN: Liturgical, 1981.
Johnson, Gord. "Our Souls Find Rest in God Alone." Unpublished lyrics, 2018.

5

Reflections on Interfaith Work and City-Building

Past, Present, and Future

Joe Mihevc

Introduction: Early Antecedents

This article, warmly nestled in the teaching, preaching and inspiration of Brian Walsh's ministry, seeks to review the long history of faith communities working for interfaith dialogue and social justice in Toronto with a view to explore where this work might venture into the future. The current City of Toronto was amalgamated on January 1, 1998, a time when a very different religious tapestry was beginning to take shape in Toronto. Before amalgamation, signs of these changes were already being felt in the former six municipalities. Of course, even before amalgamation, faith communities had an active engagement in urban social justice affairs through a variety of initiatives. It is important to review these efforts and movements, taking note of the changing religious and urban context as we seek to understand the current moment. From there, we can then build towards a sense of where this work can and should be heading.

Faith-Based Social Justice Work

Faith communities have a long history of engaging in the public sphere promoting social justice issues. Among Christians, the social gospel movement was a dominant, courageous, and persistent Protestant voice for social change in post-Confederation Canada. The movement sought to improve the social, economic and moral conditions of the urban poor. Its proponents, pastors like J. S. Woodsworth, Tommy Douglas, J. G. Shearer, and Salem Bland, to mention only a few, sought to promote social welfare reforms in an industrializing Canada. The United States had a similar movement inspired by Walter Rauschenbusch a New York pastor and theologian who pushed a "practical Christianity" of urban reforms in favor of poor people living in squalid urban living conditions.

The Canadian social gospel movement integrated spiritual development with progressive public policy. The movement founded institutions like the Fred Victor Mission (1894), the Fellowship for a Christian Social Order (1934), and supported conferences and action on child welfare, health, housing and urban reforms. The women's suffrage movement found a home in social gospel activism. Labor reforms, agrarian reforms, the Winnipeg General Strike, the formation of the United Church in 1925, and the formation of the Co-operative Commonwealth Federation (CCF) as a political party in 1932 were all associated with this faith-based movement of renewal. This period of faith-based activism laid much of the groundwork for the systems of social welfare, urban infrastructure and labor rights that Canadians enjoy today. These religious actors, movements and ideas carried political weight well past World War II as national and provincial policy built the modern welfare state.[1]

From the 1960s through to the 1990s, two movements adding to the work of the protestant churches influenced the way in which social justice work was to happen in Canada. First, the Roman Catholic Church in Canada, influenced by Vatican II and the work of the Latin American Conference of Bishops, encouraged Catholic involvement in movements for social change. Liberation theology, feminist and Black theologies, environmental ethics and spirituality all witnessed support from Catholic leadership, at least for this historic time period. Secondly, the issues that became important to faith-based Christian activism were global poverty, human rights abuses, aboriginal justice, state-sponsored oppression, and apartheid in the Global South. Twelve interchurch coalitions were formed and largely focused on issues of global peace and justice over a thirty-year time period. Today, the majority of these coalitions have been integrated under the umbrella of Kairos Canada.[2]

---

1. The authoritative text documenting this movement continues to be Allen, *The Social Passion*, 1971.

2. For a history of each of the twelve interchurch coalitions, see Lind and Mihevc, *Coalitions for Justice*.

Interestingly enough, only one of the twelve interchurch coalitions dealt with urban poverty issues in Canada. PLURA, founded in the early 1970s, represented Presbyterian, Lutheran, United, Roman Catholic, and Anglican churches. The organization funded and supported low income self-help action on poverty while also petitioning for Federal Government engagement on domestic poverty. PLURA made a point of working on addressing the root causes of poverty, actively developing networks across Canada within a solid social justice and political advocacy framework. Regrettably declining church membership in Canadian society and a small budget for domestic poverty work that spanned the entire country limited the ability of PLURA to be a potent political force.

In Toronto, the Jewish community has had a long history of social service and activism. The United Jewish Association (UJA), founded in 1917, was an amalgamation of several Jewish social welfare agencies representing a variety of Jewish denominations. The UJA brought together different religious streams of Judaism into a single agency to find and support various causes within the Jewish community and the broader Toronto community. The context for the Jewish community was very different, however, inasmuch as it was the victim of Canadian anti-Semitic actions and attitudes. As such, its posture with the larger public policy questions of the early and mid-twentieth century was largely defensive of its community and institutions.

The early days of the UJA concerned itself with mass migration, the arrival of refugees from eastern Europe, and the influenza epidemic's impact on families and children. The 1930s witnessed Jews active with Jewish-dominated garment workers seeking unionization. The post-WWII and post-Holocaust era saw the UJA direct its work towards resettlement. The fight for human rights, the rights of refugees, the battle against anti-Semitism and other forms of prejudice have continued to be prime directions of local work.

Rabbi Gunther Plaut of Holy Blossom Temple embodied this ethic. In Toronto, Rabbi Plaut became a key voice building bridges among Jewish denominations and between the Jewish community and non-Jewish communities. He was a key figure in the founding of the Urban Alliance on Race Relations in the early 1970s and served on the Ontario Human Rights Commission. His faith-based social passion also included housing and homelessness (as evident in the founding of Plaut Manor) as well as support for Holy Blossom's *Out of the Cold* program.

Interfaith Coalitions in Toronto

In terms of interfaith work on poverty and social justice issues, the most significant antecedent of current local work is the Interfaith Social Assistance Review Committee (ISARC). During the minority Ontario government of David Peterson in 1986, an independent Social Assistance Review Committee was formed to study, consult, and make recommendations on the future of social assistance in the province. Faith communities around the province formed ISARC to provide input into government policy, and to support low income Ontarians in engaging the process of reforming and upgrading social assistance. ISARC has continued and expanded its work to include poverty, hunger, homelessness, and other areas of social injustice. For the past several decades, it has organized forums and provided educational material in support of including strong social justice values in provincial level social policy development. Their website summarizes their approach: "Community development is foundational to the approach of ISARC's projects and activities to ensure sustainable, moral and ethical solutions to the systemic issues of poverty, exclusion and marginalization in our province."[3]

ISARC is important because it provided the first major effort to embed the faith-based social justice agenda within a much broader religious constituency. ISARC includes members from Buddhist, Christian, Jewish, Hindu, Muslim, and Sikh communities, to mention a few. As the work of ISARC continued into the 1990s and beyond, the face of Canada was changing, and new immigrant groups brought new religious frameworks and perspectives. ISARC was able to bring this new diversity into a common voice under the broad rubric of "faith in action."

Neighborhood-based projects across different faith groups were also evident in programs like the *Out of the Cold*, where different faith communities would join their volunteer base to provide a meal and a mat to people rendered homeless or who were marginally housed. There is also the example of the housing project co-sponsored by Darchei Noam Synagogue and St. Peter's Church that eventually became Trellis Gardens. This work added to the host of faith-specific housing projects like Micah Homes sponsored by Holy Blossom Temple, and several land donations by Christian churches for affordable housing.

A review of interfaith dialogue prior to Toronto's amalgamation needs to include the variety of organizations and relationships that brought a variety of faiths together around a common purpose. Prior to 2000, the Canadian Council of Christians and Jews, the Holocaust Remembrance

---

3. This information can be found on the ISARC website (in bibliography).

Committee, and numerous neighborhood-based interfaith groups hosted gatherings that took the form of prayer breakfasts, communal suppers for special religious events, special speaking events and preaching where faith communities would come to learn about the religious practices and values of the other. At the World Council of Churches, the work towards a goal of visible unity is often referred to as the work of *faith and order*. Analogously in Toronto-based interfaith work, groups of diverse faiths have worked together to create places for interfaith dialogue that develop mutual learning and respect without needing a social action project attached to them. Over time, relationships grew as these gatherings grew, bringing together new neighbours with different backgrounds who wanted to know more about each other. This was aided, too, as their children developed relationships with children across ethnic, racial, and religious lines. Toronto's neighborhoods, given their own ethnic, racial, and religious diversity were, and continue to be, fertile soil for the development of a deeper appreciation of what diversity could bring to daily community living.

The point of this cursory historical overview of faith-based social justice work and interfaith dialogue is that these important characteristics of life in Toronto are not post-millennial creations or developments. Rather, they have deeper roots, in some cases stretching back to Canadian confederation itself. Faith communities have a long and noble history of contributing to the common good, of paying special attention to the poorer and more vulnerable members of our communities, and of speaking religious truth to political power to develop more socially just public policy.

The Post-Millennial Context

The City of Toronto and the Greater Toronto Area (GTA) is currently in the midst of another dramatic wave of demographic change that will have significant impact on urban living. The GTA has gone from being a medium-sized region to becoming a global urban center. It has become a magnet for business and commerce, learning, arts and culture, and a refuge for people seeking a safety and a better quality of life. There are two sets of data that are critically important for understanding the opportunities and challenges for faith-based work.

Toronto is now home to residents in significant numbers from around the world. When the world experiences war and conflict, Toronto now feels this pain through relatives and loved ones who call the city their home. Certainly, the arrival of successive waves of immigrants and refugees has been wide and profound. The origins of new Torontonians include the regions of

Africa, Central and South America, the Middle East, South Asia, and East Asia. They join people of European heritage who have a slightly longer history here. Toronto also boasts the largest number of residents with Indigenous heritage. In this city, over 200 ethnic communities speak 140 languages.

The breakdown of ethnic groups in Toronto, according to Statistics Canada (2016), is as follows:[4]

European (47.7%)

South Asian (12.6%)

Chinese (11.1%)

Black (8.9%)

Filipino (5.7%)

Latin American (2.9%)

West Asian (2.2%)

Korean (1.5%)

Arab (1.3%)

Aboriginal (0.9%)

Japanese (0.5%)

Multiple visible minorities (1.8%)

Visible minority not included elsewhere (1.4%)

When in early 2017, Mayor of London Sadiq Khan made the claim that his city was the most ethnically diverse city in the world, the BBC had to take back his words in favor of Toronto owning that title. Religiously, Toronto's diversity has become equally remarkable.

National data and projections from Statistics Canada reveal that Christian denominations have decreased as a share of the Canadian population from seventy-seven percent to sixty-five percent between 2001 and 2011. In the meantime, Islam's share has grown by three hundred and sixteen percent, Hinduism by two hundred and seventeen percent, Sikhism by two hundred and nine percent, and Buddhism by one hundred and twenty-four percent. Cumulatively, this growth represents an increase from four to eight percent in non-Christian faith groups in Canada.

The data for Ontario (2011) show:[5]

Muslims   581,950 or 4.6%

---

4. Statistics Canada, *2016 Census*.
5. Statistics Canada, *2011 National Household*, Code 35 table.

Jews	195,540 or 1.55%
Buddhists	163,750 or 1.29%
Hindus	366,720 or 2.90%
Sikhs	179,765 or 1.42% of the populations

Statistics Canada projects that by 2036, non-Christian faith groups in Ontario will double in size to somewhere between thirteen to sixteen percent of the province's population. These groups represented nine percent of the provincial population in 2011. This is province-wide data, however, and the expectation is that this intensifying religious diversity will be particularly felt in Toronto as it would be in other major urban centers in Canada.[6]

The days of Toronto being an almost exclusively Christian city with a small Jewish community are clearly behind us. In its first term as a new city between 1997 and 2000, Toronto City Council wisely chose to determine that the city motto would be: "Diversity Our Strength." Rarely, if ever, in the history of humanity has this kind of ethnic, linguistic and religious diversity existed in a single urban region. It is possible that Toronto in particular, and Canada in general, could make a major mess of this. It is possible that this city and country could fall prey to tribal isolation and hostility. And yet, this city and region have had relative success in not only creating a climate of toleration, but actually a broad climate of creativity, engagement and entrepreneurship in the urban environment.

The first key learning for faith communities from this diversity is that a key piece of any work in the civic sphere must be deeply conscious of the current and emerging diversity of the city. Building on the history of ecumenical collaboration within Christianity and Judaism in Toronto that inspired social justice work and built lasting institutions, there is now an opportunity to raise the dialogue to the interfaith level. To have significant impact on achieving justice in Canadian public policy requires that multiple voices from the full breadth of Canadian faith communities be encouraged and heard.

A second key learning for Toronto-based faith communities seeking to establish a more just social vision must be the recognition of and response to the growing poverty and marginalization experienced by many of the city's residents. Toronto has clearly become one of the wealthiest and most prosperous cities in North America and the world. Using construction cranes as a unit of measurement, Toronto leads North American cities in the construction of new condo towers, numbering at least 100 cranes each year for many years and beating out cities like Seattle, New York and Los Angeles.

6. Morency et al., *Immigration*.

Despite this success in building new housing units, Toronto's housing crisis has never been worse. Toronto's vacancy rate in the rental market was one point three percent in 2017-2018. This is well below a healthy vacancy rent of three percent. As a result, rental rates for apartments have rapidly become unaffordable. Across the city 143,820 households (one in eight) are living in housing situations that are not considered suitable. Nearly half of all households (forty-six point eight percent) pay more than thirty percent of their income on rent. In the meantime, new social, supportive and affordable housing units are coming onstream much too slowly. Toronto's own goal of creating 1000 new affordable housing units each year between 2010 and 2020 has only happened once, and the overall target of 10,000 new homes will only be half met by 2020.

Toronto's own Toronto Community Housing Company lacks the financial resources to repair its own housing units and a number have been forced to close as a result. The waiting list for supportive housing numbers 14,000 households while the waiting list for social housing is over 100,000. This is a number so large that if someone registered their name on the list today, it would take them 10 to 15 years to have a unit available to them. The crisis in affordable, social, and supportive housing has meant that homelessness has skyrocketed. Shelter beds numbering 4319 in 2015 have climbed to 6588 in 2018, and that figure does not include people who could not be accommodated in existing shelters.[7]

Housing is often a symptom of the deeper malaise of lack of income, adequate employment and distribution of wealth. Toronto has become the income inequality capital of Canada, with the highest percentage of people in Canada earning more than $100,000 a year at the same time as it hosts the highest percentage of low-income earners earning less than $20,000. David Hulchanski's seminal work on Toronto's three cities shows that income inequality in Toronto grew sixty-eight percent between 1970 and 2015.[8] One in five people in Toronto lives in poverty; further, the city maintains its position as the child poverty capital of Canada with its urban child poverty rate of twenty-six point three percent. Stagnant incomes, the inability to access employment insurance, and poor social assistance rates in a very expensive city are all pushing people over the edge.

Two significant trends are important to note in understanding poverty in Toronto. First, poverty analyzed by postal code is showing that poor neighborhoods are developing in Toronto's inner suburbs while wealth is moving to the city's core and along subway and good public transit routes.

7. Toronto Foundation, *Vital Signs*, 38–40.
8. Hulchanski and Maaranen, *Neighbourhood*, 36–45.

Secondly, this poverty is concentrated in communities of color, newer immigrant groups, lone parent families headed by women, children, Aboriginal persons, and persons with disabilities.[9]

Hunger in Toronto is another sign of urban stress. In 2016 the Daily Bread Food Bank noted an overall increase of thirteen percent in client visits to Food Banks across the city. That year saw 905,970 total visits, with a markedly higher increase in the inner suburbs of Toronto. Their annual report summarizes the hunger issue this way: "Hunger in Toronto does not exist because there is a lack of food. Hunger in Toronto in 2016 is the result of high costs of housing, rapidly increasing costs of food, as well as low and stagnating incomes."[10]

The City of Toronto does have a poverty reduction strategy and has made a number of investments in areas like student nutrition programs, free access to recreation programs, increased subsidized childcare spaces, repairs to Toronto Community Housing units, and discounted TTC fares for children and residents on social assistance. Many critics have emerged claiming that the city needs to strengthen its lukewarm commitment and add significant new resources to tackling poverty in the city at the same time as urging other orders of government to do the same.

The struggle against homelessness, poverty, and inequality will clearly require the efforts of government at all orders. But it will also require a determined and vigilant civic sector pushing and lobbying, voting and organizing, visiting elected officials while also putting their own resources into the pot. As a part of this response, faith communities also need to step up their efforts to find and collaborate in identifying durable and long-term solutions to these very pressing urban problems.

Where Stand the Faith Communities?

In a fluid urban environment and in an ever-changing religious context, it is appropriate to ask where and with whom the faith communities of Toronto stand. Are faith communities understanding and appreciating the new religious tapestry with which they are living and working? Are long-established faith communities holding onto visions of a return of notions of a Christian nation? Are newer groups fearful and succumbing to the temptation to hold onto ethnic and religious customs from their country of origin? Where are the signs of religious diversity working a new magic of inter-religious dialogue and action?

9. Toronto Foundation, *Vital Signs*, 44–49.
10. Daily Bread Food Bank, *Who's Hungry 2016*, 7.

There is much vitality and energy to report here.

Toward Visible Unity

One of the most prominent groups working towards a goal of visible unity is the Toronto Area Interfaith Council (TAIC). The organization, founded in 2004, includes representatives from most major faith traditions. They have sponsored special interfaith services, educational events and conferences, dinners honoring religious traditions. Each of these has provided an opportunity to promote both awareness and a greater harmony between religious groups.

TAIC's most impressive accomplishment was undertaking the initial work of bringing the 7th Parliament of World Religions to Toronto in November 2018. Just under ten thousand participants representing 118 spiritual and secular traditions from 83 countries participated in dialogue, common prayer, the sharing of ideas and inspiration. The event positioned Toronto as an urban model for how faith communities can not only live together in harmony but can also work together on common projects.

When the massacre of Muslim congregants in Quebec at a worship service occurred in January 2017, Toronto's rabbinic leaders and synagogues opted to partner with local Imams and mosques. They organized prayer circles around places of Muslim worship during Friday prayer services. Toronto Muslim leaders returned the gesture of prayerful solidarity after Jewish worshippers were killed in October 2018 at the Tree of Life Synagogue in Pittsburgh. Building a common front around anti-hate work is driving faith communities to work more closely together.

The Toronto Area Interfaith Council is but one successful example of a movement committed to interfaith dialogue and building bridges amongst faith communities. Included in the movement are initiatives within each religion and denomination, such as within the Anglican and Roman Catholic Churches who have set up offices on ecumenism and interfaith affairs. The Noor Cultural Center provides educational programs, the Ahmadiyya Muslim Jama' organizes an annual World Religions Conference, the Intercultural Dialogue Institute of Turkish Muslims offers rich and diverse educational programming, and Scarboro Missions' promotes their Golden Rule poster and philosophy.

There are a variety of joint initiatives like the Women's Interfaith Dialogue, a coalition of Jewish, Christian and Muslim women hosting a Women's Interfaith Seder as part of its educational program. The University of Toronto's Multi-faith Center, established in 2007, focuses on students in a university environment. Since 1988, Vision TV has been an example of inter-faith television programming, the first TV station in the world of its kind. Horizon Interfaith Council has now followed that work with its media programming. World Interfaith Harmony Week, inspired by King Abdullah of Jordan, saw Toronto sponsor eight activities in 2015 alone.

Bilateral groups include the Canadian Association of Jews and Muslims, the Canadian Center for Diversity and Inclusion (formerly the Canadian Council of Christians and Jews) the Canadian Multifaith Council, Christian-Jewish Dialogue, Hindu-Roman Catholic Dialogue and many more.[11] Another grouping working on interfaith dialogue includes the myriad neighborhood associations, prayer breakfasts, dinners, walks, meetings, special events and pilgrimages hosted at the neighborhood level. These less prominent yet vital events cover virtually every neighborhood and community in the city.

Social action continues to be a part of faith communities' work. Toronto's twenty-plus *Out of the Cold* programs, run by faith communities across the city since 1988, are the most immediate and direct service provided to the urban poor and homeless. A number of programs have been running for two and three decades. The programs run once a week during the winter time and offer a meal and a mat during the coldest months for people who need the support. Originally intended to run only for a short period of time in the late 1980s and early 1990s, *Out of the Cold* is now a necessary institution in Toronto's homeless shelter winter respite program. *Out of the Cold* volunteers more recently have started political lobbying not only for public resource contributions to their work, but also to have the city consider housing rights more seriously.

When the Syrian refugee crisis became international news, faith communities rose to the occasion to raise money, find housing, and integrate new families into Toronto, as well as speak out against rising Islamophobia. This desire to help refugees echoed previous faith community efforts with Vietnamese boat people, Central American and Chilean communities, south Asian and African refugees looking for sponsors in Canada. Interesting partnerships between Muslims and Jews, Christians and Jews, community groups and faith groups emerged. The Jewish community deserves particular praise given that Syria and Israel have been officially engaged in mortal conflict for decades. Rabbi Splansky of Holy Blossom Temple was a prophetic voice reminding congregants of their own history of being unwanted refugees during the period of the Exodus from Egypt. Faith communities across Canada and certainly in Toronto deserve solid praise

---

11. Scarboro Missions, "Interfaith Directory."

for establishing the ethical contours of the Canadian conversation around refugees. The contrast with what happened in the United States during this same time period under a Trump administration is stark.

Towards Social Action and Justice

The work of Faith in the City (FITC) is worthy of highlighting as an example of direct political advocacy work when it comes to social action and justice. This group began with the clear focus of engaging social and political questions at city hall using a faith lens. A few conferences at city hall focused on how people from faith communities can engage city hall on joint projects in support of children, seniors, housing and homelessness, disadvantaged youth, immigrants and refugees, and other community services. FITC has engaged faith-filled social action work in a number of ways. From lobbying members of Council during key votes on anti-poverty and housing debates, to making deputations at committee meetings, scheduling meetings with the Mayor and members of Council, calling the media to draw attention to social justice issues, working with non-religious groups like Social Plan Toronto, they have made significant impacts on social justice issues in the city.

FITC's most notable political project was a campaign to stop a casino in downtown Toronto. The mayor of the day, Rob Ford, was looking to establish a Las Vegas-style casino in the Metro Convention Center. Las Vegas operators, along with a host of well-paid lobbyists almost had the Council votes secured for the venture. Many were convinced that the anti-casino groups were going to lose the vote at Council, given that the Mayor's office and monied investors were deemed to have the upper hand. The only major voice of opposition among staff at city hall was the Medical Officer of Health who pointed out the social ills that inevitably come with casino gambling. Even the union movement was split between those unions that were going to benefit directly from new jobs to be created by a casino versus the unions that were more conscious of the ill-effects that casinos bring to local communities. Two weeks before the debate at City Council, faith communities organized under the FITC banner held a press conference at city hall. About thirty faith leaders each dressed in the vestments of their tradition delivered a common statement. Christian clergy and bishops, a rabbi representing the Toronto Conference of Rabbis, an Imam speaking for the Canadian Council of Imams, Eastern Orthodox leaders, Sikh and Buddhist leaders, and evangelical Christians were all present. Each spoke from the heart of their religious tradition and as pastors who knew that they would be the ones cleaning up the social and familial mess caused by casino gambling.

As religious leaders, they called Torontonians and their City Council to a higher vision of what Toronto could and should be. The statement read:

> We are convinced that casinos contribute to family breakdown, depression, addiction, bankruptcies and crime, and thus are antithetical to our mission as faith traditions to strengthen individuals, families and communities.... Our governments should protect the most vulnerable in our society.[12]

The petition signed by two hundred and sixty-five Toronto faith leaders followed. One councilor became tearful when the faith leaders spoke.

When the vote at city council occurred, only 4 of 45 members of Council voted in support of the casino. The casino debate has become a prime example of how faith communities, exercising their collective voice around key urban issues, can have a powerful common good impact on public policy.

Other examples of interfaith collaboration around social justice issues include: the Multifaith Alliance to End Homelessness (housing-focused), Fossil Free Faith (ecological), Kids for Peace (youth camp), Ruah (an eco-centered community of faith), and Faith in the Common Good (peace, social justice and ecology).

The contribution of faith communities to civic life and well-being, while immense and varied, is largely invisible in civic circles. Childcare centers, seniors' programs, youth programs, arts classes, space for all kinds of community events, are an expression of faith communities contributing to the common wealth. The Halo Project most recently has sought to analyze the social and communal value of local congregations to their local communities. The monetary value contributed by local congregations to their cities is in the multi-millions of dollars. The social capital is deep, they mark the soul of many a neighborhood, and theologically are a real sign of faith communities acting out of their deepest religious convictions. The invisibility of the work is something that needs addressing in social planning circles.[13]

Prospects for Future Interfaith Work

Certainly, a lot of good has been done both when it comes to inter-faith dialogue and social action. The critical question at this juncture is to determine where this rich history is pointing and what next steps might be taken to further the work.

---

12. "Interfaith Statement Opposing Casino Expansion in the GTA," 7.
13. This work has been started by the Halo Project (website in bibliography).

The community and interfaith contexts call for this work to deepen and broaden. Religious demographics alone show an ever-increasing spectrum of faith communities settling in Canada and expanding their membership, especially in urban areas. Failure to develop ways for new and longer-term residents to understand one another will only result in the fragmentation of Toronto's social fabric. On the other hand, there is great opportunity to build a strong set of multifaith organizations committed to developing social capital from neighborhood to city to provincial and federal levels. One is left to wonder whether how much more is possible.

By building and nurturing relationships during the good times, further harm will be mitigated by the growing interdependence of these diverse religious communities during difficult socio-economic and political times. The strength of the new relationships is tested every time a hate crime is directed at a religious group.

An evaluation of the current work would certainly point to a number of weaknesses in the ways in which the work is happening. For one, the interfaith movement, both on the dialogue and the social action side, is being run largely by volunteers. Whatever structures do exist are often a function of the strength of the personalities involved rather than institutional capacity.[14] Secondly, representation at the bigger gatherings is not institutional, which weakens the power of the work. While grassroots initiatives at the community level are creatively strengthened by interfaith collaboration, a greater degree of institutionalization is clearly the call of the hour.

Institutionalization means an office with budgets and staff people. It means a level of organization and connectedness with sponsoring faith communities. Furthermore, the call for greater levels of cooperation is hard to hear in some circles that are concerned with shrinking denominational membership. Some pastoral leaders fear that mixing with others will dilute the strength of their faith's truth through some kind of syncretism or relativistic thinking.

Are there models where different perspectives, faiths, ideologies come together that might inform how the interfaith movement can be strengthened today? Can interfaith collaborators find ideas from previous movements where delicate sensitivities are held in balance?

I would propose an institutional model for future work that draws from a time when similar struggles–the desire to dialogue and the desire to build a better world–were also present. The World Council of Churches' (WCC) founding and ongoing work provides such a model. There are no doubt similar models from other faith traditions where the need arose to explore

---

14. Ijaz, "Forty Years," 197.

greater intra-denominational understanding and collaboration. I offer the World Council of Churches model for discussion.

The WCC has an amazing history and evolution. While there were a number of antecedents to the WCC prior to World War II, the first inaugural meeting was in post-war Amsterdam in 1948. The European-based world wars, with the related social and economic upheavals, gave evidence that the churches had an ambiguous, conspiratorially silent and even nasty role in the worst wars in human history. This soul-searching, coupled with a desire to be a positive presence in a post-war world, provoked a movement to better understand others' denominations and to engage social, economic, and political questions in a more ardent fashion.

The initial gathering included 147 churches, a modest beginning leading to the current total of over 350 member churches. The trajectory of the WCC has centered around two basic directions. One was around *Faith and Order* sets of issues, where churches would enter into dialogue with one another to understand the varieties of theology, religious worship, organizational structures, values, and priorities. The Council's projects have included continuing ecumenical education and formation, discussion with the Roman Catholic and Pentecostal communities who are not members of the WCC, and developing new understandings of mission and evangelization.

The Council's second basic direction focuses on the theme of "Peace, Justice and the Integrity of Creation." In short, these were the churches' actions in response to social justice issues. There is a rich history of WCC involvement in numerous issues including: refugees and stateless people, children's rights, indigenous peoples, peace in the Middle East, just relations between men and women, climate justice, HIV advocacy, nuclear arms, poverty, wealth and ecology, and human rights. The WCC maintains an office at the United Nations and is an active participant in its deliberations. In the WCC Assembly in Busan, South Korea in 2013 this work was formalized under the heading "Pilgrimage of Justice and Peace."

Can this same kind of basic structure be possible for a City of Toronto Interfaith Commission or Assembly or Council? Like the World Council of Churches, but on an interfaith scale, this entity would not be a "super interfaith" body that controls or even manages all the activities and projects that are currently happening. Rather, it would provide a forum for building individual faith traditions while in dialogue with others. Such a body would promote a goodwill understanding of the "other," while also providing opportunities to cooperate on issues of social justice that are present in the civic square. At this moment in history, the Toronto Area Interfaith Council does a marvelous job of facilitating interfaith dialogue and helping to move toward visible unity. When it comes to social action and justice,

Faith in the City performs admirably. Both need greater institutional support and ways to expand their reach.

The spirit that built the WCC globally, and the passion that energized the social gospel movement and interchurch coalitions are beckoning to consider the next phase of development in Canada. In Toronto we need a deeper understanding and appreciation of our new neighbours; at the same time the city needs to include a social ethical perspective in its public policy deliberations. In seeking to further build this movement, core funding from faith communities will need to be organized to develop an office and staff. Funding for individual projects could come from orders of government and foundations. Official representation from each faith community could be sought to ensure institutional connectedness.

The need is there; the will is there; historical antecedents are multiple; the next step is getting the job done!

Bibliography

Allen, Richard. *The Social Passion: Religion and Social Reform in Canada 1914–28.* Toronto: University of Toronto Press, 1971.

Daily Bread Food Bank. "Who's Hungry 2016: Profile of Hunger in Toronto." Toronto: 2016. https://www.dailybread.ca/wp-content/uploads/2018/03/Whos-Hungry-2016-Report.pdf

Halo Project. https://www.haloproject.ca.

Hulchanski, J. David, and Richard Maaranen. "Neighbourhood Socio-Economic Polarization & Segregation in Toronto: Trends and Processes since 1970." Lecture given at Delft University of Technology, Delft, NL, September 2018. http://neighbourhoodchange.ca/documents/2018/09/hulchanski-2018-toronto-segregation-presentation.pdf

Ijaz, Helen. "Forty Years of Interfaith Experience in the Greater Toronto Area." *Journal of Ecumenical Studies* 53.2 (2018) 183–200. https://muse.jhu.edu.

Interfaith Social Assistance Reform Coalition. https://isarc.ca/about-us.

"Interfaith Statement Opposing Casino Expansion in the GTA." Petition, 2015. https://www.toronto.ca/legdocs/mmis/2015/cc/comm/communicationfile-54042.pdf.

Lind, Christopher, and Mihevc, Joseph, eds. *Coalitions for Justice: The Story of Canada's Interchurch Coalitions.* Ottawa: Novalis, 1994.

Morency, Jean-Dominique et al. *Immigration and Diversity: Population Projections for Canada and its Regions, 2011 to 2036.* Statistics Canada. Released January 25, 2017. https://www150.statcan.gc.ca/n1/pub/91-551-x/91-551-x2017001-eng.htm

Scarboro Missions. "Toronto Interfaith History and Directory." Updated July 2016. https://scarboromissions.ca/wp-content/uploads/2015/07/Toronto-Interfaith-History-and-Directory.pdf.

Statistics Canada. *2011 National Household Survey (NHS) Profile.* Catalogue no. 99-004-XWE. Released September 11, 2013. http://www12.statcan.gc.ca/nhs-enm/2011/dp-pd/prof/index.cfm?Lang=E.

———. *2016 Census of Population Profile.* Catalogue no. 98-316-X2016001. Released November 29, 2017. https://www12.statcan.gc.ca/census-recensement/2016/dp-pd/prof/index.cfm?Lang=E.

Toronto Foundation. *Toronto's Vital Signs: Towards a More Just City Report 2017/18.* Toronto, 2018. https://torontofoundation.ca/wp-content/uploads/2018/01/TF-VS-web-FINAL-4MB.pdf.

6

Jewelry in the Apocalypse

Grant LeMarquand

Well who's that writin'? John the Revelator
Who's that writin'? John the Revelator
Who's that writin'? John the Revelator
A book of the seven seals
Tell me, who's that writin'? Ask the Revelator
What's John writin'? Ask the Revelator
What's John writin'? Ask the Revelator
A book of the seven seals.

Talkin' 'bout John the revelator
He saw Jerusalem comin' down
Yes, it was John the Revelator
And when he looked around
He saw feet like brass, eyes like fire
Heard a great voice saying, come up higher
He was John the Revelator
He wrote about the city of God[1]

—Blind Willie Johnson

---

1. Johnson, "John the Revelator." In the public domain.

The subject of this essay may seem odd for a volume in honor of Brian Walsh, of all people. Brian and jewels? Seems a strange combination. The only diamonds Brian has ever shown any interest in (as far as I know) are the ones Bruce Cockburn sings about—and they aren't *real* diamonds after all.[2] Brian probably has less bling than anyone else I know (although, to be honest, I don't actually know very many folks who wear a lot of jewelry). In fact Brian and I may be the only people I know who don't own a watch.

And yet the subject of wearing jewelry as an ostentatious display of wealth might perhaps tweak Brian's interest. Brian would certainly have an opinion or two about how the mining, production, trade, and consumption of precious metals relates to the global economy—and especially how the production of fine metals and jewels impacts the poor. And, interestingly, the book of Revelation also has an interest in such things.

Of course the network of metaphors and images in the Apocalypse is multifaceted and complex. This essay will examine just one very small word-picture—that of a woman, well really *two* women, adorned with jewels—and attempt to understand this image in the light of other references to precious stones mentioned in the Apocalypse (and other parts of the Bible and the ancient world). Our hope is that this brief review will uncover a "wealth" of significance concerning the mission of God and the mission and destiny of God's people.

The Adornment of the Whore, Babylon the Great: Revelation 17 & 18

We begin with Rev 17:1–6:

> [1] Then one of the seven angels who had the seven bowls came and said to me, "Come, I will show you the judgment of the great whore who is seated on many waters, [2] with whom the kings of the earth have committed fornication, and with the wine of whose fornication the inhabitants of the earth have become drunk." [3] So he carried me away in the spirit into a wilderness, and I saw a woman sitting on a scarlet beast that was full of blasphemous names, and it had seven heads and ten horns. [4] The woman was clothed in purple and scarlet, and adorned with gold and jewels and pearls, holding in her hand a golden cup full of abominations and the impurities of her fornication; [5] and on her forehead was written a name, a mystery: "Babylon the great, mother of whores and of earth's abominations." [6] And

---

2. See Cockburn, "All the Diamonds in the World."

I saw that the woman was drunk with the blood of the saints and the blood of the witnesses to Jesus.[3]

The identity of the famous character of "the great prostitute"[4] (17:1) and Babylon, the city she represents (17:5), has engaged and intrigued readers for centuries. Although this woman/city has been identified in the history of interpretation with various people and places (Jerusalem, the Jews, Turkey, the Turks, the Roman Catholic Church, the Pope, London, the League of Nations, the United Nations, America),[5] most contemporary readers are agreed that in its first century context, the whore of Babylon is imperial Rome. The juxtaposition of Rev 17:3 with 17:9 certainly points to the identification of the prostitute with Rome. In 17:3 the woman sits on a seven-headed scarlet beast and in 17:9 we read: "This calls for a mind that has wisdom: the seven heads are seven mountains on which the woman is seated." Rome itself, of course, sat on seven hills.[6] The identification of the woman with Rome is confirmed in 17:18 when the interpreting angel tells John the seer, that, "The woman you saw is the great city that rules over the kings of the earth." And in John's day, the city that ruled the earth was undoubtedly Rome. That the harlot sits on the beast indicates that "Roman civilization, as a corrupting influence, rides on the back of Roman military power."[7]

Since Babylon was the quintessential enemy empire of the Old Testament people of God, the empire which destroyed Jerusalem in 586 BC, so now Rome (whose armies destroyed Jerusalem in AD 70) is the new Babylon, the new world super-power— and the new imperial threat to God's

---

3. Biblical references are from the NRSV.

4. That the Revelation designates the woman in this text as a "whore" has been troubling to some interpreters. Tina Pippin has been especially vocal in her critique of the Revelation as a patriarchal document. See especially her "The Heroine and the Whore," 67–82. Pippin reads the Apocalypse as a text which excludes women. On page 79, she writes, "The tale of the Heroine and the Whore is not a tale of the liberation of female consciousness. The Apocalypse is not a tale for women. The misogyny which underlies this narrative is extreme." Susan Garrett argues that the wholly bad [women] are those whose sexuality escapes male management and manipulation". See "Revelation," *Women's Bible Commentary*, 382. Garrett's comment is surprising since the prostitute of Revelation 17 and 18 is certainly portrayed as both culpable *and* as under the control of her pimp— the dragon. For a sympathetic reading of feminist understandings of the Apocalypse see Paul Decock, "Between the Whore and the Bride," 373–99. For a different perspective on the place of women in the text see Kovacs and Rowland, *Revelation*, 188–89.

5. For details see Kovacs and Rowland, *Revelation*, 177–93.

6. Contemporaneous Roman coins depict the goddess Roma sitting on the seven hills of Rome. For an illustration see Koester, *Revelation*, 685.

7. Bauckham, *The Climax of Prophecy*, 343.

people, the church. As John reminds us, the kings of this new Babylon "will make war on the Lamb" (17:14).

For our purposes we must pay attention to what this woman/city is wearing. Her glories are first mentioned in 17:4:

> The woman was clothed in purple and scarlet, and adorned with gold and jewels and pearls, holding in her hand a golden cup full of abominations and the impurities of her fornication.

Although the woman is called a "whore" (*porné*), the word used for a low-class prostitute, as opposed to a "courtesan" (*hetaira*), her adornment, her clothing and her jewellery, is upper-class and expensive.[8]

The woman's clothing is described as "purple and scarlet." According to David Aune, the word "purple" can actually refer to a spectrum of colors including red, purple, and black. Purple garments were worn in antiquity to symbolize status and particularly royalty.[9] "Scarlet" is not so much a royal color as a mark of wealth. Both colors could only be obtained by a costly, laborious process. Purple could be obtained in two ways, one of which was from the madder plant. Since this plant was available in Asia Minor, Craig Keener suggests that Lydia, described in Acts 16:14 as a seller of purple, may have used this method.[10] This was a less expensive method than that used to obtain Tyrian purple which involved extracting the purple secretion of the murex shellfish. It is estimated that ten thousand shellfish would have been needed to produce a gram of dye.[11] Either method produced a dye which was expensive and highly valued as a status symbol. It could be that the author of the Apocalypse saw a connection between Tyrian purple and the list of luxury items which he lists as imports of "Babylon" in 18:12–14 (a list which includes "purple"), since the list in Revelation seems to have derived from a similar set of import items in Ezek 27:12–24, marketed by Tyre.[12] The prostitute John sees in his vision is clothed in the finest, most expensive of luxury clothing available.

But more important even than her clothing are her jewels. The woman is "adorned with gold and jewels and pearls" (17:4). Her adornments are a close match to the beginning of the cargo list of twenty-eight items imported by the Babylon/Rome found in 18:12–13 which begins with, "gold, silver,

---

8. See Koester, *Revelation*, 671.
9. Aune, *Revelation 17–22*, 934-35.
10. Keener, *Acts*, 2399.
11. See Keener, *Acts*, 2400, and the sources noted there.
12. Ezekiel 26–28 is an extended prophecy against economic injustices of Tyre.

jewels and pearls." Ian Paul makes it clear that Roman luxury items did not simply arrive in the capital of the empire as a result of some fair trade deal:

> ... *gold and silver* were mostly mined in Spain, while *precious metals* and *pearls* were imported from India, though lower-quality pearls came from the Red Sea. Military expansion was frequently motivated by access to metal deposits. Claudius' invasion of Britannia was largely motivated by access to deposits of copper, tin and Welsh gold.[13]

Imports of goods, in other words, was the fruit of Roman violence, and Rome's military expansion was motivated by greed for (among other things) luxury items. As one commentator says, "Gold epitomizes ostentation." Tellingly, critics such as Pliny the Elder, Strabo and Lucian "charged that Roman conquests were driven by a desire for gold."[14]

Jewels of many kinds were imported into Rome from around the empire. Ezekiel, in his own time, lists turquoise, rubies (Ezek 27:16), all precious stones (27:22), carnelian, chrysolite, and moonstone, beryl, onyx, and jasper, sapphire (this may actually be lapis lazuli), turquoise, and emerald (28:13) as among the goods of immoral Tyrian trade. In Roman times, according to both Pliny the Elder[15] and the ancient guide for sailors, *Periplus Maris Erythraei* ["The Circumnavigation of the Red Sea"],[16] these jewels were obtained from Asia Minor, Africa, and India, among other places. Rome's economic and military reach was wide. The writer of Revelation underlines Rome's global economic reach in the way that he uses the Tyrian list in Ezekiel to compose his own. As Paul points out, Ezekiel lists forty trade items, but the Apocalypse lists twenty-eight. Numbers are important for John and usually have symbolic value: twenty-eight "is 4 X 7, thus signifying Rome's total dominance (7 being the number of completion) of world trade (4 being a natural number)."[17]

In addition to jewels is the presence of pearls on both the Apocalypse's cargo list (18:12) and on the harlot herself (17:4). As Paul says,

> Roman society was obsessed with pearls, which were valued only a little less than diamonds. Wealthy women wore huge numbers of pearls, and others were known to dissolve pearls in

---

13. Paul, *Revelation*, 296.
14. Koester, *Revelation*, 702.
15. Pliny the Elder, *Natural History*, 37.79.
16. *Periplus Maris Erythraei*, 42.
17. Paul, *Revelation*, 297.

vinegar and drink them, just for the thrill of consuming something so expensive in a single gulp.[18]

Finally, as well as her adornments of fine clothing, jewels, and pearls, the prostitute carries a golden bowl. This time the writer, rather than simply listing her precious belongings, interprets the object for us: it is "full of abominations and the impurities of her fornication" (17:4). Here the woman's wealth is seen to have religious significance—her outward display attempts to mask her moral and spiritual pollution. She owns a golden cup because her profession has given her wealth. But in 17:6a the image of a wealthy prostitute with a costly drinking vessel turns violent: "And I saw that the woman was drunk with the blood of the saints and the blood of the witnesses to Jesus." The image has shifted. The woman transforms from being a prostitute bartering sexual favors for costly goods into being a demonic priestess drinking the human blood of sacrificial victims. In using religious language here, it is likely that the seer of the Revelation is alluding to the imperial cult which was pervasive throughout Asia Minor in the cities to which he is writing.[19]

For emphasis, the description of the great harlot's ornamentation which we saw in 17:4 is repeated almost verbatim in 18:16—although this time John makes it clear that it is a *city* which is adorned with this wealth:

> "Alas, alas, the great city, clothed in fine linen, in purple and scarlet, adorned with gold, with jewels, and with pearls!"

When John first encountered the woman his reaction (in 17:6b) was astonishment ("When I saw her, I was greatly amazed"). In 18:16 there is a further response. This time it is not John's reaction, but that of other witnesses, those who stand to lose from the demise of the woman/city. Their reaction is one of distress: "weeping and mourning . . . Alas, alas, the great city" (18:15-16). They weep and mourn for the fall of this empire, this Babylon, because "in one hour all this wealth has been laid waste" (18:17).[20]

But note that these witnesses are not disinterested onlookers. Revelation 18 mentions three groups of mourners who suffer regret at the fall of

---

18. Paul, *Revelation*, 296. See Pliny the Elder, *Natural History*, 9.121–122.

19. See Friesen, *Imperial Cults* and Price, *Rituals and Power*.

20. George Caird is quite wrong when he comments that, "There is a sense in which the spectators speak for the author as well as for themselves. . . . for he too was able to appreciate the glamour and brilliance [of the city]. . . . it is with infinite pathos that John surveys the loss of so much wealth." See *The Revelation*, 227. We must protest: the weeping of those who have lost a rich market for their unjust trade is not the weeping of John or of those John describes in his text as people who "follow the Lamb wherever he goes" (14:4).

"Babylon the great" (18:2). The first are "the kings of the earth"—the client-kings, who rule local areas under the patronage of Rome, and whose loyalty to Rome allowed them to "live in luxury with her" (18:9). Second are the "merchants of the earth" (18:11), also called the "merchants of these wares, who gained wealth from her" (18:15). Finally there are the (literal) captains of industry: "all shipmasters and seafarers, sailors and all whose trade is on the sea" (18:17). These three groups weep because they suffer economic loss from the downfall of this woman/city/empire. Her loss is also theirs. When the evil empire falls, she takes her clients, the merchants, down with her. The goods of this economy are described in some detail in the text:

> And the merchants of the earth weep and mourn for her, since no one buys their cargo anymore, cargo of gold, silver, jewels and pearls, fine linen, purple, silk and scarlet, all kinds of scented wood, all articles of ivory, all articles of costly wood, bronze, iron, and marble, cinnamon, spice, incense, myrrh, frankincense, wine, olive oil, choice flour and wheat, cattle and sheep, horses and chariots, slaves—and human lives. (18:11–13)

It is important to note not only how the cargo list begins—with gold and precious stones—but also how it ends. The list climaxes in "slaves" (v. 13). Two things at least need to be considered here. The first is that "slaves" are a part of the cargo, the merchandise, the items bought and sold in the Roman marketplace. John is vividly aware of the immoral and unjust nature of this imperial reality, for he does not actually call these people "slaves" (although most English translations use that word). John's wording is much more stark and reflects the view of the buyers and sellers in the slave market: they are "*somata,*" literally, "bodies." The economy of slavery has de-humanized this merchandise. They are not people. They are merely, as Aristotle said hundreds of years before the Apocalypse, "tools." The philosopher surmised that human households need tools and that "some are lifeless and some are living."[21] According to the logic of the Roman system, slaves were one commodity among many others. But John the seer perceives something different. John does not see merely "*somata,*" "bodies." Rather he sees, "*psychas anthropon*"—"human lives."[22]

John is not alone among the New Testament writers to discern a deep sickness in the Graeco-Roman system of slavery. In 1 Timothy 1, the author

---

21. Aristotle, *Politics*, 1.2.4.

22. Bauckham, *The Climax of Prophecy*, 370. Bauckham is surely correct in suggesting (with numerous commentators) that the "*kai*" (which usually simply means "and") separating "*somata*" from "*psychas anthropon*" is epexegetical and so should best be translated "bodies, that is, human souls."

asserts the goodness of the law (v. 8) and then lists numerous heinous immoral practices, a list which seems to have the decalogue as its model.[23] In this list the author implies that the worst form of breaking the commandment "you shall not steal" (Exod 20:15), is *"anthropodistais"* (1 Tim 1:10) which some translate as "kidnapping" but should probably be understood as "slave trading."[24] In the so-called household codes of Colossians and Ephesians, slaves are addressed. Some readers are troubled that these letters do not explicitly condemn slavery and openly call for its abolition. But as Brian Walsh and Sylvia Keesmaat have noted (in expounding Col 3:22–25):

> This is what Paul is really saying. . . . In contrast to the economics of the empire, Paul here proclaims a countereconomics of sabbath and jubilee rooted in the forgiving love of Jesus. By telling the slaves in our midst that they have an 'inheritance,' Paul is recalling for us the traditions of jubilee; he is reminding us that Israel's story—and now, through Jesus, our story—is a slave-freeing story. Look closely at what Paul is doing here. First he says there is no longer Greek and Jew, circumcised and uncircumcised, Scythian and barbarian, slave and free. Then he says that in Jesus' kingdom slaves who follow the messianic Master (the Lord Christ) will receive the inheritance. We are called to fill in the missing gap.[25]

Similar things could and should be said about Paul's words about slavery in 1 Cor 7:21–24 and, especially, in Philemon. No, Paul does not explicitly call for overturning of the institution of slavery in the Roman empire—but he does undermine the whole enterprise. Onesimus, the runway slave of Philemon, is to be received back "no longer as a slave . . . but as a beloved brother" (Phlm 16).[26] Onesimus is not a "living tool," he is not merely a "body" to be bought and sold. John the Revelator would agree. These commodities called slaves are "human lives" (Rev 18:13). As the South African writer and pastor Allan Boesak rightly asserts, the Christian vision of the Apocalypse is profoundly at odds with the imperial vision of Rome:

> Both slavery and racism require the fundamental dehumanization of the other in order to make the system work. At the basis of every such system, from slavery in the ancient world

---

23. The sins listed in 1 Tim 1:9–10 seem to be the author's view of the worst possible forms of breaking the 10 Commandments: thus, the worst form of dishonoring one's parents is, "murderers of fathers and murderers of mothers."

24. See Fee, *1 and 2 Timothy, Titus*, 49.

25. Walsh and Keesmaat, *Colossians Remixed*, 208.

26. Ip, *A Socio-rhetorical Interpretation of the Letter to Philemon*, 182.

to apartheid in modern South Africa, lies the assumption, the absolutely necessary assumption, that the other is a non-person, somehow less than human. This is why that person's slave status, or inferior status, is justified. John of Patmos exposes and explodes this myth even as he exposes the system that makes it necessary. But slaves were cargo, and cargo was money. And now those merchants of goods and human flesh weep, for Rome is no more: "Alas! Alas! Thou great city, thou mighty city, Babylon!" (18:10). Rubbish, says John, the merchants cry "because no one buys their cargo anymore" (18:11). The bottom line is not the splendor of Rome, it is money.[27]

Slavery dehumanizes. Slavery is based on greed. And so, because God hates such idolatry and immorality, God opposes all who uphold dehumanizing systems. God's judgment on Babylon/Rome is immensely *good* news.

But the second thing to be noted about the "slaves" in the cargo list of Rev 18:11–13 is that there is a profound connection between the end of this list and its beginning. There is a necessary interdependence between slavery and the mining for jewels and precious metals. Slavery allowed mining for precious gems to be profitable. Writing circa AD 77, very close to the time of the writing of the Revelation (c. AD 90), Pliny the Elder described gold mining by Roman slaves in this way: "the men carry the stuff out on their shoulders, working night and day, each man passing them on to the next man in the dark, only those at the end of the line see the daylight."[28] "The miners do not see daylight for many months on."[29] The cruelty of the work imposed on slaves in the mines may explain why Spartacus, the leader of the famous slave revolt of 73–71 BC, "issued an order in his camp forbidding anybody to possess gold or silver."[30]

In a recent paper Ian Paul argued that Ezek 27:13 and Rev 18:12–13 both connect mining and slavery—and that this association, so crucial in the ancient societies, continues into our modern era.[31] In many parts of Africa oppressive governments or warlords have used slave labor, or oppressive working conditions approximating slave labor, to mine jewels to fund the purchase of weapons. Paul reported that the Church of England has recently developed investment policies which regulate how it will ethically invest in mining—partly on the basis of exegetical work on Revelation

27. Boesak, *Comfort and Protest*, 121. Note: Boesak was writing this in the late 1980s during the apartheid regime.
28. Pliny the Elder, *Natural History*, 33.21.71.
29. Pliny the Elder, *Natural History*, 33.21.70.
30. Pliny the Elder, *Natural History*, 33.15.50.
31. See Paul, "The critique of slavery in Ezekiel and the Book of Revelation."

18. In his commentary on Revelation, Paul suggests that the cargo list of Rev 18:11–13 is not simply an itemization of "the indulgent consumption of the wealthy elite," although it is that. Rather, "by including slaves at the end of the list, John is emphasizing both ends of the chain of consumption: luxury and prosperity for the few has created poverty and oppression for the many. The slaves who worked in gold and silver mines [of the Roman empire], for example, had an extremely short life expectancy."[32]

John's vision of the fall of the whore of Babylon has ethical and missiological implications. To support a system which uses unjust labor to produce goods for the "indulgent consumption" of a few is to prop up a social order which is under God's judgement, an order that will fall. It is a part of the mission of God's people to "take no part in the unfruitful works of darkness, but instead expose them" (Eph 5:11). Rather than allying itself with rulers who exploit the earth and its peoples to create prosperity for the elite, John reminds his readers that these oppressive rulers will be thrown down. The wealth of Rome—or of modern superpowers—"is not a sign of God's blessing or Rome's hard work, it is directly related to the oppressive military might and economic exploitation that are the hallmarks of that society," says Boesak.[33] Rome was wealthy because of the power of the beast. But the power of the beast will, like Babylon, fall. Christopher Rowland, speaking of the text of the Apocalypse as a whole, well expresses the missiological vision presented in John's picture of the fall of Babylon: "The book of Revelation . . . shows us that the world is no longer to be accepted as it is, that what passes for reality is to be unmasked and the frequent collusion of the world of 'common sense' with evil forces to be revealed."[34]

The Adornment of the Bride, the New Jerusalem: Revelation 19 & 21

After John's disturbing vision of the fall of the whore who is Babylon/Rome, John has a vision of another woman who transforms into a city. Or perhaps we should say that in Rev 19:5–9 John has an "audition"—he *hears* about another woman, although she is not yet seen. The vision is only fully revealed in Revelation 21, but in chapter 19 John has a hint, a promise of what is to come:

32. Paul, *Revelation*, 298–99.
33. Boesak, *Comfort and Protest*, 110.
34. Rowland, *Revelation*, 3.

⁵ And from the throne came a voice saying, "Praise our God, all you his servants, and all who fear him, small and great." ⁶ Then I heard what seemed to be the voice of a great multitude, like the sound of many waters and like the sound of mighty thunderpeals, crying out, "Hallelujah! For the Lord our God the Almighty reigns. ⁷ Let us rejoice and exult and give him the glory, for the marriage of the Lamb has come, and his bride has made herself ready; ⁸ to her it has been granted to be clothed with fine linen, bright and pure"—for the fine linen is the righteous deeds of the saints. ⁹ And the angel said to me, "Write this: Blessed are those who are invited to the marriage supper of the Lamb." And he said to me, "These are true words of God."

The unseen woman of Revelation 19 is a bride, an image which recalls a number of Old Testament passages in which the covenant relationship between God and Israel is spoken of as a marriage (Isa 54:57; Hos 2:19). John is told that this bride is dressed in "fine linen, pure and bright" and that her adornment "is the righteous deeds of the saints" (v. 8). He is told that the time of the marriage supper has arrived (v. 7) and that those invited are "blessed" (v. 9), but as yet, John *sees* nothing.

In fact the promised marriage supper is interrupted in a scene of horrific judgment by a rider on a white horse who, clearly, is Jesus: he is called "faithful and true" (v. 11; cf. Rev 1:5), he wears many crowns (v. 12), he is called the "word of God" (v. 13; cf. John 1:1–18), he will rule "with a rod of iron" (v. 15; cf. Ps 2:9), on his thigh he bears the name "King of kings and Lord of lords" (v. 16; cf. Rev 1:5). How many hints do we need? Although the rider comes in judgment on the nations and wears a robe dipped in blood (v. 13), there is no battle in this scene. The blood is not the blood of his enemies, for all through the Apocalypse this rider has gone by another name: the Lamb.[35] The Lamb, John has repeatedly told us, has been slain (for example, 5:6). The blood on his robe is his own.[36] This fact does not diminish the reality of judgment, however, since the rider then invites "the birds that fly in midheaven" (v. 17a) (not to the marriage supper of the Lamb but) to "the great supper of God" (v. 7b) where they are to "eat the flesh" of the slain, including those in Revelation 18 who lamented the fall of the empire: kings, captains, and mighty men (19:18). All of this is a graphic portrayal of what comes next for, although there is no battle, the defeat of the beast and

---

35. In fact the word "lamb" (the Greek *arnion*) occurs twenty-eight times in the Apocalypse. This is a significant number: 7 x 4, the number of "completeness" multiplied by the number of "the whole world." And, as we have seen, twenty-eight is also the number of Roman import items that John lists.

36. See Gorman, *Reading Revelation Responsibly*, 109, 143, 153.

the false prophet (metaphors for Rome and its client-kings; v. 20), the defeat of Satan himself (20:1–10), and finally the "great white throne of judgment" (20:11–15) are all revealed to the seer.

Only then, only after evil and even death itself (20:14) are dealt with, is John given the *vision* of the bride in Rev 21:1–2. As with the harlot who becomes Babylon/Rome, this woman also transforms into a city, or is it the city which becomes a woman?

> Then I saw a new heaven and a new earth; for the first heaven and the first earth had passed away, and the sea was no more. ² And I saw the holy city, the new Jerusalem, coming down out of heaven from God, prepared as a bride adorned for her husband.

In the audition concerning the bride in chapter 19, we heard that she was "clothed with fine linen, bright and pure—for the fine linen is the righteous deeds of the saints" (19:8). Now, although John "sees" this time, he does not immediately describe what the bride is wearing. It is probable that the seer expects his readers to understand that a bride would have been wearing gold and jewels, given what biblical and extra-biblical texts seem to imply was the norm:

> I will greatly rejoice in the Lord,
>   my whole being shall exult in my God;
> for he has clothed me with the garments of salvation,
>   he has covered me with the robe of righteousness,
> as a bridegroom decks himself with a garland,
>   and as a bride adorns herself with her jewels. (Isa 62:10)

> I clothed you with embroidered cloth and with sandals of fine leather; I bound you in fine linen and covered you with rich fabric. I adorned you with ornaments: I put bracelets on your arms, a chain on your neck, a ring on your nose, earrings in your ears, and a beautiful crown upon your head. You were adorned with gold and silver, while your clothing was of fine linen, rich fabric, and embroidered cloth. You had choice flour and honey and oil for food. You grew exceedingly beautiful, fit to be a queen. (Ezek 16:10–13)

> He decked her in gold and pearls.[37]

> And Aseneth hurried into the chamber, where her robes lay, and dressed in a (white) linen robe interwoven with violet and gold, and girded herself (with) a golden girdle and put bracelets on

---

37. *Testament of Judah* 13.5a.

her hands and feet, and put golden buskins about her feet, and around her neck she put valuable ornaments and costly stones which hung around from all sides . . . and she put a tiara on her head and fastened a diadem around her temples . . . they saw her adorned like a bride of God.[38]

Of interest is that the word used for the adornment of the bride in Revelation 21 is the perfect *passive* participle of "*kosmeo*": she has *been* clothed. Although in 19:8 we were told that the bride's apparel would be "the righteous deeds of the saints," we were also told that "to her it has been granted to be clothed." And now in 21:2 we again encounter a passive. The woman *has been adorned*. Her raiment is a gift. Nothing could contrast more with the array of the whore of Babylon. The prostitute gained her clothing and jewels by works of injustice. Rome's imperial worship of itself is saturated in the economics of imperial violence and so its jewels are blood diamonds. But the bride is clothed in gifts which, paradoxically, are also "the righteous deeds of the saints" (19:8).

The announcement of the arrival of the adorned bride is accompanied by a three-fold proclamation of good news. This time, in contrast to the usual angelic voices heard by John, this declaration comes directly from the throne:

> And I heard a loud voice from the throne saying,
> "See, the home of God is among mortals.
> He will dwell with them;
> they will be his peoples,
> and God himself will be with them (21:3).

God with us, God with us, God with us. This is the meaning of the marriage of the bride and the Lamb. And the result of 'God with us' means, simply, an end to all suffering, all evil, all pain: "he will wipe every tear from their eyes. Death will be no more; mourning and crying and pain will be no more, for the first things have passed away" (21:4).

The vision of the bride now gives way to an exploration of the city, the New Jerusalem. Once again, as with the vision of Babylon/Rome, jewels dominate the vision. But there is a fascinating difference. The great harlot was *wearing* jewels; the New Jerusalem is *composed of* jewels.

> "Come, I will show you the bride, the wife of the Lamb." [10] And in the spirit he carried me away to a great, high mountain and showed me the holy city Jerusalem coming down out of heaven from God. [11] It has the glory of God and a radiance like a very

---

38. *Joseph and Aseneth* 3:6–4:1; cf. 18:5–6.

rare jewel, like jasper, clear as crystal. ¹² It has a great, high wall with twelve gates, and at the gates twelve angels, and on the gates are inscribed the names of the twelve tribes of the Israelites; ¹³ on the east three gates, on the north three gates, on the south three gates, and on the west three gates. ¹⁴ And the wall of the city has twelve foundations, and on them are the twelve names of the twelve apostles of the Lamb. ¹⁵ The angel who talked to me had a measuring rod of gold to measure the city and its gates and walls. ¹⁶ The city lies foursquare, its length the same as its width; and he measured the city with his rod, fifteen hundred miles; its length and width and height are equal. ¹⁷ He also measured its wall, one hundred forty-four cubits by human measurement, which the angel was using. ¹⁸ The wall is built of jasper, while the city is pure gold, clear as glass. ¹⁹ The foundations of the wall of the city are adorned with every jewel; the first was jasper, the second sapphire, the third agate, the fourth emerald, ²⁰ the fifth onyx, the sixth carnelian, the seventh chrysolite, the eighth beryl, the ninth topaz, the tenth chrysoprase, the eleventh jacinth, the twelfth amethyst. ²¹ And the twelve gates are twelve pearls, each of the gates is a single pearl, and the street of the city is pure gold, transparent as glass.

Several things should be noticed. First, the gem-like radiance of the city is described as "the glory of God" ("It has the glory of God and a radiance like a very rare jewel"; 21:11). The New Jerusalem, the bride of the Lamb, the people of God, looks like God's own glory. We will return to this point in a moment, but it is crucial to note that this radiant, gem-like glory of God is of first importance for John here.

Second, the twelve foundation stones correspond to the stones in the ephod of the high priest in the book of Exodus. The ephod stones represented each of the tribes of Israel:

> ¹⁷ You shall set in it four rows of stones. A row of carnelian, chrysolite, and emerald shall be the first row; ¹⁸ and the second row a turquoise, a sapphire, and a moonstone; ¹⁹ and the third row a jacinth, an agate, and an amethyst; ²⁰ and the fourth row a beryl, an onyx, and a jasper; they shall be set in gold filigree. ²¹ There shall be twelve stones with names corresponding to the names of the sons of Israel; they shall be like signets, each engraved with its name, for the twelve tribes. (Exod 28:17–21)

Similarly, the foundation stones of the New Jerusalem, on which the new people of God is established, are "the twelve apostles of the Lamb," each of which is one huge gem (Rev 21:14).[39]

Third, the twelve gems also correspond (roughly) to another gem list—the gems of the king of Tyre. We have already seen that John used the cargo list of the immoral trade of Tyre recorded in Ezekiel 27 as something of a model for John's condemnation of the impure trade Babylon/Rome denounced in Revelation 17 and 18. That being the case, it is at first something of a surprise to see gemstones associated with the mysterious king of Tyre in Ezekiel 28 partly reproduced in John's description of the New Jerusalem. Ezekiel 28 seems to combine a lamentation over the nation of Tyre (destroyed by Nebuchadrezzer of Babylon in 573 BC after a thirteen year siege) with a reflection on the primeval story of the garden of Eden. The resulting lament combines the story of the fallen king of Tyre with that of fallen Adam (or even a fallen angel):

> [12] Raise a lamentation over the king of Tyre, and say to him, Thus says the Lord God: You were the signet of perfection, full of wisdom and perfect in beauty. [13] You were in Eden, the garden of God; every precious stone was your covering, carnelian, chrysolite, and moonstone, beryl, onyx, and jasper, sapphire, turquoise, and emerald; and worked in gold were your settings and your engravings. On the day that you were created they were prepared.[14] With an anointed cherub as guardian I placed you; you were on the holy mountain of God; you walked among the stones of fire.[15] You were blameless in your ways from the day that you were created, until iniquity was found in you. [16] In the abundance of your trade you were filled with violence, and you sinned; so I cast you as a profane thing from the mountain of God, and the guardian cherub drove you out from among the stones of fire. (Ezek 28:12–16)

In other words, as Adam in Eden (v. 13) possessed every perfection, all wisdom and beauty, and enjoyed the presence of God (the reference to the holy mountain in v. 14), although he himself is described as having every precious stone as his covering (v. 13) and although he was blameless—yet he threw all of this over in his iniquity (v. 13). Similarly, the king of Tyre has

---

39. The correspondence between the ephod list in Exodus 28 and the foundation stone list in Revelation 21 is not quite exact for either the Masoretic text (Hebrew) or the LXX (Greek Old Testament). This may be explained by the uncertainty about what some of the Hebrew words for gems might have originally meant. For a table listing the various words used in Exodus (MT and LXX), Revelation—and Ezekiel 28—see Koester, *Revelation*, 818.

fallen because of his own iniquity: "in the abundance of your trade you were filled with violence" (v. 16). But as Dean Ulrich has commented, the pride of Tyre, "is set within the larger context of human and cosmic evil . . . Tyre's pursuit of profit became idolatrous."[40] Behind the fall of Adam, of course, is a snake. Behind the fall of the king of Tyre, demonic forces are at work. Behind the superpower of Rome's economy is the dragon ("the great dragon . . . that ancient serpent, who is called the Devil and Satan, the deceiver of the whole world," 12:9), who had given his power and authority to the beast (13:4). That the list of gemstones which are the foundation stones of Revelation 21 resembles the list of jewels found in the Edenic stones of Ezekiel 28 signifies that the New Jerusalem is (in part) a return to paradise, a return to "the garden of God" (Ezek 28:13).[41] But it is a garden now transformed into a city, a holy city, *the* holy city—a city which is itself a temple, and a temple whose gemstones form an enormous, perfect cube, a holy of holies (Rev 21:16), the place of God's presence.

Fourth, we must note the significance of some of the particular jewels mentioned in Revelation 21. "Jasper" is mentioned three times. In 21:11, the bride, the holy city has "the glory of God and a radiance like a very rare jewel, like jasper, clear as crystal"; likewise the wall of the city is "built of jasper, while the city is pure gold, clear as glass (21:18); finally, "jasper" is the first of the twelve foundation stones mentioned in 21:19. The repeated mention of jasper in Revelation 21 sends us back to the first mention of jasper in the book of Revelation in 4:3: "And the one seated there looks like *jasper* and carnelian, and around the throne is a rainbow that looks like an emerald" (emphasis added). The first gem-like description of the one seated on the throne in the Apocalypse is that God himself "looks like jasper." And now, in the ultimate vision in the book, the bride, Jerusalem is "like jasper." She looks, in other words, *like God*. The theophany, the vision of God, in Revelation 4 leads to, it seems, a theosis in Revelation 21. The bride/city radiates the glory of God, the saints of God "from every tribe and language and people and nation," (5:9; cf. 7:9; 13:7; 14:6) have taken on the character of their Creator and Redeemer.

Other jewels mentioned seem to reinforce this idea of the bride taking on God's character. The second foundation (21:19) is sapphire. In the Old Testament there are several theophanies which mention this jewel, probably because of its resemblance to the sky. On Mount Sinai the appearance of God is accompanied by a vision of sapphire: "under his feet there was

---

40. Ulrich, "Prophetic Intrusions," 107, 110.

41. There are nine gems in Ezekiel 28 rather than the twelve of Exodus. This may perhaps signify incompleteness of the riches of the king of Tyre.

something like a pavement of sapphire stone, like the very heaven for clearness" (Exod 24:10). Ezekiel's visions of God include appearances of this gem: "And above the dome over their heads [the heads of the cherubim] there was something like a throne, in appearance like sapphire; and seated above the likeness of a throne was something that seemed like a human form" (Ezek 1:26); "Then I looked, and above the dome that was over the heads of the cherubim there appeared above them something like a sapphire, in form resembling a throne" (Ezek 10:1). Once again, the foundation of the New Jerusalem shares a resemblance to God.

Two more foundation stones send us back to Revelation 4 and John's inaugural vision of God's throne. The fourth stone, according to Rev 21:19, is an emerald. In Rev 4:3, John saw around the one on the throne, "a rainbow that looks like an emerald." In the same verse in Revelation 4, John sees that "the one seated there looks like jasper and carnelian," and in Rev 21:20 carnelian is the sixth stone of the holy city. Emerald is a green stone and carnelian is red. Whether John intends symbolic significance to be given to these colors is a matter of speculation. What seems remarkable is that both God's presence (the one on the throne in Revelation 4) and God's people (the bride, the holy city) are described using these same jewels. Once again, God's people image God.

Most of all, we should note that the bride, the city, does not *have* jewels, she *consists of* jewels. She does not accumulate her glory by unjust and idolatrous forms of trade; she has "the glory of God" (Rev 21:11).

Conclusion

The Revelation's visions of the bride and the harlot, Babylon/Rome and the New Jerusalem bring together two theological themes that should not be separated: mission and spirituality.[42] The Apocalypse contends that the missional witness against the demonic powers of empire (in the Revelation's case Rome) is connected to the ultimate promise and gift of the church being characterized by "the glory of God and a radiance like a very rare jewel" (Rev 21:11). The church is called both to be a faithful witness in the world and to be a true reflection of the very life of God. Those who "follow the Lamb wherever he goes" (Rev 14:4) are those willing to witness to Jesus, even at the expense of their own lives if necessary. An example of such a witness is given in Rev 2:13 where we read of Antipas, put to death in Laodicea for his witness to Jesus. To be such a witness means taking on the likeness,

---

42. For a discussion of how spirituality and mission are linked in John's Gospel see Gorman, *Abide and Go*.

the character of Jesus. Theosis, "partaking of the divine nature" (2 Pet 1:4), is therefore not an otherworldly or merely inward enterprise. To become like Jesus, to become like God, is not only a matter of cultivating a devotional life of prayer—although the Revelation is a theocentric text full of prayer and praise. To become God-like, to become the bride, is to follow the Lamb; and to follow the Lamb includes being a public witness against the injustice of the harlot and the demonic power behind the harlot's empire. The jewel-adorned bride is that company who has borne witness against "those who destroy the earth" (Rev 11:18). The holy city is that great multitude (Rev 7:9) who bear witness that "slaves" are not just "bodies," living "tools," but human souls. They are that body of believers who did not receive the mark of the beast and so refuse to participate in the economy of an evil empire (Rev 20:4). The mission of God's people is coupled with the mission of God to judge and save the world. Therefore the character of God's people is a reflection of God's own character—they reflect the glory of the God revealed in the Lamb, the one who gives his life for others. God's people are those who reject the adornment of the great harlot of Babylon who "glorified herself and lived luxuriously" (Rev 18:7) but who receive as a gift, "the glory of God . . . a radiance like a very rare jewel" (Rev 21:11).

Bibliography

Aristotle, *Politics*: H. Rackham. *Aristotle: Politics*. Loeb Classical Library 264. Cambridge: Harvard University Press, 1932.

Aune, David. *Revelation 17-22*. Word Biblical Commentary 52c. Nashville: Nelson, 1998.

Bauckham, Richard. *The Climax of Prophecy: Studies on the Book of Revelation*. Edinburgh: T. & T. Clark, 1993.

Boesak, Allan. *Comfort and Protest: The Apocalypse from a South African Perspective*. Philadelphia: Westminster, 1987.

Burchard, C., trans. "Joseph and Aseneth." In *The Old Testament Pseuepigrapha, Volume 2*, edited by James H. Charlesworth, 2:177-248. Garden City, NY: Doubleday, 1985.

Caird, George. *The Revelation of St. John the Divine*. San Francisco: Harper & Row, 1966.

Casson, Lionel. *The Periplus Maris Erythraei: Text with Introduction, Translation, and Commentary*. Princeton: Princeton University Press, 1989.

Cockburn, Bruce. "All the Diamonds in the World." First track on *Salt, Sun and Time*. True North Records, 1974, Compact Disc.

Decock, Paul. "Between the Whore and the Bride: Apocalypse 17-22: Listening to Feminist Readings." In *Women in the Bible: Point of vue [sic] of African Biblical Scholars. Proceedings of the Fifteenth Congress of the Panafrican Association of Catholic Exegetes / Les femmes dans la Bible: Point de vue des exegetes africains. Actes du quinzieme congrès de l'Association Panafricaine des Exégètes Catholiques*.

Lusaka (Zambia), from the 5th to the 11th September 2011, edited by Jean-Bosco Matand Bulembat et al., 373–99. Abijan: APECA / PACE, 2013.

Fee, Gordon D. *1 and 2 Timothy, Titus*. New International Biblical Commentary. Peabody, MA: Hendrickson, 1984.

Friesen, Steven J. *Imperial Cults and the Apocalypse of John: Reading Revelation in the Ruins*. Oxford: Oxford University Press, 2001.

Garrett, Susan. "Revelation." In *Women's Bible Commentary*, edited by Carol A. Newsome and Sharon H. Ringe, 382. London: SPCK, 1992.

Gorman, Michael J. *Abide and Go: Missional Theosis in the Gospel of John*. Eugene, OR: Cascade Books, 2018.

———. *Reading Revelation Responsibly: Uncivil Worship and Witness. Following the Lamb Into the New Creation*. Eugene, OR: Cascade Books, 2011.

Ip, Alex Hon Ho. *A Socio-Rhetorical Interpretation of the Letter to Philemon in Light of the New Institutional Economics: An Exhortation to Transform a Master-Slave Relationship into a Brotherly Loving Relationship*. WUNT 2/444. Tübingen: Mohr/Siebeck, 2017.

Johnson, Blind Willie. "John the Revelator." Track 3 on *Bluesmen Sing Spirituals: When the Blues Go Marching In*. Sagablues, 2005, Compact Disc.

Kee, H. C., trans. "Testaments of the Twelve Patriarchs." In *The Old Testament Pseuepigrapha*, edited by James H. Charlesworth, 2:775–828. Garden City, NY: Doubleday, 1983.

Keener, Craig. *Acts: An Exegetical Commentary. Volume 3: 15:1—23:35*. Grand Rapids: Baker, 2014.

Koester, Craig R. *Revelation: A New Translation with Introduction and Commentary*. Anchor Yale Bible 38A. New Haven: Yale University Press, 2014.

Kovacs, Judith, and Christopher Rowland. *Revelation: The Apocalypse of Jesus Christ*. Blackwell Bible Commentaries. Oxford: Blackwell, 2004.

Paul, Ian. "The Critique of Slavery in Ezekiel and the Book of Revelation." Paper delivered at Society of Biblical Literature Annual Meeting, Denver, November, 2018.

———. *Revelation*. Tyndale New Testament Commentaries, 20. Downers Grove, IL: InterVarsity, 2018.

Pippin, Tina. "The Heroine and the Whore: Fantasy and the Female in the Apocalypse of John." *Semeia* 60 (1992) 67–82.

Price, S.R.F. *Rituals and Power: The Roman Imperial Cult in Asia Minor*. Cambridge: Cambridge University Press, 1984.

Rackham, H. *Pliny the Elder: Natural History*, vol. 9, Books 33–35. Loeb Classical Library. Cambridge: Harvard University Press, 1952.

Rowland, Christopher. *Revelation*. Epworth Commentaries. London: Epworth, 1993.

Ulrich, Dean R. "Prophetic Intrusions of the Final Judgment in Ezekiel's Oracles against the Nations." PhD diss., Westminster Theological Seminary, 1996.

Walsh, Brian J., and Sylvia Keesmaat. *Colossians Remixed: Subverting the Empire*. Downers Grove, IL: InterVarsity, 2004.

7

Welcome Homeless

One Village Idiot's Journey of Discovering the Meaning of Home

Alan Graham

The only memory I have of my mom and dad as husband and wife under the same roof was in 1959 when my mom was standing on her bed with a knife in her hand threatening my dad. The next thing I know my mom is in the "hospital." Thus began an odyssey of a phenomenally disruptive home environment; a journey that would take decades to unravel.

While mom was in the hospital being subjected to the most powerful psychotropic drugs combined with electroshock therapy, my workaholic father made the decision to serve her with divorce papers. This launched Armageddon: a custody battle for me and my three brothers. I was the third brother of four, ranging in age from eight to seven to four to one. For a whole year we were motherless. Although we had a roof over our heads we were, in effect, homeless. I have seen firsthand that the single greatest cause of homelessness is a profound, catastrophic loss of family.

My mom had something going for her that our friends and neighbors stranded on the street corners and living under our bridges don't have. She had a mom and dad who not only cared deeply for her, but who also had the resources to come alongside my mom to support her as she battled her mental health issues and my dad's efforts to strip her of her maternal rights. First, mom's parents were able to get her into the finest mental health facility in the world, Menninger's in Topeka, Kansas. Second, they were able to hire skilled legal counsel to ensure that my mom would never lose her rights to raise her children.

Regardless of that support, my mom was never able to conquer the mental health demons that plagued her the rest of her life. She passed into heaven in 1989. My early life was fraught with multiple institutionalizations; multiple times moving out of mom's house into dad's. Stepmother. Step brothers and sister. Unsettled. Juvenile delinquency. Drugs, alcohol, and the list goes on. There is really no way to process this as a young person. Housed yet homeless.

I finally found some clarity in 2008 when *Beyond Homelessness, Christian Faith in a Culture of Displacement* was released. This is my take on their phenomenology of home.[1]

Home Is a Place of Permanence

- Beech Street, Bellaire, Texas (11 years)
- Huisache Street, Bellaire, Texas (1 year)
- Braes Meadow Drive, Houston, Texas (2 years)
- Nairn Street, Houston, Texas (six months)
- Hobbs Road, Alvin, Texas (3.5 years)
- Piefer Home, Alvin, Texas (six months)
- Garage Apartment, Alvin, Texas (six months)
- Apartment, Alvin, Texas (six months)
- Cleveland Street, Alvin, Texas (1.5 years)
- Syracuse Cove, Austin, Texas (2 years)
- Multiple Apartment Complexes (2 years)
- Old Quarry Lane, Austin, Texas (2 years)
- 1408 Redbud Trail, West Lake Hills, Texas (34 years)

I wasn't settled in any one place until I planted my roots at 1408 Redbud Trail. It was here that I began to fully develop my understanding of the meaning of home. Even then, such understanding took time. A lifetime of being unrooted and constantly uprooted took its toll. Living as I did in a culture of displacement, it was difficult to begin to recognize the effects of living without deeply planted roots. Displacement is a growing problem in Western culture, and I've seen it firsthand. In my daily life, I can see the internal

---

1. The remaining section headings are taken from the eight characteristics outlined as core elements of the phenomenology of home in Bouma-Prediger and Walsh, *Beyond Homelessness*, 56–64.

struggle play out when folks first come to the *Community First! Village* in Austin, Texas. You can tell by the look in their eyes that there is a missing link. That link is community, a longing for a place of permanence.

Home Is a Dwelling Place

I love to marinate in the word "dwell." Its poetry rolls off the tongue. When I think about the words dwell, or dwelling, they conjure up a vision of crossing the threshold of our family home, instantly liquifying and filling every nook and cranny of that dwelling place. Settled in one place for 34 years, you can find Graham family DNA in every corner of this place we called home. Of course, some of those nooks and crannies were created in fits of disruption. But it was in those disruptive moments that the doors of forgiveness, reconciliation, and healing were opened. To dwell is to be settled. And yet, to get there requires openness to the possibility of many unsettling moments.

Home Is a Place of Embodied Inhabitation

When I give talks on the phenomenology of home, I often find myself dwelling on Bouma-Prediger and Walsh's notion of embodied inhabitation. For thirty-four years, our home was filled with the embodied life of the Graham family. These walls saw the kiln-fired hand prints the kids brought home from pre-school and the hand-made Father's Day mug that never held a liquid. When speaking of home, I talk about the measuring ruler hanging on the wall in the kitchen. This is where we used to measure the children's annual growth. This ruler now provides a different memory when the children, now grown, offer to measure me to see if I have (once again) shrunk. I can visualize each of the dogs, cats, gerbils, hamsters, sugar gliders, and other assorted pets who made their way in and out of our lives. I can still see, as if only yesterday, the playscape, zipline, fort and playhouse. Our home of 34 years was a place of embodied inhabitation. Even so, it took me years to plant roots. While we have since moved to a new house, we carry the things of that home with us into our new community.

Home Is a Place of Hospitality

We have four biological children. Prior to each birth we held stork-watching parties. We invited everyone we knew to come celebrate with us. We prepared large and abundantly. That was simply our philosophy. In many ways, you can see this hospitality flowing out of Jesus' miracle of the multiplication of the loaves and fishes. Jesus desires to give abundantly even when there appears to be a lack of abundance. That philosophy continues to this day and is one of the driving forces behind Mobile Loaves & Fishes, the outreach ministry I started with some friends back in 1998. As we work towards empowering communities into a lifestyle of service with the homeless, we seek to inspire people into a lifestyle of abundance. We do this by modelling and inviting others to give their best first.

This philosophy was accentuated in 2006 while on pilgrimage in Mexico. Along with a couple of mendicant friends, I was invited into the home of a poor rural family, who then invited us to lunch. What came next was one of the best meals I have ever eaten. This spirit of abundant hospitality emerged, surprisingly, in surroundings that suggested a lack of abundance. I've come to understand that hospitality is not economic. It is spiritual. Abundance flows from the heart, not from the pocket. The spirituality of fundraising at Mobile Loaves and Fishes flows this very perspective. We describe it in a formula that we call the HP ratio (Heart over Pocket) where "H" (Heart) is the numerator and "P" (Pocket) is the denominator. We then raise its value exponentially to the power of "G," where "G" stands for God.

$(H/P)^G$ = Unstoppable Momentum

Hospitality opens your heart. When your heart opens, abundance flows.

Home Is a Place of Safety and Refuge

We refuse to be victims of the fear mentality so pervasive today. When we purchased our home in 1984, we spent quite a bit of money rehabbing it. The renovations included the installation of a high-tech security system. Not only did we buy into the notion of needing to protect our lives, but we also bought into the need to protect all of our stuff. Over time, that kind of security became a burden. Within five years, we not only abandoned that fear-driven need for a false sense of security, we also abandoned the keys to our doors. For nearly 30 years, no one had a key to our home. The doors were open 24/7. We raised our family without fear or an overly disordered attachment to our possessions. This philosophy allowed us to open our doors to folks one would not normally open one's doors to. People without homes, people who had been in prison, those who battled mental health issues, and addictions, you know, "those people." We welcomed the people we had learned to seek safety from.

What happens when you bring people who have nothing into your home of abject abundance? Well, a few things go missing.

I'll never forget being asked one day to go to the garage to get a tool to tighten up a door knob. This was not a job I normally did. As I opened each drawer in search of the tool, I found, instead, several pieces of serving silver in one. They had been hidden away. One of my friends from the streets who had been staying with us was the culprit. Over thirty years we learned something profound: don't be so attached to your stuff that it will prevent you from welcoming the kingdom of God into your home. We must learn to differentiate between ordered and disordered attachments. We don't miss the silver. In the moment, we felt violated and disappointed in our friend. And yet, in the end, our lives were made far richer by opening our doors to the stranger. Once we let go of disordered attachment, it is amazing how ordered life can become.

Home Is a Place of Stories and Memories

I love the quotation from John Berger in *Beyond Homelessness* where the author writes:

> the mortar that holds the impoverished 'home' together—even for a child—is memory. . . . To the underprivileged, home is represented, not by a house, but by a set of practices. . . . Home is no longer a dwelling, but the untold story of a life being lived.[2]

On another trip to Mexico City, this time with the Urban Land Institute, we toured the redevelopment of a large landfill. This tour showcased trash turning into treasure. The metaphor was awesome. While shopping centers, office buildings and homes were being built, the landfill on the same patch of land was still operating. I stood to watch the contrasting images of a new development emerging from the landfill. At the same I noticed a garbage truck backing into the landfill to unload its own treasures. As garbage poured out of the truck bed, twenty people surrounded the newfound treasure to begin digging. They searched, looking for anything of value. There in the middle, a family of many generations. Children ran around barefoot, as their parents searched, accompanied by seniors in the last days of life. There was laughing, celebration, scolding, and crying. The stuff of life. In the midst what seemed to be extreme poverty, a smile came to my face. Life was, well, just life. When

---

2. Berger, *And Our Faces, My Heart, Brief as Photos*, 64 quoted in Bouma-Prediger and Walsh, *Beyond Homelessness*, 58.

evening arrives, when folks relax and start going down memory lane you will always hear someone say, "remember when?"

To be at home is to build those "remember when" moments. 1408 Redbud Trail has been that place for my family and me. It has been that place for a very long time. Our lives are often so un-rooted and rushed that we never take the time to build those memories. To feel truly at home, we need to place the storied mortar into the crevices of our lives.

Home Is a Place of Orientation

As I write these words in celebration of the gifts of Brian Walsh to my life, I am on a train with my family, traveling from Berlin to Amsterdam. It is the thirteenth day of a sixteen-day journey, and I've caught myself longing for home! My inner compass is oriented to Austin, Texas, and specifically, the *Community First! Village* where Tricia and I now live. Our roots are there now. Although we left our deepest tap root at 1408 Redbud Trail, we have learned that home is far, far more than just a place. Home is our "magnetic north." It is all of these characteristics rolled up into one big joyful bundle. The longing is deep and internal. The longing for home is in each of us, however misguided the orientation. I was able to escape the misguided orientation of my early years to discover my own rootedness, my own orientation. Now, on this train, towards the end of this trip, I just want to be transported home, to my place of re-orientation. I want to be in that little village that I hope is creating a similar place of orientation for others.

I was recently on a playground with my goddaughter. She was spinning some kids around on a small merry-go-round. After multiple rotations, the kids would come off disoriented and barely able to keep themselves grounded. This lack of orientation seems to be how many of us feel in this Western culture of displacement. We stumble and wobble around looking for a place to settle. For some reason we just continue to spin round, and round, and round.

Home Is a Place of Affiliation and Belonging

I find it interesting living in a country that has, over many decades, tried to engineer affiliation and belonging, even as we humans tend to gravitate to folks who are a whole lot like us. For the most part, I don't think that opposites actually attract. We want to be around people that have shared similar values. It's not that we want to segregate. And yet, our close inner circle of relationships often mirrors our own values.

My country has something to learn from those who are chronically homeless. I offer this as a concluding example, having spent decades living and serving amongst those who have experienced homelessness. Among people who are chronically underhoused, I have found many common traits: profound and catastrophic loss of family, mental health issues, addictions, intellectual disabilities, job loss, and communities with a lack of affordable housing. This combination of factors can bring about a beautiful gift for all of humanity. And yet, in this society, folks who share these experiences can be misunderstood and stereotyped, excluded, and seen as something bad. It can be difficult for people to understand these values. In a polarized world it is increasingly difficult to affiliate and belong with those so different from us. This goes both ways.

When people get curious about the *Community First! Village*, they often ask if we are merely creating ghetto places for poor people to live. Reflecting on my experiences in Mexico, I have come to understand that if you uproot people from their affiliation and sense of belonging, there is significant psychological collateral impact. The work of Mobile Loaves and Fishes, and *Community First! Village* is not a matter of keeping people in poverty. Quite the opposite. We should do everything possible to create opportunity for folks to get out of poverty. All too often, however, we equate material wealth with happiness. Places like the *Community First! Village*, that are built for folks who live in extreme poverty can be places where everyone wants to live. We have proven that. When you affiliate and belong, it turns out you begin to care.

This all flows right out from that one simple scripture, "Then the Lord God took the man and settled him in the Garden of Eden to cultivate and care for it" (Gen 2:15).[3] Pretty dang simple isn't it? We need to be settled so that we can discover our God-given gifts to do purposeful work, and then share that with others in community.

Brian, you put skin on this idiot's skeleton, helping me to understand the meaning of home. Not only have you had a profound impact on me personally, but I have no doubt, through the movement we have created, that your fingerprints will echo throughout eternity. Your book sits prominently on the window sill of my office. *Beyond Homelessness* inspired the *Community First! Village*, our movement and my book. From the depths of the cave of my heart, thank you! You are a difference maker!

---

3. Scripture quotations taken from NAB.

Bibliography

Bouma-Prediger, Steven, and Brian J. Walsh. *Beyond Homelessness: Christian Faith in a Culture of Displacement*. Grand Rapids: Eerdmans, 2008.
Graham, Alan, and Lauren Hall. *Welcome Homeless: One Man's Journey of Discovering the Meaning of Home*. Nashville: W Publishing Group / Nelson, 2017.

8

Voices from the Ragged Edge

The Gritty Spirituality of the Lament Psalms[1]

—— J. Richard Middleton ——

In the movie *The Princess Bride* there is a conversation between the princess, who has been kidnapped, and her rescuer (the Dread Pirate Roberts), in which she says: "You mock my pain." He replies: "Life *is* pain, highness; anyone who says differently is selling something."[2]

A Multifaceted World of Suffering

Without being quite as cynical as that, most of us can affirm that pain or suffering is an indelible fact of human existence, as we know it. We live in a world racked by suffering.

Many marriages, despite our best intentions, fall apart. Close friends die of suicide or of cancer. And we're confronted in our inner cities with

---

1. I take great delight in contributing this essay in honor of my friend Brian Walsh, who has taught me so much, not least about the subject of lament. This essay is the fruition of numerous Bible studies, class lectures, and talks I have presented on the lament psalms since the late nineteen-eighties. The title ("Voices from the Ragged Edge") was developed in dialogue with John Garner, pastor of Harbour Fellowship Church, St. Catharines, ON, when he invited me to preach on the lament psalms in 1993. At the invitation of John Franklin, I summarized that sermon in a short meditation on lament for the newsletter of the Canadian Theological Society (1994), which was reprinted in *Perspective* (1995), the bulletin of the Institute for Christian Studies.

2. From scene 20, *The Princess Bride*. The movie is based on William Goldman's 1973 novel of the same name.

hollow-eyed street people, casting furtive glances in our direction, in the hope of a handout.

Meanwhile the victims of political violence and terrorism pile up as so many dead bodies in the streets of city after city, and country after country—every decade the names change, but the suffering continues. And we wonder if there will ever be a lasting peace agreement between Israel and the Palestinians.

As earth's climate warms (precipitated by human action), we are overwhelmed by massive and more frequent tsunamis, earthquakes, and hurricanes, which wreak destruction all over the globe, with a devastating loss of life.

Meanwhile the planet groans in the thrall of our pollution of air, water, and land, with huge floating continents of plastic in the Pacific, widespread rainforest depletion, and the destruction of species at an alarming rate in our own time.

The suffering of the world is multi-faceted, and it is massive.

Tragic as this massive suffering is, the tragedy is compounded by the church's paralysis. As a people called by God to respond in compassion to the pain of others, we find, if we are honest, that we lack the energy for this mission. Many would-be followers of Jesus are too spent just coping with the ordinary crises of life to give much of ourselves to others. So we pull back self-protectively into a defensive posture, avoiding even eye contact with the street person, unable to bear such exposure to the world's wounds.

I believe that the roots of our paralysis lie in the church's own pain that has never been adequately processed.

The church has a very hard time dealing with pain. We prefer to accentuate the positive. But the positive—praise and celebration—isn't always appropriate.

When Praise is Inappropriate

Imagine barely surviving a car-crash, perhaps being the only survivor, badly injured, in hospital; then your pastor comes to visit you and reads Psalm 150.[3]

> [1] Praise the LORD!
> Praise God in his sanctuary;
>   praise him in his mighty firmament!
> [2] Praise him for his mighty deeds;
>   praise him according to his surpassing greatness!

3. All biblical quotations, except for Psalms 30 and 39, are NRSV.

> ³ Praise him with trumpet sound;
>   praise him with lute and harp!
> ⁴ Praise him with tambourine and dance;
>   praise him with strings and pipe!
> ⁵ Praise him with clanging cymbals;
>   praise him with loud clashing cymbals!
> ⁶ Let everything that breathes praise the Lord!
>   Praise the Lord!

Well, *your* pastor wouldn't do that.

Or suppose you are in the middle of a tragic divorce; or you've just been downsized (you've lost your job), and you're not sure how your family is going to survive, given the mortgage payments and other bills. And someone says to you (as a friend of mine used to say in every situation): *Just praise the Lord anyway, brother*!

But how *can* you praise God when you're suffering from the shock of disorientation? How could you, if you were an Israelite, newly exiled to Babylon, sing one of the songs of Zion? Psalm 46 is a classic Zion song, celebrating God's presence in the midst of Jerusalem. It opens with this confident assertion: "God is our refuge and strength, / a very present help in trouble" (Ps 46:1). Because God is in the midst of the city, the psalmist affirms that it shall never be moved (Ps 46:5).[4] Except the city now lies in ruins.

So a later psalmist, writing in the midst of the exile, sings, not a Zion song, but a lament—a communal complaint: "By the rivers of Babylon— / there we sat down and wept, / when we remembered Zion" (Ps 137:1).

And Psalm 137 goes on to ask: How can we sing the Lord's song (like Psalm 46 or Psalm 150) in a strange, alien land? (Ps 137:4) And any time you're suffering, you are in an alien land, alienated from the reality of flourishing that God intends for this good creation.

In the song "These Plastic Halos," Mark Heard describes the difficulty of many churchgoers to be honest about their pain.[5]

Heard uses the metaphor of "plastic halos" to describe the masks Christians often wear in church, behind which "lurks a scarred and fragile face." These masks serve to hide our pain because we "think our tears / would provoke holy wrath." The result of our "stone-gray silence" (our inability to "face our fears") is that "we press on / with feeble cheer," "refusing comfort unawares."

---

4. Verse references to the psalms are given for the English text. Many psalms have different verse numbering in in the Hebrew Masoretic Text, which typically treats the superscription to the psalm as the first verse, whereas the English starts verse numbering after the superscription.

5. Heard, "These Plastic Halos."

In the final stanza Heard characterizes this approach to masking suffering as a "protocol" that we learn, in which we praise optimism and denigrate sorrow. The song ends with these words: "As we watch / the world turn to dust / the tears of God fall for us."

It is my thesis that the lament psalms provide an *alternative* protocol for addressing suffering, a protocol that is both existentially healing and deeply rooted in the redemptive sweep of the biblical narrative.[6]

The "Problem" of (Explaining) Evil

But sometimes it isn't the focus on praise and celebration in the church that prevents our dealing with pain. Sometimes well-meaning Christians stop us short from hosting disorientation, from being fully honest about our suffering, by providing a quick (and ultimately superficial) *explanation* for suffering—much like Job's comforters.[7]

Most of us are familiar with the traditional "problem of evil."

1. We believe that God is good and loving (God *doesn't want* evil and suffering).

2. We believe God is sovereign or all-powerful (God *could remove or prevent* evil and suffering).

3. Yet evil exists.

This certainly seems like a contradiction. And there are various ways to resolve it.

We could say, *There is no God* (that would certainly solve the logical problem). Or we could say that *God isn't totally good or trustworthy* (we

---

6. My initial insights into lament as an alternative protocol began with a course I took on the Psalms taught by Werner E. Lemke at Colgate Rochester Divinity School in 1986, at which time I read Walter Brueggemann's *Message of the Psalms*. These initial insights were deepened through a weekend workshop on the Psalms that Brueggemann led at St. Andrew's Presbyterian Church, Kitchener, ON, in April 1989. Brueggemann's helpful categories of *orientation*, *disorientation*, and *new orientation*, which are central to *The Message of the Psalms*, form the framework for this essay. Brian and I made extensive use of these categories in our analysis of the postmodern condition, in *Truth Is Stranger than It Used to Be*, and in many other places.

7. I use the metaphor of "hosting" disorientation to suggest that it is not optimal for disorientation to invade the "house" of our lives in a permanent takeover; but neither should we slam the door on suffering, since it ends up coming in the back window anyway. Rather, we need to be hospitable to our suffering, addressing it through the protocol of the psalms, until it is ready to leave, and we begin to shift to a new, transformed, orientation.

could deny the first premise). Or we could say that *God isn't totally sovereign*; God just can't do anything about it (we could deny the second premise).

We could even say that *evil doesn't really exist*; it is an illusion—which is affirmed by some Eastern religions.

However, by far the most common solution in the history of Christian thought is to claim that God has a "good reason" for allowing evil and suffering. Or, as Augustine and some of the early Church Fathers put it, there is a "greater good" that God has in mind that could not be accomplished without all the evil and suffering in the world. This is a Christian version of denying the third premise. In other words, what we *think* is "evil" is not really, ultimately evil, since it is necessary for the best of all possible worlds. This keeps God technically blameless, since God needed to allow all the bad stuff that has actually happened in order to accomplish this greater good (whatever it is).[8]

There are many examples of *prima facie* evils that actually do serve a greater good. For example, there are times I have had to work hard on a lecture or a talk when on the surface it seemed like "an evil" to me; I would much prefer to be out walking in the woods or riding my bicycle. But I've buckled down to write the talk, since I judged it was a greater good that couldn't be accomplished if I slacked off.

Or suppose you were wounded on the battlefield, without antibiotics, and the wound became infected with gangrene. Perhaps your leg had to be amputated to save your life. Normally, amputating a leg would not a good thing; but in this case it serves a greater good (saving your life), which could not be accomplished without it.

The trouble with the greater good defense as a global solution to the problem of evil is that it requires us to say that *all* the bad stuff that happens in the world (every bit of it) is necessary for some greater good that God couldn't accomplish without it.

Perhaps the primary example of the greater good that has been proposed to explain why God allows suffering is free will. The free will version of the greater good defense claims that God values free will so much that even if it results in terrible evil—including terrorist bombings, the Holocaust, ethnic cleansing in Rwanda and Bosnia, and so forth—then, so be it. It is all required (and worth it, from God's perspective) for us to have free will.

My point is not to discuss the merits of the free will argument, but to note that we find many examples of this greater good *approach* among Christians who attempt to give an explanation for why someone suffers.

---

8. For a formal analysis and critique of the greater good defense, see Middleton "Why the 'Greater Good' Isn't a Defense."

Have you ever been at a funeral and heard someone say that God had a reason for taking the person? Even if we don't know what that reason is, it is very common for Christians to claim that there must be some purpose for our suffering.

Two Approaches to Suffering in the Writings of C. S. Lewis

C. S. Lewis articulated a variant of the greater good defense in his famous book *The Problem of Pain*, originally published in 1940.

At one point in the book Lewis explains that people often are not aware that they are in a state of rebellion against God, especially if all is going well with them. "But pain," he notes, "insists upon being attended to."[9]

This leads to his famous statement:

"God whispers to us in our pleasures, speaks in our conscience, but shouts in our pain: it is His megaphone to rouse a deaf world."

What happens once we find that pain has "roused" us from our slumbers, when we become aware that we are "not in accord with the universe," that there is a reality that impinges upon us, which we do not control? Lewis suggests we have two options: we might rebel against God (with the possibility of repentance later on) or we begin a process of turning to God.

"No doubt," Lewis admits, "pain as God's megaphone is a terrible instrument; it may lead to final and unrepented rebellion. But it gives the only opportunity the bad [person] can have for amendment. It removes the veil; it plants the flag of truth within the fortress of a rebel soul."

Pain, or suffering, in other words, is a *wake-up call*. It is needed in the world since it shocks at least *some* people into turning to God (which is the greater good). Of course, not all repent. But the implicit argument Lewis is making here is that there is a reason for suffering that justifies it.

That was in 1940.

Yet about twenty years later (in 1961) Lewis wrote a book called *A Grief Observed*. He wrote it under the pseudonym N. W. Clerk because he couldn't come right out and contradict (in his own name) what he had said in *The Problem of Pain*. But contradict it he did. In this new book he rejected entirely the greater good argument to explain evil.

At one point Lewis wonders about God's presence—or rather God's felt absence.

---

9. This quote and those that follow are from Lewis, *Problem of Pain*, 83.

> Meanwhile, where is God? This is one of the most disquieting symptoms. When you are happy, so happy that you have no sense of needing Him, so happy that you are tempted to feel His claims upon you as an interruption, if you remember yourself and turn to Him with gratitude and praise, you will be—or so it feels—welcomed with open arms.
>
> But go to Him when your need is desperate, when all other help is vain, and what do you find? A door slammed in your face, and a sound of bolting and double bolting on the inside. After that, silence.
>
> You may as well turn away. The longer you wait, the more emphatic the silence will become. There are no lights in the windows. It might be an empty house. Was it ever inhabited? It seemed so once. And that seeming was as strong as this.

Lewis concludes this line of thought with two questions. First, he asks simply: "What can this mean?" But then, alluding ironically to Psalm 46:1 (much as Job 7:17–18 may be an ironic comment on Ps 8:4 [Heb 8:5]), Lewis asks: "Why is He so present a commander in our time of prosperity and so very absent a help in time of trouble?"[10]

This is certainly far removed from any version of a greater good argument. So what happened between *The Problem of Pain* and *A Grief Observed*?

Lewis experienced the joy of marriage (having been a bachelor for over fifty years); shortly after, his new and beloved wife, Joy Davidman, was diagnosed with cancer. There was a time of remission; then the cancer returned, and she died three years after the original diagnosis.

When Explaining Suffering Is Unacceptable

It is one thing to articulate a theoretical position about suffering serving a greater good; it is quite another to still believe this when suffering (and death) hits someone you know and love.

This is vividly portrayed in the 1993 movie *Shadowlands*, which depicts the life of C. S. Lewis, especially his marriage to Joy Davidman; the movie draws on *A Grief Observed*.[11]

---

10. These quotes are from Lewis, *A Grief Observed*, 9.

11. The 1993 movie *Shadowlands* was a remake of the original 1985 made-for-TV movie and a 1989 play of the same name. Anthony Hopkins plays the character of Lewis; Debra Winger plays his wife.

There are three illuminating scenes (one right after another) that illustrate the shift that Lewis (known as Jack to his friends) went through after his wife died.

In the first scene, after Joy's funeral is over and Lewis is walking out of the church, the priest who just conducted the service says, "Thank God for your faith Jack; it's only faith makes any sense of times like these." Without uttering a word, Lewis's body language speaks volumes. He briefly glances at the priest and continues walking, with his jaw set, as if he simply can't countenance this attempt at comfort.

In the second scene, Lewis is at home, after the funeral, with his older brother, Warren (known as Warnie). After a time of silence, he muses: "So afraid of never seeing her again, thinking that suffering is just suffering after all—no cause, no purpose, no pattern." His brother answers: "I don't know what to tell you, Jack." To which Lewis responds: "There's nothing to say; I know that now. I've just come up against a bit of experience, Warnie. Experience is a brutal teacher, but you learn, by God you learn."

In the third scene, Lewis re-enters the social scene at Cambridge University. When asked by a sympathetic colleague, "Anything I can do?" he responds: "Just don't tell me it's all for the best, that's all."

The priest (Harry) who had conducted Joy's funeral is there and offers a pious comment: "Only God knows why these things have to happen." To which Lewis responds, getting to the crux of the matter: "God knows, but does God care?" The dialogue then comes fast and furious.

"Of course, we see so little here. We're not the creator," says Harry.

"No we're the creatures, aren't we," rejoins Lewis. "We're the rats in the cosmic laboratory." At this point Harry shakes his head, but Lewis won't be stopped. "Have no doubt the experiment is for our own good, but that still makes God the vivisectionist."

Harry tries to interject, "Jack . . . ." But Lewis responds by shouting, "NO! It won't do. It's a bloody awful mess and that's all there is to it."

The Honesty of the Psalms

Interestingly, what Lewis articulates in *A Grief Observed* (and what his movie character articulates in *Shadowlands*) against those who would "explain" evil is very similar to what many psalmists articulate in lament or complaint psalms, as well as the prophet Jeremiah in his anguished prayers (for example, in Jer 20:7–18), not to mention Job the sufferer throughout the book that bears his name.[12]

---

12. Whereas many commentators suggest that God shuts Job down for his audacious

Lament psalms, which make up over one-third of the Psalms (compared to hymns of praise, which are less than a quarter), are honest, abrasive prayers, which squarely face up to the dark side of human experience; and so they can provide for us guidance (a "protocol") for how to "host" and process disorientation.

I want to focus on two psalms here—Psalm 39 (a psalm of lament) and Psalm 30 (a thanksgiving psalm).[13]

I'm going to start with Psalm 30, the thanksgiving psalm. Although we use terms like thanksgiving, praise, and worship often interchangeably, the genre of thanksgiving psalms is somewhat different from the genre of hymns of praise in the Psalter. Hymns of praise describe what God typically does. Thus they praise God in more general ways for characteristic attributes or actions—usually in the present tense. Take, for example, Psalm 103:

> [2] Bless the LORD, O my soul,
>   and do not forget all his benefits—
> [3] who forgives all your iniquity,
>   who heals all your diseases,
> [4] who redeems your life from the Pit. (Ps 103:2–4a)

Another example is Psalm 117:

> [1] Praise the LORD, all you nations!
>   Extol him, all you peoples!
> [2] For great is his steadfast love toward us,
>   and the faithfulness of the LORD endures forever.
> Praise the LORD! (Ps 117:1–2)

Whereas hymns of praise (like Psalms 103 and 117) describe God's typical actions, a thanksgiving psalm tells a story in the past tense. It thus looks back on an event in which God did something wonderful for the psalmist.

Up from the Abyss—
A Story of Deliverance (Psalm 30)

Here is the text of Psalm 30, along with my schematic, interpretive outline.[14]

---

prayers that challenge divine justice, I have argued that God validates Job's lament. See Middleton, "Does God Come to Bury Job or to Praise Him?"

13. Here I need to thank Brian Walsh for an insightful Bible study he led on these two psalms, which sparked my interest in exploring them further.

14. All quotations from Psalm 30 here and later in this essay are NIV.

Thanksgiving for rescue: the story summarized (1–3)

¹ I will exalt you, Lord,
 for you lifted me out of the depths
 and did not let my enemies gloat over me.
² Lord my God, I called to you for help,
 and you healed me.
³ You, Lord, brought me up from the realm of the dead;
 you spared me from going down to the pit.

Invitation to the community to join in thanksgiving (4–5)

⁴ Sing the praises of the Lord, you his faithful people;
 praise his holy name.
⁵ For his anger lasts only a moment,
 but his favor lasts a lifetime;
weeping may stay for a night,
 but rejoicing comes in the morning.

The Story Expanded (6–12)

Orientation: security and presumption (6–7a)

⁶ When I felt secure, I said,
 "I will never be shaken."
⁷ Lord, when you favored me,
 you made my royal mountain stand firm;

Disorientation: crisis (7b)

but when you hid your face,
 I was dismayed.

Disorientation: lament (8–10)

⁸ To you Lord, I called;
 to the Lord I cried for mercy:
⁹ "What is gained if I am silenced,
 if I go down to the pit?
Will the dust praise you?
 Will it proclaim your faithfulness?
¹⁰ Hear, Lord, and be merciful to me;
 Lord, be my help."

New Orientation: transformation and renewal (11–12)

¹¹ You turned my wailing into dancing;
 you removed my sackcloth and clothed me with joy,
¹² that my heart may sing your praises and not be silent.
Lord my God, I will praise you forever.

Psalm 30 is a psalm of new orientation. The psalmist has experienced a renewal, an encounter with God, which has brought significant transformation in his life. That's why he praises God at the beginning of the psalm. I called on you, he says, and you healed me; you brought me up from the realm of the dead and you spared me from going down to the pit. Sounds like a contradiction, doesn't it? You brought me up; you spared me from going down. But this isn't literal description. This is poetry. The psalmist is bursting with gratitude. The point is: God rescued him. He doesn't say from what. It could be from sickness, from war, from persecution, from poverty—we don't know exactly what the problem was. He says God protected him from enemies, but doesn't expand on it.

The psalms are full of images like the grave, or Sheol, the pit, the miry ground, my enemies (also described as dogs or bulls), who have surrounded me. But they rarely get more specific than that. It is almost as if the psalmist (and the God who inspired these psalms) wants the language open and porous enough so that we (whoever we are) can read *our own* troubles through these prayers, so they can be serviceable for our encounters with God.

The story of a thanksgiving psalm usually has two parts—what went wrong in the psalmist's life (the disorientation) and how God intervened to bring healing or deliverance (the new orientation or renewal).

A lament psalm is really half of a thanksgiving psalm. A lament psalm is a prayer for help from the bottom of the pit; but a thanksgiving psalm is a prayer of gratitude offered once you're back on solid ground.

On Top of the World—Orientation

Psalm 30 is slightly different from most thanksgiving psalms in that it doesn't just tell the story of disorientation and the renewal that happened; but it goes back *before* the disorientation, to the prior orientation that got "dissed."

> ⁶ When I felt secure, I said,
>   "I will never be shaken."
> ⁷ Lord, when you favored me,
>   you made my royal mountain stand firm. (Ps 30:6–7b)

Those are words of assurance, and security, and confidence. And we all need orientation, a secure sense of place and direction in the world. C. S. Lewis had an orientation in *The Problem of Pain* (this allowed him to explain why we suffer).

Psalm 1 (a wisdom or *torah* psalm, a psalm that instructs us in how to live) is a classic example of a psalm of orientation, which is probably why it has been put at the beginning of the Psalter. Its message is very simple: Blessed are those who walk in the way of righteousness; they shall be secure and fruitful, like a tree planted by streams of water. But the wicked (and those who follow their path) are not so. They are unstable and transitory, like the chaff the wind blows away.

Nothing could be simpler. There are two moral or religious directions in life: good and evil. You follow one path, you are secure and blessed by God. You follow the other, and you don't last. That's the covenantal structure of life; that's the basic "orientation" of Scripture. That's kid's stuff! In the good sense of the term, that's Sunday-School faith. Every child (and every Christian) needs a clear-cut sense of what life is all about, a basic orientation that makes sense of things.

And, you know, it often *does* work that way. You work hard in school, and you often do get good grades, and even a scholarship, maybe a good job. You apply yourself on the job, and often you get a raise, and maybe a promotion (which, of course, you deserve).

You work hard at a relationship and it turns into a marriage. And you work hard at marriage, and it endures. And you put a lot of energy into your kids, and they turn out alright. You work hard at a church, you're as faithful as you can be, and you have church growth (numerical and spiritual) and church unity.

"Orientation" works. Sometimes.

And when it does, you feel on top of the world.

From Confidence to Dismay—Disorientation

But this psalmist's world came crashing down; or, to continue the psalmist's own metaphor, *he* came crashing down from the mountaintop.

His memory of God's favor (in verses 6 and 7) is pervaded by a profound sense of loss. The psalmist tells of the withdrawal of God's presence and the disorienting fall from the heights into the abyss. "But when you hid your face, / I was dismayed" (Ps 30:7b).

He gives no specific details, but it felt like God was gone. This is exactly what C. S. Lewis experienced in *A Grief Observed*.

Like the psalmist (and like Lewis), many in the church and in our society at large have *experienced* the absence of God and are consumed by a sense of betrayal, with neither hope for the future nor energy for significant living. Pain has overwhelmed joy. Although this pain is often caused by large family or personal crises, much of it is the result of the accumulated frustrations of a life which does not seem to work out as it is supposed to. And this certainly amounts, in the end, to a large crisis.

What are we supposed to *do* when the "orientation" doesn't work the way it's supposed to? What was C. S. Lewis supposed to do? Say: It's all for the best? God has a greater good that required this? Is *that* what we should tell victims of a terrorist bombing or a natural disaster?

We will come back to Psalm 30. But first we will turn to Psalm 39, an individual lament prayer, told from the bottom of the pit.

From Silence to Speech (Psalm 39)

Whereas Psalm 30 is instructive for us by going back before the disorientation to the prior orientation, Psalm 39 is also instructive for us, because the psalmist tells us the story of how he came to lament.[15]

The Difficulty of Honest Speech

> [1] I said, "I will watch my ways
>   and keep my tongue from sin;
> [2] I will put a muzzle on my mouth
>   while in the presence of the wicked." (Ps 39:1–2)

His first impulse is to silence. Voicing his pain honestly in public, and especially to God, would be inappropriate. This psalmist decides to keep quiet about his suffering and "muzzle" his mouth since "the wicked" were around (verse 1) and he wanted a good testimony. He says, in effect: I was taught that a truly spiritual person should speak only nice, edifying words. Presumably he did not want to display a lack of trust in the presence of unbelievers. So he said: My lips are sealed! Thank you, Jesus![16]

The Difficulty of Prolonged Silence

But the longer he kept quiet, the more agitated he became.

> [2] So I remained utterly silent,
>   not even saying anything good.

---

15. All quotations from Psalm 39 are NIV.

16. My thanks to Walter Brueggemann, who put the matter in this colorful way in his 1989 workshop on the Psalms.

> But my anguish increased;
> ³ my heart grew hot within me.
> While I meditated, the fire burned; (Ps 39:2–3a)

Like many in the church, this writer bottles up his pain until it grows into a raging fire within and he is ready to explode. Then he speaks (39:3b). But it doesn't come out all at once.

Testing the Waters

This is what he starts with:

> ⁴ Show me, LORD, my life's end
> and the number of my days;
> let me know how fleeting my life is.
> ⁵ You have made my days a mere handbreadth;
> the span of my years is as nothing before you.
> Everyone is but a breath,
> even those who seem secure.
> ⁶ Surely everyone goes around like a mere phantom;
> in vain they rush about, heaping up wealth
> without knowing whose it will finally be. (Ps 39:4–6)

Perhaps he's not sure what God can handle. So he tests the waters, musing in a general way about human mortality and asking a safe, disinterested question about how long he has to live (39:4-6): I've noticed that people die and I was wondering if you could (maybe) tell me how long I've got.

What Is Really at Stake

And God doesn't strike him down. So he gets bolder. From safe musings and disinterested inquiry, he moves to an honest admission of need. "But now, Lord, what do I look for?" (39:7a) Not how long I'm going to live. What do I *really* look for? What do I *really* hope for? "My hope is in *you*!" (39:7b) And he pleads for deliverance.

He addresses seven imperatives to God, telling God what to do:

- Save me (39:8a)
- Don't make me the scorn of fools (39:8b)
- Remove your scourge from me (39:10)
- Hear my prayer (39:12a)

- Listen to my cry (39:12b)
- Don't be deaf to my weeping (39:12c)
- Look away from me (39:13)

Why couldn't the psalmist have *started* with this? What held him back?

In his new-found honesty, he tells God why. "I was silent; I would not open my mouth, / for *you* are the one who has done this" (39:9). The problem is that his pain came from God; he perceived his suffering as *God's fault* and was, understandably, slow to voice this. But whereas Psalm 30 faults God for abandonment, Psalm 39 goes considerably further. "Remove your scourge from me; / I am overcome by the blow of your hand" (39:10). Now a "scourge" is a whip. So the psalmist says, in effect: Stop hitting me! I'm exhausted. This psalmist accuses God of violence against him and pleads for an end to the pain because he can't take it any more.

The Power of Honest Speech

Now, it certainly isn't "theologically correct" to accuse God of doing evil, as this psalmist has done. This is a statement made in extremity, out of desperation. But it is not unique in the Psalter. There are many psalms of lament that make similar statements. From Psalm 22, which Jesus prayed on the cross ("My God, my God, why have you forsaken me?"), to Psalm 88, which of all the psalms seems most bereft of hope ("I suffer your terrors; I am desperate"; Ps 88:15), we are bombarded with voices from the ragged edges of life that articulate pain honestly to God. These abrasive prayers all complain about suffering as intolerable and implore God for deliverance. Indeed, many lament psalms, along with portions of Jeremiah and Job, are prayers in which life is experienced as so raw and so fickle, where the pain and suffering are so massive, that the supplicant ultimately experiences *God* as fickle and dares to voice this in prayer.

I think we can learn from the honesty of the psalmists. For when the pain and disorientation are that great, we have only three options.

Bottle It Up

We can bottle it up inside, nursing it until we self-destruct and it explodes into violence and abuse against those around us, especially those most vulnerable. I believe that a great deal of spousal and child abuse is rooted in accumulated suffering which, instead of being articulated, is kept within, and has nowhere to go. And when we have nowhere to direct our pain except at those around us, we can't even perceive, much less begin to respond to, their suffering.

Denial

Or, we can piously deny the pain and maintain the theologically correct status quo. We can sing hymns of praise in church and say, "God is good—all the time," though we don't, in our bones, believe a word of it. And then we become numb to our pain, and numb to God. And we certainly become numb to the pain of others.

Lament

Or, following the lead of the psalmists, we can take our anger, our doubt—all the dismay and the terror of life—and we can put it at the feet of the Most High. We can bring our pain to the throne of God and say, "You're supposed to be faithful, but I don't see it! You're supposed to be good, but I don't experience it."

And, contrary to appearances, that desperate, honest voicing of pain to God is not blasphemous, but is a holy, redemptive act. Prayers of lament are radical acts of faith and hope, because they *refuse*, even in the midst of suffering, to give up on God.

Notice how desperate—even childish and regressive—the speech of the psalmist becomes in Psalm 30:

> What is gained if I am silenced,
>   if I go down to the pit?
> Will the dust praise you?
>   Will it proclaim your faithfulness? (30:9)

Here the psalmist mounts an argument for why God should save him. I'm going down for the count, he says. I'm about ready to die, and they don't praise you in the grave. Don't you want me to praise you? Then save me quickly!

This childish, desperate outburst is actually a radical confession of faith; the psalmist, even in his desperation, knows that help lies in God alone. None other can deliver.

That is why Psalm 39 is peppered with imperatives, commands address to God. You have to be desperate to address imperatives to the Creator, to tell God what to do. But that is the inherent boldness of supplication or petitionary prayer. And lament is supplication with an edge.

The fact is that silence will not get us through the pain. Only speech addressed to God gets us through—speech that summons God into our suffering, which says to God, as the writer of Psalm 30 did, "Hear, Lord, and be merciful to me; / Lord, be my help" (30:10). Or, even as the writer of Psalm 39 did in his impropriety, "Look away from me, that I may enjoy life again" (39:13). It doesn't have to be theologically correct speech. But it has to be gut-honest speech.

The Biblical Story as Paradigm

When we have the audacity to lay our pain at God's feet, to summon the Most High into our suffering, something remarkable happens. God comes.

The Exodus

Lament psalms have their roots, ultimately, in the exodus, the central and founding event of the Old Testament, when Yahweh delivered the Israelites from Egyptian bondage. Central to the story as it is told in the Bible is the Israelites' primal scream of pain to God. Between centuries of accumulated suffering and God's decisive intervention, we find this remarkable statement:

> The Israelites groaned in their slavery, and cried out. Out of the slavery their cry for help rose up to God. God heard their groaning, and God remembered his covenant with Abraham, Isaac, and Jacob. God looked on the Israelites, and God took notice of them. (Exod 2:23b–25)

This agonized cry of pain at the heart of the exodus echoes resoundingly throughout the psalms of lament. Lament is redemptive, therefore, not simply because the supplicant clings to God in desperate faith; that is certainly significant. But, more fundamentally, lament is rooted in the very pattern of the biblical story, at the hinge—even the fulcrum—between bondage and deliverance. This is true both in the Old Testament and in the New.

Jesus

Jesus, in the garden of Gethsemane, as he faced his time of disorientation, cried out in sorrow, sweating blood (Luke 22:44), and pleaded with his

Father to "remove this cup from me" (Luke 22:42). And on the cross, in the midst of his disorientation and agony, he cried out in agony, quoting Psalm 22, "My God, my God, why have you forsaken me?" (Matt 27:46; Mark 15:34)

The disorientation of the death of Jesus was so massive, says the New Testament, that when he died the earth shook (Matt 27:51); creation itself reeled in a kind of cosmic sympathy with the Son of God. And Jesus was plunged into the abyss of disorientation, even death. He was crucified, dead, buried, says the Apostles Creed; he descended into hell, into Hades, into Sheol, into the pit. But his cry, even of abandonment, went up to God. And three days after his disorientation and his agonized cry, God answered his cry, and raised him from the dead.

All Creation

But more than this, the cross itself was God's response to the lament of all creation. For creation itself, says Paul in Romans 8, is groaning in its bondage to corruption, subject to futility, and yearning eagerly for redemption (Rom 8:19–22). And we ourselves groan inwardly, says the apostle (Rom 8:23). I submit that our articulation of these groanings into prayer, even ragged prayers on the boundary of propriety, has the potential to unleash the power of the resurrection, leading to new creation.

But we have to cry out. What unites these three pivotal events is the pattern of calling on God. The watchword of lament prayer could well be the words of Joel 2:32 (quoted by Peter on the day of Pentecost in Acts 2:21, and by Paul in Rom 10:13): "Everyone who calls on the name of the LORD shall be saved."[17] But we have to *call out* to God.

The Psalms as Models for Processing Pain

In conclusion, I want to suggest that silence about pain in our society and in the church conveys the message that God simply doesn't care about suffering. Too many Christians have had to suppress their pain to sing glib hymns of praise and thanksgiving, when what was really needed was closer to a primal scream of rage. And hurting visitors are effectively excluded from participation in worship by invocations that enjoin the congregation to put aside their problems and come and worship God.

---

17. Joel 2:32 in English Bibles is equivalent to Joel 3:5 in the Hebrew Masoretic Text.

But if the church took seriously the psalms of lament as model modes of speech (an alternative "protocol") in its communal life and processed the pain of its members in liturgy and public worship, it would convey the quite radical message that our suffering matters to God. Indeed, it matters so much that he bore it in his own body on the tree.

And if our suffering matters to God, then we might begin to believe—and feel—that the suffering of others matters too. Voicing our pain to God might then be redemptive not only for ourselves, but ultimately for the world. As the hinge or fulcrum, which unleashes the power of the resurrection, lament has the potential to generate genuine thanksgiving for the grace of God, thus energizing the church in its vocation in a suffering world.

Bibliography

Brueggemann, Walter. *The Message of the Psalms: A Theological Commentary*. Minneapolis: Augsburg, 1984.

———. Psalms Workshop. St. Andrews Presbyterian Church, Kitchener, ON, April 1, 1989.

Goldman, William. *The Princess Bride: S. Morgenstern's Classic Tale of True Love and High Adventure*. New York: Harcourt Brace, 1973.

Heard, Mark. "These Plastic Halos." *Eye of the Storm*. Bug 'n Bear Music, 1983.

Lewis, C. S. *A Grief Observed*. Greenwich, CT: Seabury, 1963 [orig. Faber & Faber, 1961].

———. *The Problem of Pain*. New York: Macmillian, 1947 [orig. The Centenary Press, 1940].

Middleton, J. Richard. "Does God Come to Bury Job or to Praise Him? The Significance of Yhwh's Second Speech from the Whirlwind." *St. Mark's Review* 239 (March 2017) 1–27.

———. "Voices from the Ragged Edge: How the Psalms Can Help Us Process Pain." *Canadian Theological Society Newsletter/Communiqué de la société théologique canadienne* 14.1 (November 1994) 4–7.

———. "Voices from the Ragged Edge: How the Psalms Can Help Us Process Pain." *Perspective* 29.1 (March 1995) 4–5.

———. "Why the 'Greater Good' Isn't a Defense: Classical Theodicy in Light of the Biblical Genre of Lament." *Koinonia* 9.1&2 (1997) 81–113.

Middleton, J. Richard, and Brian J. Walsh. *Truth Is Stranger than It Used to Be: Biblical Faith in a Postmodern Age*. Downers Grove, IL: IVP Academic, 1995.

The Princess Bride. Directed by Rob Reiner. Screenplay by William Goldman. Twentieth-Century Fox, 1987.

Shadowlands. Directed by Richard Attenborough. Screenplay by William Nicholson. Savoy Pictures, 1993.

9

Iris and Nereus Here and Now

Greg Paul

A short time ago I arrived at Sanctuary on a Monday morning to hear that Dana, a member of our community in the early days and for a long time after, had died. He was forty-nine, which meant I'd first gotten to know him when he was in his early twenties. Dana was a genuine street tough guy; he'd been incarcerated for the first time at nine years of age for stealing a car. Mom looked after him, though, smuggling dope to him while he was inside. He was homeless through all of the decade and a half that I'd been close to him, addicted to crack and then shifting to booze—mostly Listerine—fighting a lot, in and out of jail. I had more than a few go-rounds with him myself, back in the day, but a strange sort of friendship survived all that.

He seemed to have been doing better when he died. He'd been housed for a few years (our own Greg Cook moved him in); he'd reconnected with his baby's mother, and despite the abusive character of their earlier relationship, they apparently went out to dinner and a movie now and then. He knew and visited his daughter with some regularity. So, it was sadder than usual to hear that he'd died alone in his room, of "natural causes," and his body had not been found for two or three weeks. That always seems especially tragic to me: to have a place with a door on it and a bed in it, but nobody close enough to know when you've died, let alone be there as you're leaving.

Dana's was one of two community voices that defined Sanctuary as a church back when the rest of us were trying to figure out just what we were. A group of mostly middle-class church people like me along with a sprinkling of street folks sat around in a circle debating whether or not we should meet weekly for communion, prayer, teaching, and so on. Someone used the word "congregation," perhaps sardonically, to describe our little group. Dana, sitting there with his arms crossed (tattooed to the knuckles; not tasteful sleeves, but the smudgy blue-green prison-tat variety), leaned forward and spat, "Congregation! This ain't a congregation . . . This is a family."

I thought it took a substantial amount of grace for him to embrace a bunch of wealthy do-gooders as brothers and sisters.

The other foundational voice belonged to Richard, also now gone, "If we don't do this [he meant meet weekly for worship], we'll die." He didn't mean the group would wither and fall apart. He meant that he and Dana would soon be found dead in an alley nearby.

I don't remember a word any of the middle-class church folk spoke, but I'll never forget those prophetic utterances of Dana and Richard. With two pithy phrases, they revealed to us who we were, and what we were called to be: home to a diverse and dysfunctional family whose only hope for real life was to be found in rooting that life in relationship with the One who made us. In Brian's turn of phrase, we've been "home-making" ever since.

You'll understand, then, when I say that the news of Dana's death hit me hard. There have been too many griefs among my people for me to process properly, and the weight of sorrow inadequately expressed has in recent years grown, at times, to crushing proportions. Every new death triggers painful memories of those who have passed before.

A couple of hours later that same morning, I met with another friend from the community who is suffering with cancer. We had hardly sat down in the café when he said, "You know I'm not going to last long," and began to weep. Well, so did I.

"How am I supposed to do this?" he asked.

"I don't know," I answered. "I've never done it before."

He laughed. And then he began to recount, not his woes, but his gratitude for the family he's found in our community. He talked about specific people, wondering why they cared for him so much, and about the sense of deep belonging he has in the community as a whole.

"They love you," I said. "That's why they're sitting with you in the hospital at three in the morning. It isn't because of the job. They love you, and you love them, and they know that."

So we talked about that, too, how loving and being loved changes you.

"If I'd had people like you in my life when I was young, I never would have ended up here," he said. "But I wouldn't have met you guys later on, either!" He laughed again, pleased by the conundrum.

We laughed and cried and sipped coffee.

By the time I left for home at day's end, I was exhausted. On the subway, in an effort to distract myself from the endless list of names of my departed brothers and sisters and the awful circumstances of their demises swirling around in my mind, I hauled out my phone and began on a whim to read *Romans Disarmed* again, from the beginning. I honestly hadn't thought about how it starts and what I'd find there; in my distracted state, it was a surprise. It was almost like reading it for the first time, and it did me in in much the same fashion.

Those observations in the first chapter about the interdependence of grief and joy that night, lament and celebration, and the way Frenchy led us through them, provided exactly the unflinching excision of the wound I needed, along with a reminder of why it is all so precious. As I snuffled my way homeward, I found a measure of release, healing, and much-needed perspective. Iggy's death is at the center of that tale, of course, and reflecting on it sent me off in another direction.

I was at a retreat center on a little lake in Australia's Snowy Mountains when he left us. It had felt impossible to get on a plane when I knew he'd die before I got back home again; it was soul-wrenching to wake up that morning and read the news half an hour before I was supposed to speak to a conference of Salvation Army officers. I wept. I questioned what on earth I was doing at a time like this half a world away from the people I loved most. I was angry and resentful and bitterly sad. But also, I read in that email what you later observed in your book: Iggy passed away in a hospital room absolutely jammed with people who loved him. One of whom was you.

There's no rational explanation of what I'm about to say, which is perhaps why I've never said it to anyone else before. Somehow, knowing that Brian was there made it a little easier for me that morning, and also when I reflected on it later. While he was clearly present because of the depth of his own relationship with Iggy, in some strange fashion it felt to me as if he was also there by proxy for me. I don't know why—maybe it has something to do with both of us being the geezers in our respective tribes. Nevertheless, it was oddly comforting.

I'd apologize for this shaggy dog tale, but really, it's a microcosm of the story of Brian's relationship with the Sanctuary community—a long, winding yarn full of obscure connections and moments of brilliant clarity. I've seen the list of other contributors to this *festschrift* and we both know I don't have those kinds of academic theological chops. What little theology I have is of the lunch-bucket praxis sort; it's been tested and articulated to me mostly by people like Dana, Richard, Frenchy, Angela, and Iggy. Fortunately, I know that Brian knows that it's relationships like those that put the boots on the gospel. He's honored such wrestling and wandering in me and others in a way that is tremendously encouraging.

In the end, it really is all about home, isn't it? Brian and his partners have been writing about it for decades. We've been trying to live it day by day here at Sanctuary for almost thirty years. In other words, all this time he's been explaining to us what it is that we're trying to do, and challenging us to go farther. To build a bigger house, a longer table, to cook and share together a richer, more nourishing meal. To cultivate a farther field, to think more deeply and act more decisively to respect and protect the wilderness that surrounds and sustains us. To resist the temptation to flee from lament too quickly. To live daily the redemption that is yet to come in its fullness; to do so remembering that "trailing clouds of glory do we come / From God who is our home."[1]

Brian's had a profound effect on me personally; if theology is, in part, the house we build so our minds can have a home in this world, what he's done is constructed more than a few walls in my dwelling place. I've treasured those times when, as two people who have been battered by life for a couple of decades longer than most of the people we hang with, we've been able to care for each other in an intimate, pastoral way. No wonder there is a bond between us. But I'm so thankful that it's been more than just personal. I can't think of anyone who isn't a daily inhabitant of our community who has done more to shape it. And I do mean "who has done," not just "who has written."

In general, academia seems almost to have barricaded itself off from the real world and, especially in the "developed" world, from the daily realities of living kingdom justice. I don't know anybody else who has so determinedly and graciously pierced those walls, and pierced them again and again, and created a widening, increasingly well-traveled path between the two. Wine Before Breakfast and the community about it that has grown like a pearl around a grain of sand has not only been such a source of sustenance and hope, respite and challenge, for staff and other anchoring members of our community—it has, in truth, been a home. We all need more than one, don't we? Any healthy soul finds perhaps several homes, some distinct and others overlapping. A farmhouse, a college building, an old downtown church. These of course are only the physical walls and boundaries within which the life of the home has its being, and that life is found in the lives within. I speak selfishly but gratefully when I say that the life my younger Sanctuary staff colleagues and other anchoring members of our community have found in that office and the Wycliffe chapel has held, nourished, and even healed them; in some ways, they've grown up there. The academic environment (if you'll forgive me for using such a constrained term to describe the sub-world Brian's created at Wycliffe) is so different than ours that it has provided them with new fields to explore

---

1. Wordsworth, "Intimations," ll. 65–66.

and revealed to them that yes, they can thrive beyond our own somewhat pungent ecosystem, as well as providing them with enough distance to better appreciate what we have at Sanctuary.

It's also hard to overstate what it has meant for people like Iggy, Chris, and others from our core community. Through Brian and his crowd, they've been given an inkling of the breadth and vitality and joyful graciousness of the true church, and a little foretaste of the kingdom where the meek (the sat-upon, spat-upon, shat-upon) are no longer shoved to the perimeter, but are free to roam throughout God's good earth. They've been delighted to find themselves among bright, beautiful young people of privilege and realize they can be at home there. Imagine their delight at the Consummation of All Things when they find themselves at the center and realize it's up to them to welcome in the marginal people like you and me!

That's an image that holds within it a balm for my own traumas these many years, having witnessed so many of my brothers and sisters die young and in tragic, often horrific circumstances. Walking alongside them in the midst of lives wrecked by layers of oppression has been beautiful—enough so that I never want to leave it—but also difficult spiritually, morally, materially, philosophically . . . well, it's just not been easy. Again, *Romans Disarmed* especially (but also *Colossians Remixed* and *Beyond Homelessness*) give me language, ideas, a paradigm that helps me decode our world. Iris and Nereus may be constructs to help with historical fidelity, but they're my people here and now. The clarity of the picture drawn of the reality of first century church life reminds me that our struggles and sorrows are not new, nor are they in the historical or global context unusual—and it's for this Jesus came, lived, taught, suffered, died, and rose again.

As I write this, just days after hearing about Dana, we're reeling from the news of Dallas's death by overdose. (Emperor Doug Ford, the first of his name, has just de-funded more overdose prevention sites.) Two more are in hospital; one may survive, the other will pass in a matter of months if not sooner. Iggy, Dana, Dallas, and dozens upon dozens more now populate for me what has become a great and growing cloud of witnesses; when I wake in the night, one or another often looms out of that cloud and I feel their own present *shalom*, their blessing on me, their encouragement to keep running the race. What a privilege as priests of the Most High God to have had a hand in establishing a couple of little cities of refuge for the likes of them—the ones who have been hunted mercilessly throughout the land by the avenger of blood. They'll be waiting for us one day, brother, and as priests they'll welcome us refugees home. There are times I can hardly express how eager I am to get there.

City of Refuge[2]

There's a city 'cross the river
and it's shining from within
People are dancing on the ramparts,
beckoning to you to come on in
To the city of refuge

You better run, you better hide
Stay low on the saddle as you ride
There's one more river you got to cross
Got to bear the weight of what you've lost
That river is hungry, jealous as the grave
Got to let go of the things you want to save
but there's a city 'cross the river . . .

I love the dark, I love the night
I feel so naked when the sun is shining bright
I wash my hands, can't get them clean
My mind replays every sordid scene
That river wails a mournful tune
A song as cold and lonely as the moon
but there's a city 'cross the river . . .

Now saddle up, it's time to go
I love you more than you could ever know
I'm by your side—no, you're not lost
Every man got to carry his own cross
So pick it up, let go your pride
I swear I'll meet you on the other side
'cause there's a city across the river . . .

Bibliography

Red Rain. "City of Refuge." Track 3 on *A Night at Grace's*. Self-published, 2006, Compact Disc.
Wordsworth, William. "Ode: Intimations of Immortality." In *The Norton Anthology of English Literature,* edited by Meyer Howard Abrams, 2:175–80. 3rd ed. New York: Norton, 1974.

---

2. Red Rain, "City of Refuge." Used with permission.

10

Hospitality as Hermeneutic and Way of Life

Rachel Tulloch

When I was married in 2010, Sylvia and Brian gifted us a beautiful handmade pottery bowl. It is quite broad, much too large for our family to use on our own. "Because a home is for hospitality," they wrote on the gift tag. For me, this sums up the ethos and the politics of Brian's extended reflections on homemaking in his writing and in his teaching. Home as fleshed out in the biblical narratives is not cozy and insular like the modern nuclear family. Rather, home is a guiding metaphor for enduring covenantal relationships, the building of a life-in-common rooted in memory and oriented toward a shared hopeful future. Thus homemaking is an ongoing vocation that involves attentiveness to the places in which we dwell and all of the creatures we share these places with. It also requires an openness to others, even strangers, who call us to continually extend the boundaries of our care and concern and who contribute to the homemaking process through the gifts and challenges they bring. Hospitality is not just one function of home; it is constitutive of home.

What stands out to me about Brian's academic career is how difficult it would be to talk about Brian's work without talking about his life. Brian's thought is rooted in the material engagements of his life as a pastor, teacher, husband, father, farmer, advocate, participant and supporter of community initiatives. These engagements are not supplements to his academic work; rather they are what make sense of it. For Brian, abstract and disengaged theology is self-contradictory. One can never do theology well without being rooted in both place and practice or without considering the embodied implications of one's thought. Theology done from a posture of engagement does not eschew reason or abstract thinking (indeed, thought is impossible without employing categories and some degree of abstraction), but it refuses to let theological reflection linger in those airy spaces without coming down again and again into the earthiness of daily embodied life. If the Word became flesh and dwelt among us, making home, tabernacling, this ought to be the paradigmatic movement for our thinking and living as Christians, followers of this way.

And for this Word-made-flesh, this first century rabbi and his odd band of followers, homemaking does not resemble the exclusionary white picket fences of the American dream nor the shiny condos emblematic of urban Canada's faux self-identity of diversity and progressiveness. Homemaking is, rather, a courageous enterprise. It is a shared vocation which includes in its very nature the imperative persistently taught and modeled by Jesus of Nazareth to continuously stretch the boundaries of our natural impulses in order to welcome those who are different and who challenge our given or preferred identities and affinities. Again, hospitality is not a voluntary addition to the core vocation of biblical homemaking but is essential to what homemaking means. Hence the importance of "the stranger" in the Bible's moral imagination.

In the apocalyptic scene of the judgment of the sheep and the goats in Matthew 25, Jesus famously identifies himself with the stranger in need of welcome, making the welcome of the stranger one of the main criteria dividing the faithful sheep from the unfaithful goats: "I was a stranger and you welcomed me" (25:35).[1] In what follows, I speak of "the stranger" not as a label intended to objectify anyone or to romanticize poverty and marginalization. Rather, the stranger is a figure of disruption, more a role rather than an identity. Strangers are not just recipients of hospitality or donation but are bringers of gifts both welcome and uncomfortable. They are crucial for the ongoing shared project of life together.

What these gifts are cannot be anticipated nor their scope determined in advance. In contrast to friends or family members, with whom we largely know what we are getting when we show hospitality, strangers are strangers to the extent that we do not know what they bring with them. Their world, knowledge, experiences, and expectations are unknown to us. Therefore, welcoming strangers is risky by its very nature, and the gifts the stranger brings are not always easy to receive. Thomas Ogletree notes that in order to receive these gifts, those who are at home must be willing to have their place of comfort and security unsettled by someone else's world. The giving and receiving of stories and the consequent sharing of "worlds"

---

1. All scripture citations are from the NRSV.

is one of the concrete ways in which this exchange happens and in which some of the power imbalances inherent in the exercise of hospitality are thrown out of joint:

> Concrete interactions invariably have asymmetrical elements. When the stranger stands before me in his vulnerability, there is at least an inequality of power in our relationship. He has need of my recognition and service; I have at my disposal support systems which already suffice for my needs. I am "at home" in my world; he is in an unfamiliar place and does not know what to expect. However, when the stranger begins to tell her stories, a new kind of asymmetry appears. With regard to the world of meaning which she is uncovering, she enjoys a level of authority that wholly surpasses my own. I am the novice, she the expert. I can only sit at her feet to learn.... My readiness to welcome the other into my world must be balanced by my readiness to enter the world of the other.... What do my stories say when they are told in a strange household?... In short, the ramifications of hospitality are not fully manifest unless I also know the meaning of being a stranger.[2]

For Brian, home and hospitality are at once hermeneutical and practical. Indeed, both are required. As hermeneutic, Brian's use of the categories "home, homelessness, and homecoming"[3] to frame the biblical narrative endows the meaning of home with cosmic dimensions, widening it far beyond its usual reference to include all of creation in the scope of its vision of life together. And since hospitality is constitutive of home, this cosmic home-making can never be a homogenizing erasure of difference, a projection of the ideal modern home onto the whole world. Since narrative and tradition are integral to humankind's way of seeking to make ourselves at home in the world, hospitality describes a posture of reflective engagement with one's traditions, texts, and guiding narratives in light of the presence of difference or otherness, what is outside or left unaccounted for in one's current framework. It calls for attentiveness, grace, receptivity, and transformation.

Furthermore, there is no truthful use of this hermeneutic which does not issue forth in hospitable ethical and political practices. Hospitality is not just a way of thinking but a way of life. In *Beyond Homelessness*, Brian and Steven Bouma-Prediger write that "Christian sojourners are, first of all, people of the Book, who, second, love one another, and, third, entertain angels: these three characteristics can be summarized as memory, community,

---

2. Ogletree, *Hospitality to the Stranger*, 3–4.
3. See, for instance, Bouma-Prediger and Walsh, *Beyond Homelessness*, 14–15.

and hospitality."⁴ The idea of sojourning as they develop it in the book weaves together concepts more commonly associated with dwelling—care and attentiveness to place—with concepts more commonly associated with journeying—non-possessiveness and an orientation towards a longed-for future. The church as a sojourning community must embody both the dwelling and the journeying since it is a people who are in a very real sense both in exile and at home. This is fleshed out in the three characteristics of the sojourning community named by Bouma-Prediger and Walsh: *memory, community,* and *hospitality.* Memory and community are essential aspects of homemaking, ways of making a home in the world through the formation of habits, shared understandings, and practices. They foster a sense of belonging and identity. However, they can easily become exclusionary. That is why hospitality is not only an essential third characteristic of a sojourning people, but it changes the very nature of what the memory and community of this people looks like. This memory and this community are formed in the context of ongoing encounters with the stranger and they look very different as a result. Rather than a homogenous community forming a primarily stable identity, the habits of a hospitable community are subject to disruption by the unknown, unexpected, or previously excluded.

The Gifts of the Stranger: Habits and Disruption at Sanctuary

> Old and New Testament stories not only show how serious our obligation is to welcome the stranger into our home, but they also tell us that guests are carrying precious gifts with them, which they are eager to reveal to a receptive host. . . . Thus the biblical stories help us to realize not just that hospitality is an important virtue, but even more that in the context of hospitality guest and host can reveal their most precious gifts and bring new life to each other.⁵
>
> —Henri Nouwen

Brian has been one of the main influences and supports for my commitment to do theological reflection out of a community of praxis. In Natalie

---

4. Bouma-Prediger and Walsh, *Beyond Homelessness,* 297.
5. Nouwen, *Reaching Out,* 66–67.

Wigg-Stevenson's words, "rather than reflecting *on* Christian community or *on* Christian practice," since my earliest days as a member of Sanctuary and as a student of Brian's, I have felt called to do "theological reflection *in* Christian community and *as* Christian practice."[6] I have been a member of the Sanctuary community since 2003 when I first moved to Toronto to study theology. Sanctuary is an eccentric church in downtown Toronto whose shape is determined by its stated intention to have people who are marginalized by society at the center of its life and worship practices. This is motivated by a theological imagination in which the poor and excluded are, in fact, central to the gospel, and their location in the world is a sign of where God has chosen to be present in a definitive way. The community includes people from a diversity of backgrounds and levels of societal power and privilege, but with the stated priority that those who are "poor and excluded" are "particularly valued."[7] In addition to lively and participatory worship together on Sunday evenings, "church" at Sanctuary is about a diverse community of people from both poverty and privilege eating together, making art, playing games, grieving sadness and loss together, accompanying each other through struggles, offering each other practical help, and advocating for each other within the systems of power that threaten the city's most vulnerable people.

Because Sanctuary is a community made up of many people who have rarely if ever known a secure sense of home and also other people whose lives have been primarily settled and safe, it is a good example of a sojourning community. Sojourning is a way of life somewhere between being settled permanently and wandering aimlessly. Many of us come from settled places and have been unsettled by new friendships forged with people whose lives are so different from our own. Others come from very unsettled places of wandering and homelessness and find themselves drawn toward a place of more safety and permanence. In between the settled and the unsettled is the space of sojourning, which we now inhabit together. This is where we can meet and walk together and be changed by each other as our lives intersect in various ways.

In what follows, I want to reflect on how hospitality as a defining feature of a church community affects its liturgical habits. Disruption is one of the more distinctive features of Sanctuary's worship, and while I do not wish to suggest that all churches must tolerate the level of disruption in their communal worship that Sanctuary does, I want to consider this feature of Sanctuary's worship as analogically related to the relationship between,

---

6. Wigg-Stevenson, *Ethnographic Theology*, 82.

7. Sanctuary's statement of identity reads, "We are becoming a healthy and welcoming community where people who are poor and excluded are particularly valued. This community is an expression of the good news embodied in Jesus Christ."

or perhaps the tension between, habits and disruption in the moral formation of the church. Learning to receive the gifts of disruption is crucial for the church if its habits and practices are to be receptive and vulnerable, subject to challenge, critique and reform, and open to the arrival of unanticipated gifts. At Sanctuary, this disruption happens in very visible ways during the communal worship. I want to suggest that it has become, mostly unconsciously, a liturgical performance of the practice of "welcoming the stranger," and that it trains the community in the skills of humility and receptivity which enable it to receive the gift of disruption that the stranger often brings. By stranger, I do not necessarily mean someone unfamiliar, since many of the disruptors at Sanctuary are known and loved within the community. The stranger in this sense is one who brings something unexpected, often uncomfortable, into the realm of the habitual, the predictable, the settled and secure. Emmanuel Katongole and Chris Rice illustrate this point in their discussion of the Gospels' story of the woman who interrupts a meal to anoint Jesus' feet and thereby,

> confirms that the church is an interrupted gathering of a beloved community. The dinner party is interrupted by the unwelcome presence of a stranger. In fact, it is through this interruption that the beloved community is called to see more clearly that we are not a lifestyle enclave. The community of Jesus is not a spiritual gated community or a ghetto of moral righteousness. Instead the stranger constantly interrupts our life. Hospitality, openness and an ongoing engagement with the stranger are hallmarks of our life together.[8]

At Sanctuary, both communion and preaching are regularly disrupted, often in small ways, but sometimes quite dramatically. The following three stories are events I have witnessed over my time worshipping on Sundays at Sanctuary, which provide a sense of how unusual the type of "liturgical" disruptions experienced at Sanctuary are in the life of the wider church and also how they force this particular community to adjust its habits, to create new ones, and sometimes to take itself less seriously.[9]

1. Nancy—One Sunday evening, during the teaching of the scriptures, a commotion was heard in the stairwell leading from the front door up into the worship space. A young woman suddenly burst into the room and headed for the preacher, running into his arms for protection. Her angry partner, a young man who was also part of the community

---

8. Katongole and Rice, *Reconciling All Things*, 116.
9. Pseudonyms used.

but whose violence made his presence at community events difficult, followed her as far as the entrance of the room, shouting threats and waving his fist in the air from the doorway. The sermon was abruptly ended for the week as the preacher and other community members responded to shield Nancy, escort her partner out, make a plan for her further safety, and debrief with the rest of the congregation who were somewhat shaken by the event.

2. Brandon—Another Sunday evening before the communion, a street-involved man whom I had known from early on in my time at Sanctuary as a prankster, agitator, and brilliant poet stumbled into the center of the room. His face was painted white, layered with the garish makeup of Christopher Nolan's version of the Batman villain "Joker." He shouted, "I am a social outcast! I will never fit in this place! God might as well just beat me up!" He then alternated between laughing loudly and falling on the floor shaking violently and begging for an exorcism. Another young street-involved woman who had entered with him knelt over him, weeping and praying earnestly for his healing and salvation. Gradually, a couple of the worshippers who knew both of them well managed to slowly walk them to the edge of the worship space so that the communion time could proceed.

3. Jason—The third instance involves a long-time community member who had undergone an unusual amount of trauma and loss over the previous few years, even by the standards of this suffering-filled community. As I entered the room one Sunday, he was sitting just inside the entrance, weeping. I hugged him, and he kissed my cheek and ruffled my three-year-old son's hair. However, he became increasingly more agitated as the worship proceeded. During one of the songs, he jumped out of his chair and stumbled toward the communion table. Shouting indecipherably through his tears, he raised the glass goblet of wine, drank it all, and smashed the empty goblet on the table, sending shards of glass into the communion bread and into the flesh of his own hand. Two people cleaned up the table and the shards of glass and went out to retrieve more bread and wine. Someone else followed the man outside, where he could be heard yelling and banging throughout the rest of the communion time.

The nature of each of these incidents is quite different. The first involves a woman running to the safest place she knows for protection and care. The second is a kind of performance art, which the man continued to practice at the Sanctuary worship service for years before his violent and untimely death. The third is an eruption of anger and anguish directed against the symbols of hope and communion which form the symbolic center of the community. However, each of these stories indicates just how disrupting to the conventional habits of liturgy it can be to take the presence of people who are poor and marginalized seriously in worship. Each of these events can also be interpreted theologically as performing something which goes beyond the intentions and awareness of the particular actors involved.

1) The first was a performance of the church as a literal "sanctuary," a place of safety and refuge. This is a role the community takes quite seriously, and one of the favorite songs during Sunday worship for many years is called "City of Refuge." The lyrics of the chorus are as follows:

> There's a city 'cross the river
> And it's shining from within
> People are dancin' on the ramparts
> Beckoning to you—come on in
> It's a city of refuge[10]

This reflects a deeply biblical imagination of the church as sanctuary. It is an imagination formed by the hindsight of the Old Testament tradition whereby certain cities were designated for accused murderers to seek asylum from blood vengeance.[11] It is also formed by the foresight of the eschatological city of Jerusalem, where God has promised to forever dwell among people, wiping the tears from their eyes and making death, mourning, crying, and pain a distant memory.[12] In the interim, the church rightly seeks to become a place of refuge itself. It does not promise immunity to violence, since when it is at its most faithful, the church often attracts such violence against itself; and when it is unfaithful, the church is often complicit with or itself becomes the perpetrator of violence. Nonetheless, communal practices of care for and attentiveness to those who are victimized and excluded provide the backdrop against which the first scene I described becomes intelligible. The woman's interruption of the sermon and clinging to the preacher was predicated on prior relationships of nurture and care, in which she had developed at least some level of trust with the community and with the preacher in particular. Therefore, this event represents the ordinary politics of Sanctuary, even as it disrupts the liturgical habit of the preaching of the word.

---

10. Red Rain, "City of Refuge." Used with permission.
11. See Exod 21:12–14; Num 35:1–34; Deut 19:1–13; Josh 20:1–9.
12. See Rev 21:3–4.

2) The second event was more self-consciously a performance or even an antic, and the man who dressed as the Joker on this occasion was one of the church's more frequent liturgical disruptors, who delighted in the shock-value of his actions. How does this type of behavior feature in a discussion of the *gifts* of the stranger? His behaviors were not habits encouraged by the community as they could be overly distracting or attention-seeking. He was regularly walked outside for the remainder of the worship time. But he always came back. He was loyal and loving, fond of giving giant bear hugs and composing poetry on the spot. He told the truth in his own way, and his formation into the kind of person who felt compelled to do so occurred through the hard knocks of life. This formation did not produce what is typically recognized as virtuous character, but it did produce a character whose whole life was a form of protest art, who could speak jarring truths that forced people out of their comfort zones. His irreverence challenged the church's right to take itself seriously given the brutal realities of those who have suffered on the underside of its power (like the Indigenous peoples of North America of which he was a part). And yet, there was a clear sense of loyalty even within this irreverence. He felt that he had a claim to this particular place or perhaps that it had a claim on him, this table of bread and wine and the rag-tag worshippers that gathered around it. His pain and protest belonged here somehow more than anywhere else. Since his tragic death, worship runs more smoothly but his presence is deeply missed.

3) The final instance described was especially difficult for many in the gathering because of their own deep reverence for the communion table; however, this event too performed something at the heart of the gospel, something true to the tearing of flesh and spilling of blood enacted weekly at the table. Presumably, Jason did not intend to do anything theological. As a friend commented to me after, the event was like a fight at the family dinner table, an outburst of anger and anguish directed against what is central and valued by the gathered loved ones. And indeed, the communion table at Sanctuary is like a family dinner table in many ways. It is at the center of the room literally and symbolically. It is the point of gathering and the focus of attention. It is the place where people bring their gratitude, their memories, their hopes, and their pain. However, since this particular table is also the place where God has promised to be available in a particular embodied way, these personal offerings are taken up into the larger story of God's redeeming and reconciling love and forgiveness enacted on the cross. In the same way, Jason's offering of anguish and pain is also taken up into the larger story of the cross.

In his discussion about the theology and politics of hope in Africa, Emmanuel Katongole speaks of lament as a theological practice of "dwelling in the midst of ruins," a practice in response to the worst violence and trauma that rips apart social fabrics and leaves individuals and communities in ruins. The practice of lament offers a glimpse that, " . . . even in the midst of such unimaginable violence (as in Congo) there might be a way of speaking about hope."[13] This is "[n]ot hope as a consolation but as the anguished discipline of *turning to and around God*."[14] Thus, this event, this act of lament, is included within the larger story of God's own identification with the deepest pain and agonized godforsakenness in the world. Jürgen Moltmann reminds us in *The Crucified God* that Jesus' cry of dereliction on the cross was a literal abandonment of God by God, so that in Christ, "God has identified himself with the godless and those abandoned by God."[15] Hence theology " . . . must come to terms with the cry of the wretched for God and for freedom out of the depths of the sufferings of this age."[16] This coming to terms "depends less upon the openness of theologians and their theories to the world and more upon whether they have honestly and without reserve come to terms with the death-cry of Jesus for God. By the standards of the cry of the dying Jesus for God, theological systems collapse at once in their inadequacy."[17] Over the years, there have been many expressions of lament, grief, and protest directed at the eucharistic table at Sanctuary. Moltmann's theological discussion of the cry of dereliction is a reminder that God definitively identifies with these cries: " . . . the crucified God is near to him in the forsakenness of every man. There is no loneliness and no rejection which he has not taken to himself and assumed in the cross of Jesus. . . ."[18] Moreover, because the table is the site of God's presence in the midst of the gathered community, regardless of each individual's own conception of what they are doing, by bringing their laments here, they are in fact "turning to and around God." Jason's iconoclastic display, right down to the cry of godforsakenness and the bloody hands, represents the very heart of the gospel proclaimed in the ritual he is attacking. Thus, without knowing it (in fact, precisely *because* he does not know he is doing it), he preaches the gospel to us.

While these disruptive events are difficult in the moment, with time they can be received as gifts. Habits by their very nature are predictable, and in order to be receptive and reform-able, a community's habits must be subject to disruption. Otherwise, the temptation to reinforce one's individual

---

13. Katongole, *Born from Lament*, 19.
14. Katongole, *Born from Lament*, 19, (italics mine).
15. Moltmann, *The Crucified God*, 19.
16. Moltmann, *The Crucified God*, 153.
17. Moltmann, *The Crucified God*, 153.
18. Moltmann, *The Crucified God*, 277.

or communal virtuous self-conception is strong. On the other hand, if such disruptions themselves become habits, which is a constant danger in a context like Sanctuary's, then they lose their unsettling power and can become simply destructive. If the communion goblet gets smashed every week, then there is no longer any meaningful practice to be disrupted.

Furthermore, what might on first glance appear to be a lack of discipline actually requires a peculiar form of discipline. As Stanley Hauerwas and William Willimon have written, "To be disciplined means to make our lives vulnerable to friends."[19] Welcoming, listening, and being open to discomfort are rather difficult disciplines. They are disciplines that the Sanctuary worshipping community has had to develop over many years in order to learn how to discern the gifts of disruption.

Only through hospitality does the church learn to be a people capable of receiving the gift of being disrupted, challenged, unsettled by God and by others, both inside and outside the church. And, as Katongole notes, it is this bodily knowing which comes only through unscripted encounters with "the stranger," which enables the church in turn to become an unsettling presence in its social context: "For the church to be capable of interruption, we must exist as a community that is willing to adjust itself to the constant interruption of the stranger. The church is not only an interrupt*ing* community: we are ourselves always interrupt*ed*."[20] If the church is meant to be, in Frederick Bauerschmidt's words, "a distinctive, and discomforting, social presence in the midst of the nations,"[21] then perhaps because of their social location, the poor, oppressed, and excluded are especially suited to become the distinctive and discomforting social presence for the church.

In conclusion, I want to express my gratitude for all I have learned from Brian's guidance and example. I have also been a recipient of the hospitality of his classroom, his family's home, and the liturgical proclamation and embodiment of God's strange and gracious hospitality at Wine Before Breakfast. All those who have benefited from this hospitality know that it is not always nice and comfortable; there is always a prophetic edge to it. But it is a taste of the hospitable, quirky, beloved community called into being by Jesus—the community which will only be fully realized in the renewed creation when we are all finally at home.

---

19. Hauerwas and Willimon, *Where Resident Aliens Live*, 111.
20. Katongole and Rice, *Reconciling All Things*, 114.
21. Bauerschmidt, *Julian of Norwich and the Mystical Body*, 11.

Bibliography

Bauerschmidt, Frederick Christian. *Julian of Norwich and the Mystical Body Politic of Christ*. Notre Dame: University of Notre Dame Press, 1999.

Bouma-Prediger, Steven, and Brian J. Walsh. *Beyond Homelessness: Christian Faith in a Culture of Displacement*. Grand Rapids: Eerdmans, 2008.

Hauerwas, Stanley, and William H. Willimon. *Where Resident Aliens Live: Exercises for Christian Practice*. Nashville: Abingdon, 1996.

Katongole, Emmanuel. *Born from Lament: The Theology and Politics of Hope in Africa*. Grand Rapids: Eerdmans, 2017.

Katongole, Emmanuel, and Chris Rice. *Reconciling All Things: A Christian Vision for Justice, Peace, and Healing*. Downers Grove, IL: InterVarsity, 2008.

Moltmann, Jürgen. *The Crucified God: The Cross of Christ as the Foundation and Criticism of Christian Theology*. Translated by R. A. Wilson and John Bowden. London: SCM, 1974.

Nouwen, Henri J. M. *Reaching Out: The Three Movements of the Spiritual Life*. Garden City, NY: Image/Doubleday, 1986.

Ogletree, Thomas W. *Hospitality to the Stranger: Dimensions of Moral Understanding*. Philadelphia: Fortress, 1985.

Red Rain. "City of Refuge." Track 3 on *A Night at Grace's*. Self-published, 2006, Compact Disc.

Wigg-Stevenson, Natalie. *Ethnographic Theology: An Inquiry into the Production of Theological Knowledge*. New York: Palgrave MacMillan, 2014.

11

Springtime in Cape Town

The Sacramental, Prophetic Imagination of Desmond Tutu

Stephen Martin

B rian Walsh has been identified with the idea of worldview ever since the publication of *The Transforming Vision* in 1984.[1] But the idea of worldview is also contested in Brian's later work, not because it is conceptually incoherent but because it is theologically incomplete. And that incompleteness can create a vacuum that transforms worldview into repressive ideology. Thus, rather than enacting the servanthood of a suffering Messiah, Christians become culture warriors, seeking to "make America [or Canada] great again." This is why Brian always taught that worldview must be paired with cross-shaped discipleship. Such discipleship is a way of life evident neither in narrow, moralistic terms nor in how one thinks abstractly about questions of the day, but in concrete, specific practices. It can be discerned in what one throws in the garbage, where one chooses to live (and shop), and even the arrangement of furniture around a television.[2] With his partner, Sylvia Keesmaat, Brian has demonstrated what this looks like in the urban space of Toronto and most recently in a (nearly) off-the-grid organic farm.

---

1. Co-authored with J. Richard Middleton.
2. Walsh, "Transformation." I'm aware that the Reformational tradition from which Brian speaks always—even if not always consistently—paired "world and life-view." Even this sounded too intellectualist, which is why "[from] worldview and [to] way of life" became the common phraseology around The Institute for Christian Studies during his time there.

But there is another side to Brian's thought, a side perhaps masked by his association with Reformed Christianity (and his vocation as a campus minister in the Christian Reformed Church). That is, Brian has an affinity for the sacramental. I think this reflects the Anglicanism that has been his ecclesial ethos for many years and is particularly evident in his work on Bruce Cockburn.[3] It is embodied communally in his *Wine Before Breakfast* gatherings at Wycliffe College, an Anglican college at the University of Toronto. Though he has also woven it into sermons and meditations,[4] it is not a dimension of Brian's thinking to which many have drawn attention. In a Reformed understanding, *sacrament* is equivalent to the two ordinances of baptism and the Lord's Supper. The sacraments are added

> to the Word of the gospel to represent better to our external senses both what God enables us to understand by the Word and what he does inwardly in our hearts, confirming in us the salvation he imparts to us.[5]

A *sacramental* view, however, understands the ordinances as clue to a wider vision of the material world as bearer of the divine presence. In the words of another Anglican, it is expressed in the idea that

> the very life of God ... [is] be communicated through the mundane: everyday material things. Bread, water, wine, oil, human hands—prompting Archbishop William Temple to declare that Christianity was the most materialistic of the great religions. Ours could not be a faith so otherworldly that it was of no earthly good.[6]

It is this other side that I want to take up, paired conceptually with another key idea in Brian's work: the prophetic imagination.[7] This term became his keynote in the late-1980s. It captures well the interface of worldview and discipleship, but in a way that allows the witness of the biblical prophets to contest afresh the captive imagination characterizing those choosing conformity to transformation.

I will also add a word not often used in Brian's work (despite his Anglicanism): *spirituality*. Aware of the assumption that prophetic Christianity replaces piety with activism, Brueggemann counters that social radicalism

---

3. Walsh, *Kicking at the Darkness*, 50–52; 69–70.
4. See his beautiful meditation, "Iggy's Gift."
5. *The Belgic Confession*, Article 33.
6. Tutu, "Dark Days," 33.
7. The term comes from Brueggemann, *The Prophetic Imagination*. Brueggemann's writings have been ubiquitous in Brian's work since the late-1980s.

without spirituality "is like a cut flower without nourishment, without any sanctions deeper than human courage and good intentions."[8] Spirituality is important. However, the term is fraught in the Reformational tradition. It evokes criticisms of escapist dualism, as if it is opposed to materiality, or privatistic pietism, as if opposed to public witness. In what follows, I will use it to mean a particular set of practices more attuned to the monastic life than most classical Protestants would be comfortable, but which I think might be embraced if understood properly.[9] Indeed, the figure I shall treat below, Archbishop Desmond Tutu, cannot adequately be understood without taking into account the spiritual and sacramental practices that root his public and prophetic witness. That will be my thesis, at any rate. At the end I will bring the discussion back to the overall theme of this volume: a sort of homecoming.

Forming a Sacramental, Prophetic Imagination

When Desmond Tutu talks about growing up in white-dominated Johannesburg, he tells two stories. The first involves his father, a school principal and a proud man "being humiliated by a young white shop assistant . . . being addressed, 'Ja, boy?' by one much younger [and far less educated] than himself, and being forced to swallow his pride." The second involves his mother, a cleaning woman at a school for the blind. One day young Desmond was walking down the street with his mother when they saw a white man approaching them wearing the black cassock of the Resurrection Fathers. But *this* white man doffed his hat and bowed to Desmond's mother as he passed. Tutu recalls that he

> was relatively stunned at the time, but only later came to realise the extent to which it had blown my mind that a white man would doff his hat to my mother. It was something I could never have imagined. The impossible was possible.

---

8. Brueggemann, *The Prophetic Imagination*, 8.

9. Within the broader Reformational tradition James K.A. Smith tries to reconnect spirituality as a set of practices shaping subjects for the Kingdom. See Smith, *Desiring the Kingdom*. Part of my agenda in the first section following is to address the question of where such an imagination-forming spirituality might originate, and in the second to speak of its public display in counter-cultural gatherings that contest public space and display the subversive Kingdom of God. I will go beyond the idea of spiritual (and liturgical) practices as forming individual subjectivity to forming an alternative community.

This is how Tutu met "the man who changed my life."[10] In that one, simple action Trevor Huddleston subverted the racialized script governing relations in 1940s South Africa.[11] Tutu would later learn of the imagination that stood behind Huddleston's action: that where other whites saw a black woman of the lowest class, this white man saw a bearer of God's very image in her singularity, a presence lamp before which to genuflect.[12] Tutu's encounter permitted him to see that, even in white-dominated South Africa, "The impossible was possible."

This encounter not only began a life-long friendship between Tutu and Huddleston, it moved him into the orbit of the Community of the Resurrection (CR), an Anglo-Catholic order founded by Charles Gore in 1892 and centered in England's industrial north.[13] The CR had come to Johannesburg shortly after the South African (Boer) War. Their special focus was on educating African children, and Tutu's family, though originally Methodist, would soon send their children to be educated by the CR. Sometimes known as the Mirfield Fathers, the CR were known for their devotion to daily prayer and the Eucharist, and for their social activism. Their transforming vision was to reproduce the life of the early church pictured in the book of Acts in the modern world. Taking seriously the apostolic injunction to hold all things in common, its members lived out a vow of poverty (through a common purse), chastity, and obedience—a renunciation of the respective entanglements of money, sex, and power. As well as the daily Eucharist, the common life of the CR centered the offices which divided the day into disciplined and regular times of communal gathering, and individual prayer. The outward manifestation of this shared, inward life was in the works of mercy, particularly among the poor where Christ was found.

---

10. Tutu, "The Man."

11. While the ideology of apartheid was imposed by D.F. Malan's Akrikaner National Party in 1948, the policies and practices it scripted into law owe their origins to British colonial rule.

12. Tutu would later explain, "When we [in the Anglo-Catholic tradition] pass in front of an altar we normally reverence the altar with a bow, but before the reserved sacrament we usually genuflect," as quoted in "The Challenges of God's Mission" in Battle, *Reconciliation*, 105. This is the key to understanding the significance of Huddleston's bowing to Aletta Tutu. An ordinary cleaning woman is a "Presence Lamp," a bearer of the divine presence. A sacramentally-formed imagination like that of Trevor Huddleston could recognize Aletta transfigured into a living temple.

13. The definitive history of the CR is Wilkinson, *The Community of the Resurrection*. See also Lee, *Compromise and Courage* and Clarke, *Anglicans Against Apartheid*. For Huddleston's story, see Huddleston, *Naught for Your Comfort*; Denniston, *Trevor Huddleston*.

While as a married (non-celibate) priest he never joined the CR as a brother, its formative power is profoundly evident in Tutu's Christianity. "It is from these remarkable men," he has written,

> that I have learned that it is impossible for religion to be sealed off in a watertight compartment that has no connection with the hurly burly business of ordinary daily living, that our encounter with God in prayer, meditation, the sacraments, and Bible study is authenticated and expressed in our dealings with our neighbor, whose keeper we must be willy nilly.[14]

Tutu is seen globally as a social activist and a champion of progressive causes, from Palestinian liberation to LGBTQ inclusion. He is stereotyped as a liberal whose relation to Christianity is mere contingency at best, and deception at worst.[15] Even at home, "many South Africans," says journalist Alistair Sparks, "believe to this day that Tutu was primarily a political activist who used his pulpit as a platform." In fact,

> The opposite is the truth. It was the depth of his spirituality that drove him to political activism. He was not a politician with a strategy but a churchman with a mission—a mission he believes was given to him by God "to work for the realisation of something like his kingdom in this country."[16]

Tutu's roots in the soil of Anglo-Catholic spiritual practices is unquestionable, and accounts for his energy as an activist:

> It would be impossible to engage in the kind of public life I have had if this was not undergirded by the spiritual life. Our [Anglo-Catholic] tradition is one where we have, as far as possible, a daily Eucharist, and an extended time of quiet and meditation, and at mid-day we have to pause for the Angelus.[17]

---

14. Tutu quoted in Wilkinson, *Community of the Resurrection*, 299.

15. Ironically, this "liberal" understanding of Tutu is similar to the apartheid regime's accusation that he was a covert Marxist, hiding "behind the structures and the cloth of the Christian church." ("State President's Letter" in "Documentation: The Church-State Confrontation," 73.) Recent works on Tutu's prophetic ministry continue to miss or minimize the formative significance of his Anglo-Catholic spiritual practices: Cilliers, "Between Separation and Celebration"; Judex Kaunda, "'A Voice Shouting in the Wilderness.'"; Maluleke, "Desmond Tutu's Earliest." The best account of Tutu as Anglo-Catholic is Battle's *Reconciliation*.

16. Sparks, et al., *Tutu*. The quote is from Lelyveld, "South Africa's Bishop."

17. Allen, *Rabble-Rouser for Peace*, 66.

Tutu's priestly ministry began in 1960, the same year as apartheid exploded onto the world news wires with the Sharpeville massacre, which saw 69 unarmed protesters shot by police. In response, protests spread across South Africa, most notable was the one led by Philip Kgosana to Cape Town's Parliament. But the rest of the decade saw a brutal repression and virtual silencing of black opposition movements, and the arrest, banning, or exiling of their leadership. There was also a growing awareness that the parliamentary opposition was merely giving legitimacy to the regime. But it was also a time when signs of transformation were beginning in the South African churches. New organizations were emerging such as the Christian Institute (CI), led by the dissident Afrikaner cleric Beyers Naudé. The CI was characterized by an ethos of listening to the voices of black South Africans (something white liberals had an unfortunate habit of *not* doing). The South African Council of Churches (SACC) published the watershed "Message to the People of South Africa" in 1968. A remarkable experiment called The Federal Theological Seminary (FEDSEM), an interdenominational community bringing black and white Christians together, sought to transform theological education to address specifically the context of oppressive South Africa. Tutu would become an associate of Beyers', and deeply interested in the Black Consciousness Movement that coalesced in the CI. He rose to General Secretary of the SACC, which gained international profile (and increasingly became a local target) through his strong association with it. And he taught and administered at FEDSEM. Through all this ecumenical and multiracial activity, his catholicism only deepened, as did his commitment to non-violent engagement of the regime.

Appointed as first black Dean of Johannesburg in 1975 and bishop of Lesotho in 1976, Tutu's episcopal ministry coincided with the final push to end apartheid which began in the Soweto uprisings of 1976. Like Sharpeville, Soweto was marked by a brutal police action, this time against protesting schoolchildren. But unlike Sharpeville, the aftermath extended far into the future, spawning new movements of resistance throughout the 1980s. On the eve of those student protests, Tutu sent a prophetic letter of warning to Prime Minister John Vorster. Its plea included these words,

> I am writing to you, sir, because I have a growing nightmarish fear that unless something drastic is done very soon then bloodshed and violence are going to happen in South Africa almost inevitably . . . I am frightened, dreadfully frightened, that we may soon reach a point of no return, when events will generate a momentum of their own, when nothing will stop their reaching a bloody denouement which is 'too ghastly to contemplate'.[18]

18. Tutu, *Hope and Suffering*, 32.

The letter was published for the world to see, and Tutu's pleas would soon turn to the international community for economic sanctions to bring a peaceable end to a conflict that was exploding across the country, and indeed throughout the region. While dismissed by many whites at home as a "rabble rouser", Tutu's star waxed abroad, eventually earning the Nobel Peace Prize in 1984. He became an icon of the anti-apartheid movement around the world. The Anglican Church of the Province of Southern Africa made Tutu Archbishop—the first black Archbishop in the church's history—in 1986.

As Archbishop of Cape Town, Tutu's sacramental imagination transfigured space, turning staid spaces into anticipations of the Kingdom of God. His official residence in the wealthy, white suburb of Bishopscourt and the colonial St. George's Cathedral in downtown Cape Town became transgressive spaces of celebrative, multi-racial gathering.[19] At the same time as he was dominating headlines for his advocacy of economic sanctions, he was establishing The Institute for Christian Spirituality. Headquartered at Bishopscourt, its first director (and Tutu's confessor), Fr. Francis Cull, was housed in the former slave quarters (an irony that was not lost on Cull, who delighted in telling visitors that "the black man now lived in the big house . . . and the white man in the eighteenth century slave quarters.")[20] Tutu's imagination also refigured relationships. While the dour, stereotypically Calvinist imagination of successive Prime Ministers and Presidents saw Tutu as an imposter, a communist in Christian dress, Tutu saw them as baptized Christians toward whom he bore pastoral responsibility. "Mr Botha," he said later of the former State President, "is a member of my family, and God will ask me, 'What did you do to help redeem my child?'"[21] It took "prophetic imagination" and "transforming vision" for the tiny archbishop (barely five feet tall) to confront these imposing figures in their offices with the words, "You know you have lost."[22] After all, coming at peaceful people with force of arms was proof positive that the regime was devoid of any true, moral authority.

This is a sacramental, prophetic imagination. To one particular instance of that imagination I now turn.

---

19. To be fair, this transformation had begun under his immediate predecessors, but Tutu embodied what only a black person ascending to one of the most prominent public positions in South African life could.

20. Quoted in Allen, *Rabble-Rouser for Peace*, 276.

21. Quoted in Allen, *Rabble-Rouser for Peace*, 357.

22. Allen, *Rabble-Rouser for Peace*, 302.

Performing a Sacramental, Prophetic Imagination

September is springtime in Cape Town. And September 1989 was looking to be a crucial month for the blossoming of a post-apartheid South Africa. The ruling party was in upheaval. P.W. Botha had been forced out as leader of the National Party and replaced by F.W. de Klerk as interim party leader and acting State President. Elections were scheduled for September 6. Outside the system, the South African Council of Churches' Standing for the Truth campaign had reached its climax.[23] A series of rolling mass actions (strikes, stayaways, and boycotts) had been engaged for the six weeks prior to the elections. These had included open defiance of apartheid laws, including segregated amenities, beaches, and other public places. The global boycott of South Africa and immanent collapse of the economy had put the regime under tremendous pressure. The violence of the state had also mobilized again to counter. Many feared a final, bloody confrontation.

Everything was meant to climax in a series of marches on September 2. Three separate marches from three locations were to converge on Parliament. As the crowd gathered in Cape Town's city center the police arrived in armored vehicles and ordered the gathered to leave. When the crowd refused to disperse, the police fired streams of purple dye at the crowd, followed by tear gas. Protesters were beaten and whipped. In the ensuing panic as protesters fled the police arrested anyone with purple on their clothing. Hundreds took refuge in St. George's Cathedral. Fearful and discouraged, they were addressed by Tutu:

> Say to yourselves, 'God loves me.' In your heart: God loves me, God loves me. . . . I am of infinite value to God. God created me for freedom. . . . My freedom is inalienable. I don't go around and say, 'Baas [Boss], please give me my freedom. . . .' My freedom is God-given! Right! Now straighten up your shoulders, come, straighten up your shoulders like people who are born for freedom! Lovely, lovely, lovely![24]

It's hard not to recall the two encounters described in the previous section. The police had treated the demonstrators as the shop assistant had treated Tutu's father. But now, huddled in St. George's Cathedral, Tutu called on them to recognize the "presence lamp" in each other. The

---

23. The churches stepped forward in 1988 after the umbrella United Democratic Front was outlawed and its leadership arrested. Because South Africa was ostensibly a "Christian" country, the overt action of churches identifying themselves with the liberation movement was a significant line that was crossed. State action against the churches made visible the either-or of the gospel in judgement of the Christian regime.

24. Quoted in Allen, *Rabble-Rouser for Peace*, 307.

freedom of an image-bearer of God was not earned, nor was it granted by the powerful who thought they determined such things. It was a birthright to be recognized and lived into. Later that evening someone sneaked back into town and spray painted on the wall of one of the civic buildings the phrase, "the purple shall govern."[25]

The wake of the march saw a brutal crackdown on dissent, especially in the townships. The police interrupted services the following week at St. George's Cathedral. On Monday, Tutu and other clerics were trapped inside Central Methodist Church by police and arrested. On the day of the elections, twenty-three protesters were shot dead by police. Tutu burst into tears on hearing the news. Despairing, he retreated into his chapel at Bishopscourt, deep in prayer.

He emerged the next day "with a clarity of mind he says he had not experienced since writing his letter to Prime Minister Vorster on the eve of the Soweto uprising in 1976."[26] After drawing on that depth of which Brueggemann speaks, Tutu's imagination was renewed. At a memorial service for the dead, he announced that there was going to be another march—an idea greeted with surprise by the advisors and leaders of the Mass Democratic Movement, who had not been consulted and who now urged him to reconsider.[27] Surely this was a time to consolidate and regroup rather than to provoke, they said. Convinced that "God had told him" to march, Tutu was insistent. When the march was announced, public response was overwhelmingly in favor. There were voices of wide support inside and outside the country, including Cape Town Mayor Gordon Oliver, opposition MPs, and business representatives. Global leaders, including Prime Minister Thatcher and President George H.W. Bush, urged the regime to accede. Johan Heynes, Moderator of the Dutch Reformed Church, offered to mediate between Tutu and de Klerk to negotiate permission for the march. In the end, de Klerk (who was now President-Elect) announced that, "the door to a New South Africa is open, it is not necessary to batter it down."[28] In what then Cabinet Minister Gerrit Viljoen would later call, "a more fearful leap into the dark" than even the release of Nelson Mandela a few months

---

25. A variation on the words of the 1955 Freedom Charter and which had been a popular slogan since, "The People Shall Govern." See Smuts, et al., *The Purple Shall Govern*. More information is available at The Sunday Times' Heritage Project Site.

26. Sparks et al., *Tutu*, 181.

27. Tutu recalls, "When Cheryl Carolus, one of the United Democratic Front leaders, asked who had given me the mandate to call for a march, I replied without presumption that God had told me; and in her impish way she retorted that no one dare take God on." Desmond Tutu, "Dark Days," 37.

28. Allen, *Rabble-Rouser for Peace*, 310.

later,²⁹ the march was allowed for Wednesday, September 13. The proviso was that it be "lawful" and "peaceful."

While Tutu had expected "perhaps a thousand" to come, "what followed was a spectacle not seen in South Africa since young Philip Kgosana's mass march on Parliament twenty-nine years earlier.

> An estimated thirty thousand people of all races, including bishops and parliamentarians, workers and businessmen and women, students and children in their school uniforms, marched in a huge column nearly a mile long . . . to the Grand Parade . . . There were no police in sight: UDF marshalls with 'colored' armbands directed the march and controlled the traffic. They were in charge.³⁰

The "they" is ambiguous. Arguably it was the people who were "in charge." The banners and colors of banned organizations such as the ANC and UDF were freely displayed. People marched as if the New South Africa was already present and on view. A tremendously diverse group—students and professionals, labor and civic leaders, and thousands of ordinary people, black and white, men and women, rich and poor—converged on the Grand Parade in front of the old, colonial City Hall. In his introductory remarks, Rev. Allan Boesak proclaimed, "a victory for our people!"³¹ He named the two imaginaries around the march. He recalled the proviso of President de Klerk, insisting that to the contrary the gathering did not take place within the bounds of the Apartheid state, but in defiance of that authority. Indeed, "this is our city, this is our country [and] this parliament ought to be our parliament."

When it came time for him to speak, Tutu changed the pace. He greeted the crowd and smiled. Surveying the gathered, he named what was happening in front of him as a "victory for peace" and "for common sense." It was a victory for all. Then he addressed not the crowd, but de Klerk on behalf of the crowd. "We want to say to Mr. de Klerk," he bubbled, ". . . come and see!"³²

> Come here and see *peaceful* people! [Then to the people] Show Mr. de Klerk your hands. They are empty hands, Mr. de Klerk! [Again, to the people] Let's show Mr. de Klerk that we are a

---

29. Quoted in Allen, *Rabble-Rouser for Peace*, 312.

30. Sparks et al., *Tutu*, 183.

31. What follows is transcribed from raw footage of the gathering from Brian Tilley and Lawrence Dworkin, prod., Cape Town Peace.

32. c.f. John 1:39

disciplined people. Let's keep quiet! [The people immediately grow silent] Did you hear a pin drop, Mr. de Klerk? [One more time to the people] We want to say to Mr. de Klerk, come and see *Technicolor*! They tried to make us one colour, purple. We say 'we are the Rainbow People! We are the new people of the new South Africa!'

I want to suggest that there are three things of relevance to Tutu as purveyor of a sacramental, prophetic imagination here. The first is the way Tutu gestured to the crowds gathered in all their diversity as a *people*. The question of what constitutes a people is one of the classic questions of political theory. What differentiates, for instance, "the masses," "the multitude," or "the mob" from a *res publica*, a properly political entity? Taking its point of departure from a perversion of Kuyperian Sphere Sovereignty[33], the politics of Apartheid South Africa was obsessed with policing boundaries, boundaries both of *volk* and of institutional type. Thus the sight of church leaders conducting crowds of racially-mixed political protesters was doubly transgressive of public space. Indeed, these transgressions had been deliberately and strategically planned throughout the defiance campaign. They were a people without need (or desire) for a state to shape or control them. The kind of people they were was more akin to St. Augustine's definition as "a gathered multitude of rational beings united by agreeing to share the things they love."[34] This gathering and sharing "goods in common" was evident in their desire for a future in which each person was allowed to display their giftedness as the building-up of a social body (see 1 Cor 10:16–17; 12:4–31; Rom 12:3–13). It was a people gathered in diversity and blessed and soon to be sent forth to the townships and factories, to the churches and the schools with a new identity.[35]

The second thing of relevance concerns the *manner* of their gathering. They were a people gathered as liturgical performance, a liturgical performance of the very thing de Klerk expected to be negotiated and decided with the regime at the head of the table. This was a people who in Tutu's terms were constituted by *diversity* ("Technicolor") under *discipline* ("did you hear a pin drop?"), a people who gathered with empty hands, in *peace*. In the oft-quoted hinge-point of St. Paul's letter to the Romans, the apostle says,

---

33. See Kuyper, "Sphere Sovereignty." A good overview of the South African [per] version and its church-state mapping is Baskwell, "Kuyper and Apartheid." See also Thom, "Between Priestly Identification." As well: Kinghorn, "Social Cosmology."

34. *City of God* xix. 24. See also Martin, "Sacramental Imagination."

35. As Boesak anticipated in his speech before Tutu's.

> I appeal to you therefore, brothers and sisters, by the mercies of God, to present your bodies as a living sacrifice, holy and acceptable to God, which is your spiritual worship. Do not be conformed to this world, but be transformed by the renewing of your minds, so that you may discern what is the will of God— what is good and acceptable and perfect. (Rom 12:1–2)[36]

Saint Paul has for eleven chapters told the story of that people created, called, and redeemed by the God of creation in deliberate contradistinction to that people shaped by the rebellious powers, including Caesar. Now he demarcates that people as those who refuse conformity to this age,[37] who are "transformed" by a new mentality in their relationships, and who display the peaceable virtues of the true new age in contrast to the violent virtues of the regime.[38] Those who were seemingly "on the wrong side of history" were thus enabled "to live in the light of deeper realities than those that surrounded them. This made possible, "the sharing of a communal life that would normally be counterintuitive for those at the heart of an empire like Rome."[39] All this was a worshipful response to "the mercies of God," a "living [offering] of their bodies" as one "sacrifice."

Finally, this was a performance of the new South Africa that was given a name: "the Rainbow People." The image of the rainbow is of course a deeply biblical symbol: it was given after the judgment on human violence in the Genesis flood, a symbol of new beginnings, of a new covenant, of "never again." He then led the crowds (holding hands) in a litany that repeated those words uttered at the Cathedral ten days earlier under very different circumstances: "our march to freedom is unstoppable!" Looking at the jubilant people now transfigured into signs of God's presence, Tutu finished, laughing: "Mr. de Klerk, please come."

It is difficult to imagine a more powerful demonstration of a sacramental, prophetic imagination. What happened on September 13, 1989 on Cape Town's Grand Parade was a parable of the Kingdom of God, a taste of God's future. It was orchestrated by a man who had fifty years earlier seen "the impossible become possible" as a white priest bowed to an African woman, whose understanding of what it was to be human was forged in prayer and nurtured in the Eucharist. It was the outcome of an imagination that saw

---

36. All biblical citations are from the NRSV.

37. See the note in NRSV which offers an alternative translation of *tō aeōni* as "age." Sylvia Keesmaat suggests that the entirety of Romans 12–13 is "framed by an apocalyptic . . . challenge to the 'New Age' of the Empire." "If Your Enemy is Hungry," 143.

38. See Keesmaat, "If Your Enemy is Hungry."

39. Keesmaat, "If Your Enemy is Hungry," 144.

God's possibility in the midst of oppressive reality. It was an imagination that knew God—who make ordinary things into extraordinary—transfigure the latter into the former.

In South Africa "the purple" did govern, and sooner than the watching world expected. The elections of September 1989 were the last to elect an all-white Parliament. Five months later, the liberation movements were unbanned, and Nelson Mandela was released. It was unsurprising that he spent his first night of freedom in Bishopscourt. Less than five years later, people of all races, colors, and cultures streamed to voting stations for the first non-racial, democratic elections.

It was said by some that that day in April 1994 was the birth of the new South Africa. The world certainly thought so as it viewed, with astonishment, the snaking lineups of voters. The newly minted President Nelson Mandela said as much when he stood not far from the place the purple had been baptized in dye, and the exact spot where Tutu had addressed the crowd in the aftermath. Mandela said in his speech that here, at the southern tip of Africa, a fateful convergence 300 years ago between Africa, Europe, and Asia had gone horribly wrong.[40] The rainbow—now a synonym for the new South Africa—carried the promise of that narrative being rewritten, with justice established. In his inauguration, Mandela picked up the never again: "Never, never and never again shall it be that this beautiful land will again experience the oppression of one by another and suffer the indignity of being the skunk of the world."[41]

But others claimed that the rainbow nation had been born much earlier, on the streets of Cape Town and other places of gathering to perform a new society.[42] While some hailed the release of political prisoners and the unbanning of the liberation parties as the turning point, others insisted that the people had unbanned themselves long before, simply by refusing to live by the rules laid down by the regime. They were living the liberating future even in the midst of the oppressive present. The regime had simply yielded to the inevitable, finally (recalling Tutu's terms), "joining the winning side."

Those who joined in the protests became more than the sum of their individualities: they became a people. Their coming together was not simply to express an idea they all agreed on or to put forth an agenda they all shared. It wants to offer their bodies to a cause. And sometimes that offering meant suffering detention and abuse at the hands of the regime.

40. Mandela, "Nelson Mandela on the Occasion."
41. Mandela, "Nelson Mandela at His Inauguration."
42. Here I speak anecdotally, since "others" include my colleagues at the University of Cape Town, who contested the idea that "Freedom Day" should be associated with an election.

In occupying the streets of Cape Town, in joyously defying unjust laws and refusing to recognize illegitimate authority, they transformed public space, making it a stage for the performance of a different story: not a story of people divided by their differences but a people united in their diversity, like the colors of the rainbow.

And at the head of this procession was that tiny priest, Desmond Tutu.

The Ongoing Challenge of a Prophetic, Sacramental Imagination

I would not want to gloss over the many challenges facing South Africa in the present moment. Indeed, the rhetoric of "the miracle of the new South Africa" veiled for some time the limitations of any political newness within the regime of global capitalism. The very international order that Tutu was able to mobilize to pressure the apartheid regime soon enfolded that noble experiment into neo-liberalism. The moral character of The Rainbow Nation was deeply compromised by the arms deal (which has embroiled members of the new political elite, including the previous President, in legal battles to this date). The "never again" of the rainbow looks increasingly like "more of the same"—to the point that Tutu himself vowed to "pray against" the ANC government.[43]

Brian Walsh never tired of reminding us as his students that it is of the essence of idolatry to identify any one movement as the Kingdom of God. The Kingdom is always to come. All homecoming within history is "a *sort-of* homecoming." But the Kingdom is *also* always on the way, and sometimes it breaks through the intransigent hard-heartedness into the here and now.[44] It finds cracks even through a regime convinced of its own righteousness, that it ruled the peoples of the southern tip of Africa by divine right. The Kingdom makes its presence known in movements that, "like grass through cement," insinuate themselves into the paved stones of the modern world. Indeed (since this is an article dedicated to Brian), we might invoke the lines of Bruce Cockburn, whose imagination allowed him to see a small uprising in a Chilean shanty town coinciding with the bells of First Mass as heralding the dawn of a new world.[45] That's also what happened half a world away in September 1989. Such insinuations are "parables of the Kingdom"—not mere symbols, but material manifestations of its reality. It was Brian Walsh

---

43. See Martin, "A New Kairos"; Martin, "Thuma Mina."

44. Walsh, "Derrida and the Messiah," 29–33.

45. See "Santiago Dawn," from the album *World of Wonders* (True North Records, 1986). Also see Brian's exposition in *Kicking at the Darkness*, 78–79.

who first taught me to discern this. And so, may God bless him as he continues to inspire us to see the green shoots emerging in the cracks of wintery empire as assertions of springtime grace.

Bibliography

Allen, John. *Rabble-Rouser for Peace: The Authorized Biography of Desmond Tutu*. New York: Free, 2006.
Baskwell, Patrick. "Kuyper and Apartheid: A Revisiting." *HTS Teologiese Studies / Theological Studies* 62.4 (2006) 1269–90.
Battle, Michael. *Reconciliation: The Ubuntu Theology of Desmond Tutu*. Cleveland: Pilgrim, 2009.
Bratt, James D., ed. *Abraham Kuyper: A Centennial Reader*. Grand Rapids: Eerdmans, 1998.
Brawley, Robert L., ed. *Character Ethics and the New Testament: Moral Dimensions of Scripture*. Louisville: Westminster John Knox, 2006.
Brueggemann, Walter. *The Prophetic Imagination*. 2nd ed. Minneapolis: Fortress, 2001.
Cilliers, Johan. "Between Separation and Celebration: Perspectives on the Ethical-Political Preaching of Desmond Tutu." *Stellenbosch Theological Journal* 1.1 (2015) 41–56.
Clarke, Bob. *Anglicans against Apartheid, 1936–1996*. Pietermaritzburg: Cluster, 2008.
Christian Reformed Church. "The Belgic Confession." https://www.crcna.org/welcome/beliefs/confessions/belgic-confession.
Denniston, Robin. *Trevor Huddleston: A Life*. New York: St. Martin's, 1999.
"Heritage Project Site." The Sunday Times. http://heritage.thetimes.co.za/memorials/wc/ThePurpleShallGovern/article.aspx?id=568880.
Huddleston, Trevor. *Naught for Your Comfort*. London: Fontana, 1956.
Kaunda, Chammah Judex. "'A Voice Shouting in the Wilderness': Desmond Mpilo Tutu's Contribution to African Theology of Public Prophetic Preaching for Social Justice and Wholeness." *International Journal of Public Theology* 9.1 (2015) 29–46.
Keesmaat, Sylvia. "If Your Enemy Is Hungry: Love and Subversive Politics in Romans 12 & 13." In *Character Ethics and the New Testament*, edited by Robert L. Brawley, 141–58. Louisville: Westminster John Knox, 2006.
Kinghorn, Johan. "Social Cosmology, Religion and Afrikaner Ethnicity." *Journal of Southern African Studies* 20.3 (1994) 393–404.
Kuyper, Abraham. "Sphere Sovereignty." In *Abraham Kuyper: A Centennial Reader*, edited by John Bratt, 461–90. Grand Rapids: Eerdmans, 1998.
Lee, Peter. *Compromise and Courage: Anglicans in Johannesburg 1864-1999*. Pietermaritzburg: Cluster, 2005.
Lelyveld, Joseph. "South African's Bishop Tutu." *New York Times Magazine*, March 14, 1982, quoted in Allister Sparks, Mpho A. Tutu, and Douglas B. Abrams. *Tutu: Authorized*. New York: HarperOne, 2011.
Maluleke, Tinyiko. "Desmond Tutu's Earliest Notions and Visions of Church, Humanity, and Society." *Ecumenical Review* 67.4 (2015) 572–90.
Mandela, Nelson R. "Nelson Mandela at His Inauguration as President of South Africa, Pretoria." May 10, 1994. http://www.mandela.gov.za/mandelaspeeches/1994/940510_inauguration.htm.

———. "Nelson Mandela on the Occasion of His Inauguration as State President, Cape Town." May 9, 1994. http://www.mandela.gov.za/mandela_speeches/1994/940509_inauguration.htm.

Martin, Stephen W. "A New Kairos for South Africa." *Political Theology Today*, July 4, 2017. https://politicaltheology.com/a-new-kairos-for-south-africa-stephen-w-martin.

———. "Sacramental Imagination and Ecclesial Transformation." *Journal of Theology for Southern Africa* 139 (2011) 42–57.

———. "Thuma Mina—A New Beginning for South Africa?" *Political Theology Today*, February 27, 2018. https://politicaltheology.com/thuma-mina-a-new-beginning-for-south-africa.

O'Donovan, Oliver, and Joan Lockwood O'Donovan, eds. *From Irenaeus to Grotius: A Sourcebook in Christian Political Thought, 100–1625*. Grand Rapids: Eerdmans, 1999.

Smith, James K. A. *Desiring the Kingdom: Worship, Worldview, and Cultural Formation*. Grand Rapids: Baker Academic, 2009.

Smuts, Dene, Margaret Nash, and Shauna Westcott, eds. *The Purple Shall Govern: A South African A to Z of Nonviolent Action*. Cape Town: Oxford University Press, 1991.

Sparks, Allister, et al. *Tutu: Authorized*. New York: HarperOne, 2011.

"State President's Letter to Archbishop Desmond Tutu dated 16 March." In "Documentation: The Church-State Confrontation. Correspondence & Statements February—April 1988." *Journal of Theology for Southern Africa* 63 (1988) 68–87.

Thom, Gideon. "Between Priestly Identification and Prophetic Confrontation: The Roots of the Volkskerk in Afrikaner History." *Studia Historia Ecclesiastica* 18.2 (1992) 149–61.

Tilley, Brian, and Lawrence Dworkin, dir. "Cape Town Peace March, 1989." Cape Town: Afravision, 2004. https://vimeo.com/29303438.

Tutu, Desmond. *Hope and Suffering*. Grand Rapids: Eerdmans, 1984.

———. "Dark Days: Episcopal Ministry in Times of Repression, 1976–1996." *Journal of Theology for Southern Africa* 118 (2004) 27–39.

———. "The Man Who Changed My Life." *Cape Times*, June 17, 2013. https://www.iol.co.za/capetimes/the-man-who-changed-my-life-1533199.

Walsh, Brian J. "Derrida and the Messiah: The Spiritual Face of Postmodernity." *Re.generation Quarterly* 5.1 (1999) 29–33.

———. "Iggy's Gift." *Empire Remixed* (blog). May 16, 2015. http://empireremixed.com/2015/05/16/iggys-gift.

———. *Kicking at the Darkness: Bruce Cockburn and the Christian Imagination*. Grand Rapids: Brazos, 2011.

———. "Transformation: Dynamic Worldview or Repressive Ideology." *Journal of Education and Christian Belief* 4.2 (2000) 101–14.

Walsh, Brian J., and J. Richard Middleton. *The Transforming Vision: Shaping a Christian World View*. Downers Grove, IL: InterVarsity, 1984.

Wilkinson, Alan. *The Community of the Resurrection: A Centenary History*. London: SCM, 1992.

12

The Wit(h)ness of Suffering Love

James Olthuis

In their 1995 preface to *Truth Is Stranger Than It Used to Be*, Richard Middleton and Brian Walsh emphasize that "truth is sought and found only in community."[1] Not only is good vision crucial in any search, a map of the territory is highly desirable. Indeed, with that in mind, Brian and Richard in 1984 had written *The Transforming Vision*, an eloquent and influential articulation of a biblical vision *of* the world as a vision *for* the transforming of that world. It was—and still is—an important book.

At the same time, although the details remain blurry, I do recall that soon after its publication, Brian pointed out what to him was a serious shortcoming in the book: its deafness to suffering. Consequently, it is no surprise when in the opening paragraph of the abovementioned preface, the authors call this inattention to the "rootedness" of a biblical worldview "in God's response to human suffering ... a serious lacuna."[2] In *Truth is Stranger Than It Used to Be*, they made "*a radical sensitivity to suffering* that pervades the biblical narrative from the exodus to the cross"[3] an overarching theme.

Sensitivity to suffering with its commitment to "fostering justice and compassion" involves "the 'embrace of pain,' since it involves forthright honesty about (rather than denial of) suffering."[4] Walter Brueggemann refers to this biblical trajectory as the "prophetic imagination," for it is the prophets who par excellence "give voice to the suffering of the people, and even ... to

---

1. Middleton and Walsh, *Truth*, 5.
2. Middleton and Walsh, *Truth*, 4.
3. Middleton and Walsh, *Truth*, 87.
4. Middleton and Walsh, *Truth*, 94.

the suffering of God."[5] In the New Testament the focus is on the life, death and resurrection of Jesus, as the Way, the Truth, and the Life by whom and through whom redemption is achieved. It is the prism or lens through which Christian identity is shaped. As God-is-with-us (Emmanuel), so we are to *be-with* others. In a world broken by suffering and evil, we are to be compassionate as God is compassionate. Hence, following Jesus asks for what Middleton and Walsh so aptly call "a praxis of suffering love."[6]

However, practicing suffering love is no small challenge. My goal in this paper is to deepen our understanding of the nature of trauma[7] (radical suffering) and to emphasize the crucial role of witness in healing from the effects of trauma. My hope is to help give shape to theology as a healing discourse, to speak of the creating/healing/transforming love which is God and which leads to transforming change in the practices of life. This seems particularly fitting in a book honoring Brian, whose passion in life is and has been to bear witness of, offer testimony to, and embody the healing power of suffering love.

Sensitivity to Suffering

Suffering, particularly human suffering, has always been a focus of theologians. How are we to relate God to suffering? Such discussions, known as theodicies, were attempts to justify the ways of God in a broken and evil world. Why did an all-powerful and all-good God not create a world in which humans would freely choose to do the right thing? Why does an omnipotent God decide to allow so much horrific suffering? The questions multiply.

Since I already have a paper arguing the urgency of understanding God's sovereignty, not as sheer, omnipotent, power-*over*, but as the invitational, evocative power-*with* of love, engaging in that discussion will not be my focus here.[8] It is, however, of importance to note that the explanations offered by theodicies have rather served to aggravate rather than alleviate the pain of the suffering. How is a person suffering from torture, abuse, or dying from cancer comforted by being told suffering is the result of sin? How does this not blame the victim and compound the suffering? Does it help to tell a father whose son committed suicide that it was the will of God? How do such accounts show sensitivity to suffering and support the healing process? If God is in charge, and nothing happens without the will of the Father, why

5. Middleton and Walsh, *Truth*, 94.
6. Middleton and Walsh, *Truth*, 161.
7. Trauma is from the Greek word literally meaning "wound."
8. See Olthuis, "Thinking God Otherwise," in process of publication.

does God allow heinous atrocities such as the Holocaust? Wendy Farley says it well: "The phenomenon of human suffering continues to bleed through the explanations that attempt to account for it."[9]

Thankfully, in the second half of the twentieth century the theological focus on suffering was dramatically altered by increased recognition that "suffering belongs to the person and purpose of God."[10] Abraham Heschel's *The Prophets* led the way: "Pathos, concern for the world, is the very ethos of God."[11] Old Testament theologians Walter Brueggemann and Terence Fretheim, theologians Eberhard Jüngel and Jürgen Moltmann, along with feminist theologians such as Elizabeth Johnson[12] joined in. Fretheim's *The Suffering of God* was particularly helpful. "The wounds of God" from broken relationships "are manifold."[13] His detailed attention to the biblical material made clear that denying the reality of the suffering of God is "a violation of biblical language."[14]

However, although there is increased recognition of the suffering of God, many Christians read the Creation-Fall-Redemption-Consummation narrative in linear fashion. This tempts them to envision the crucifixion (and suffering) as something of the past beyond which we have moved to the new life of the resurrection (and relief from suffering). The result can be a kind of triumphalism focused on heaven and its absence of suffering which detracts from, minimizes, or downplays the horror and anguish of earthly suffering. In some circles the dominate emphasis is stiff-upper-lip endurance, put trauma behind you, forget it and get on with your life. If or when they do not experience healing, ill people may even be chastised for their lack of faith. Believers are exhorted to accept and even welcome suffering: Jesus suffered, therefore, followers of Jesus will suffer. Such glorification of suffering has at times served to support the "perpetuation of oppressive systems for persons and communities on the margins."[15] I remember only too well in 1980 being angered listening to a black pastor in South Africa admonish his parishioners not to protest apartheid because being Christian means suffering.

---

9. Farley, *Tragic Vision*, 19.

10. Fretheim, *The Suffering*, xii.

11. Heschel, *The Prophets*, 24.

12. See Brueggemann, *The Prophetic Imagination*; Jüngel, *God as the Mystery of the World*, trans. Darrell Guder; Moltmann, *The Crucified God*, trans. R.A. Wilson and John Bowden; Johnson, *She Who Is*.

13. Fretheim, *The Suffering*, 116.

14. Fretheim, *The Suffering*, 67.

15. Rambo, *Spirit*, 5.

In this regard, the development of the dispensational theology of Darby and Scofield in nineteenth century North American evangelical circles with its emphasis on the next life in heaven has been particularly damaging. Through attending to the lives of Darby and Scofield, Christian psychoanalyst Marie Hoffmann has indicated how dispensationalism developed as a defensive strategy to justify and excuse the put-down of feelings and inattention to experienced trauma.[16]

Instead of understanding the biblical Creation-Fall-Redemption-Consummation as a linear sequence, it needs to be envisioned as a four-theme spiraling narrative: Love Incarnated (Creation), Love Wounded (Fall), Love Re-Incarnated (Redemption), Love Consummated (Eschaton). The ongoing energy and flow of love in the flux of the universe is a zig-zagging movement of differentiation/integration, despite and in struggle with the parasitic, destructive forces of evil. The four motifs continually interweave and overlap in a cosmic rhythmically (dis)continuous spiral. In its advancing historical movement, God's suffering love is the energizing surge of the cosmos, not in distance from, but as the cosmos's intimate, indwelling, generative and regenerative dynamic.

God, as the letting-be of love, indwells the cosmos. Creation is God's home. When evil happens, God does not flee but remains true, unwavering, steadfast, suffering-with the creation. God, the Compassionate One, in embrace of and in solidarity with the pain of the universe, as the Word Made Flesh lived, died, and resurrected. "The steadfast love (*chesed*) of the Lord never ceases, his compassions (*rachamin*) never come to an end; they are new every morning, great is thy truth (*emunah*)" (Lam 3:22–23).[17] *Rachamin* is the Hebrew word for compassion, from *rechem* (womb or uterus). Literally, the meaning of compassion "is the womb pained in solidarity with the suffering of another."[18]

In the brokenness of life, compassion is our calling. As God suffers and mourns with those who mourn and suffer, so we are called to suffer-with and mourn-with those in sorrow and pain. Suffering-with, it needs to be emphasized, is not suffering-from and involves no glorification of suffering. Suffering-with is voluntary, a witness and protest against suffering. Suffering-with is compassion, loving service, not only on behalf of fellow humans, but on behalf of all creatures, including the earth itself. We are "heirs of God and joint heirs with Christ—if, in fact, we suffer with him so that we may also be glorified with him" (Rom 8:16). In Matthew 25 Jesus indicates that

---

16. Hoffman, *When the Roll*, 4–5.
17. All scripture quotations are from the RSV.
18. Purves, *The Search for Compassion*, 69.

"just as you did it [feed the hungry, give drink to the thirsty, clothe the naked, welcome the stranger, visit the sick] to one of the least of these who are members of my family, you did it unto me" (v. 40). In Phil 3:11 Paul explains his motivation: "I want to know Christ and the power of his resurrection and the sharing of his sufferings by becoming like him in his death, if somehow I may attain the resurrection from the dead." In his letter to the Colossians, Paul explains what is at stake in such suffering-with—and it's monumental. "I am completing what is lacking in Christ's afflictions for the sake of his body, that is the church" (Col 2:24). Walking in Jesus' steps does not mean trying to copy the details of his life—an obvious impossibility. It means that each of us, in our uniqueness, in the particular needs of our time and place, are called to follow Jesus and have compassion. In the Greek to have compassion is a verb—*splanchnizomai*, used only of Jesus in the Gospels—which "literally means to have one's bowels turned over."[19] We are called to compassion (as a verb), to go where it hurts, to share in the pain of the wounded, to cry with those who mourn, to comfort those in misery, to protest with those who starve, to join with those at the margins of society.

Trauma

So, that is our question and challenge. How, in a world awash in suffering and woe, so often overrun with atrocity and anguish of nearly every kind, are we to foster and nourish a praxis of suffering love. To begin with, I think it's important to appreciate the fundamental difference between the kind of stress, hassle, or frustration that is part and parcel of ordinary life, and the radically different distress and affliction of suffering that is trauma. Unlike the vexation and annoyance of commonplace misfortunes, our ordinary cuts and bruises, trauma wounds radically. Trauma severely impairs a person's ability to process or integrate what has happened. Trauma assaults our fundamental sense of self, undermines our ways of viewing the world, and shatters our usual ways of operating in the world.[20] And, globally, trauma cripples and blunts an entire society's ability to process and integrate what has happened. Trauma reshapes a community's sense of identity, forever modifying its *modus vivendi*. Think only of the ongoing subliminal effect of the Civil War in the United States, or the Holocaust not only on the Jewish people but all peoples. Trauma with its post-traumatic aftereffects is the suffering that on multiple levels does not go away. Life is never the same again—for everyone, for every nation, for the earth.

19. Purves, *The Search for Compassion*, 74.
20. Herman, *Trauma*, 51.

Traumatic events are unusual, not because they are rare, but because they do not stay in the past. A traumatic event is horrific and shocking. It is too much to bear, too much to process, and impossible to take in and integrate at the time of its occurrence. The full impact only manifests itself later, often years later.[21] Unbearable, unsayable, uncontainable, trauma has what is now referred to as a double structure: its initial incidence, and the return of the unfinished event at various times and in various ways. Trauma repeats.

Since trauma overwhelms, its victims internally disconnect, or dissociate. They displace, block, repress, numb, deny, or bottle up the painful affect in an effort to survive and move beyond the trauma. For some, in particular veterans of war or victims of extreme violence, a random sensation or image stirs up the memory of the trauma to the point that they believe they are reliving the terrible event. Some dissociate to the point that the original wounding itself remains unregistered in the conscious memory. What has happened is, as it were, "forgotten." However, for all victims, unattended pain, even when sealed off outside of a person or community's awareness for years and years—even for generations—does not disappear or dissipate on its own. The body remembers, and unconsciously, imperceptibly, the painful affect influences, colors, and affects every activity and every relationship experienced. As long as the hurt is unattended, uncared for and unintegrated, it continues to intrude, retraumatizing.

The effect of unresolved early childhood trauma is particularly instructive in this regard. When young children feel unworthy, unacceptable, inadequate, unlovable, when they lose a parent or caregiver or are humiliated, used, or abused, in deep pain they retreat and pull back. Fearful, distrustful, and angry, with inner selves walled off for protection, they construct adaptive selves.[22] The hope is to in this way manage life without exposing themselves to further deep hurt. Some become "pleasers," willingly deferential in order to receive love and acceptance. Others turn themselves into "intimidators," whose one and only goal is never to be a loser again. Still others posture themselves as "indifferent," fine, untroubled, and untouched by what has happened—pretending it doesn't really matter anyway. The same process, *mutatis mutandis*, happens on a national and international level as groupings and nations adjust, and realign, to find their places internationally.

However, so long as the original wounding remains unattended, it continues to rankle and fester, asking to be noticed, wanting nursing and

---

21. For history of trauma studies, see Herman, *Trauma*, chapter 1, and Caruth, *Trauma*.

22. See Olthuis, *The Beautiful Risk* for an extended discussion of this process.

care. Even though compensatory strategies enable trauma survivors to get on with their lives, unconsciously they are reenacting and replaying their childhood, ethnic, or national script. And unconsciously, no matter how successful they are, they do not flourish but remain wounded and bruised as individual people and as peoples. Pain isolates, and the longer it continues unabated the more unreachable and desperate those who suffer become inside, as the free-floating, sealed-off affect continues to irritate and torment. For some people being frantic—hectic on the outside, hurting on the inside—remains the story of their lives. Others fumble along, inwardly resigning from life. Some resort to addiction, uppers and downers. Others become walking time-bombs. For some, deep despair leads to suicide, and on and on. Again, *mutatis mutandis*, the same holds true on the corporate national and international levels.

Trauma is Contagious

There is still another dimension which plays itself out in all this. Trauma is contagious. It wreaks havoc not only in the life of its first victims, but indiscriminately in the lives of many others to the third and fourth generation. Untreated, free-floating emotional pain leaks out and finds its way into others. Like sponges, people unawares can soak up, and absorb the anxiousness, helplessness, despair, or anger from people they meet. Unwittingly, someone else's distress has spread and become their own. Trauma claims new victims.

This feature came into public awareness particularly after World War II. It was discovered that a sizeable number of people suffering from depression, anxiety, paranoia, and other maladies had absorbed the bottled-up, raw, unworked-through feelings from their war veteran fathers. This same process is always at work politically and culturally. When world leaders act out their unresolved childhood scripts and/or their unresolved national scripts ("I/we will never again be humiliated, abandoned, abused, whatever!") in the guise of particular programs and policies, they foment societal turmoil and discord everywhere and on multiple levels. Via the multi-peopled, multi-layered character of political, social, and economic interaction, individual trauma can easily become contagious and go viral, precipitating cultural crisis. A recent experience of mine is a small-scale example of how this works. A middle-aged man obviously troubled began making a disturbance at a Starbucks in Toronto to the dismay and gathering discomfort of all the patrons. As the manager approached, the man stood up, looked straight into the manager's eyes and said: "If President Trump can rant and rave, so can I" and quietly walked out. Nothing more was said—nor needed to be said.

Wit(h)nessing

It is precisely because trauma spells disaster on many levels that it is difficult to process and work through. But for the same reason, unless we do recognize it, and work it through, the undertow of the trauma will haunt us in nightmarish ways. Trauma will then own us, our community and nation even in the face of defiant insistence that it belongs to the past. In addition, perpetrators of atrocities as well as proponents of policies that hurt and marginalize certain groups will do everything to escape accountability, questioning the credibility of the victims, promoting forgetting. What is needed, in the words of Judith Herman, is a "social context that affirms and protects the victim and that joins victim and witness in common alliance." For the individual the important context is a network of caring and compassionate relationships. For the society at large, "the social context is created by political movements that give voice to the disempowered." Without such movements, "the active process of bearing witness inevitably gives way to the active process of forgetting. Repression, dissociation, and denial are phenomena of social as well as individual consciousness." Herman's apt observation: In studying the nature of psychological trauma, we come face to face not only with human vulnerability but "with the capacity for evil in human nature."[23]

Suffering-With

Three inter-related considerations call for comment in our desire to develop a spirituality of compassion. First of all, as previously mentioned, for followers of Jesus the only perspective is suffering with victims of trauma individually, but also society-wide, and globally. Secondly, trauma calls out to be witnessed. Healing happens in-relation. Without acknowledgment, there is no healing. The healing pathway neither sidesteps trauma nor denies it. And thirdly, the crucial importance of concomitant and supportive political and social witness in the healing process. These key features are the focus of concern in what follows.

Suffering-with is far from an easy process. As vulnerable human beings, we don't want to suffer and try to avoid it at all costs. Yet, in suffering-with

---

23. Herman, *Trauma*, 7–9.

we willingly join with and share in another's pain and suffering. It is impossible to take away the pain, but its impact can be lessened and shared through support and encouragement. Pain isolates in aloneness. Compassion connects.

Now comes the main point. Joining with others in the depths of their aloneness and suffering calls on us to be open to our own hurts and wounds. If we do not feel our own pain, if we blunt our own suffering through apathy (*a-pathos*), we will be quick to downplay, minimize, or ignore the suffering of others, unable to exercise compassion (*com-pathos*).[24] It is a dangerous fantasy to imagine that we can walk intimately with people in their woundedness if we have not embraced our own woundedness. Only when we are in touch with our own suffering, individually and corporately, aware as Henri Nouwen would say that we are "wounded healers,"[25] will we enjoy the generosity, sensitivity, and compassion of spirit needed to accompany others in their suffering.

This is crucial because suffering-with begins precisely by acknowledging the horror of the trauma to its very victims. This may seem so self-evident as not to be necessary. Of course, they know what has happened to them. But that is the question: do they? A person's, a nation's first thoughts, first words are querulous: what is going on? What happened? Knocked for a loop, numbed, victims search for words, wildly trying to get a grip and make sense of what is happening. Precisely because trauma disorients and renders powerless, it needs to be validated. A witness, as truth-teller, plays an important role in this. Not acknowledging the trauma implicitly says it's either so bad we dare not acknowledge it, or it's not "that bad," why are you/we so upset? This helps explain why, for example, in the shooting tragedy in Columbine High School twenty years ago, the word "death" was initially never mouthed. It was, simply, too hard to accept.

Responses of this order actually stifle and repress healing on every level. "Cared" for in such ways makes victims feel unheard and unsupported. It prompts them to either numb themselves even more or to feel guilty or ashamed for being so weak. Just when the wounded need support in accessing the extent, parameters, and scope of their wounds, to help them find ways to contain or restrict its effect, they are left to suffer alone. Without encouragement in facing trauma head-on, the danger grows that the injured will either turn inward to themselves, sinking into depression, shame, and despair, or turn outward, nursing anger and plotting revenge.

---

24. Soelle, *Suffering*.
25. Nouwen, *The Wounded Healer*.

Yes, the trauma happened in the past, can never be undone, and victims long to forget it. However, it's debilitating effect invades the present, threatening the future. A witnessing presence helps victims work through trauma's impact by helping them reconnect with the world. By assuring victims that they are not alone, the witness encourages survivors to let themselves feel the hurt and process the wounding and thus begin the long, hard work of recovery.

There are huge gaps between victims and witnesses, gaps of time and space. There are also gaps of time, recall, perception, and memory for the victims themselves between the occurrence of the trauma and any telling or retelling. Victims are no longer the same persons. Even if the memory of the trauma has not been blocked, the recall of its impact and the details will invariably fluctuate from day to day. These gaps can never be eliminated but they need to be traversed. This makes witnessing, as Shelly Rambo names it, "a middle activity" which "allows the witness to see, but never directly; to hear, but never directly; and to touch, but never directly."[26]

As a middle activity called to bridge or span the gaps, witnessing is a particularly sensitive undertaking. When and if the witnesses reach out to the wounded victims with empathy, a with-experience is created, and mutual trust develops, easing and dispersing feelings of isolation and fear. Openness-to-the-other, listening with non-judgmental acceptance, affirming, and confirming develops a sense of connection and mutual understanding. The aggrieved, experiencing the openness, begin to trust that they will be heard and believed. Feeling heard and believed, victims enjoy a sense of validation and reorientation. Victims become survivors. As survivors they are emboldened to let themselves feel the depth of their hurt. And letting pain be pain begins the process of working through the pain. *Baring* one's pain in a community of loving support helps with *bearing* the pain.

The suffering-with of witnessing works optimally for healing in a surround of mutual trust and love, that is in a network of caring relationships. Witnessing on a national and international plane is in this regard of a quite different nature due to its multi-layered, multi-interested, multi-regional involvements. On those levels the relative success or failure of such witnessing largely depends on the degree of personal rapport and trust of the relevant spokepersons.

In suffering with victims on a personal as well as a national or international level, witnesses are not detectives on fact-finding missions to determine guilt or innocence. The goal is not to uncover all the facts nor is it to forget the particulars. Among acquaintances, a witness is an empathic

---

26. Rambo, *Spirit*, 40.

companion and compassionate ally. On an institutional, political level, a witness is an open-minded advocate concerned to facilitate a full telling of the events. In both cases, it involves truth-telling. Yes, you have been undone! The wounding was serious, and the suffering is very real. It should not have happened. True! But it is also true: you are not now alone. We are in this together, meeting-in-the-middle, bearing the suffering together in hope of future flourishing. On the personal level the focus of the truth-telling is validation, reassurance, and reorienting of the victim; on the societal level, the truth-telling is integral to a reconciliation process.

Suffering Love and Personal Recovery

Although everyone's pain and suffering is intricately interwoven with the world in which they live, the journey of individual healing is different in character and shape from institutional, societal, or planetary renewal. At the same time, the inward journey of personal healing is essential for the outward journal toward social renewal.

A first step in recovery for individuals is naming and owning the suffering. The overwhelming impact of "the intense arousal evoked in trauma . . . impair efforts to formulate the traumatic event into an explicit narrative." Many traumatized survivors "suffer from alexisomia, the inability to put words to sensation."[27] Finding a language to articulate what happened assists the process of filling out and integrating what is often a dissociated or skewed memory. In the process of storying, a victim regains some sense of personal power by giving borders and a beginning sense of containment to the event.

The empathic presence of a concerned witness serves to create a safe space for finding the right words to narrate the trauma. In the back and forth, the wounded victim begins to reorient, feel less alone, and gain a companion for the journey of recovery. In the retelling and relistening again and again, the victim, feeling heard, remembers even more and a story takes shape. "Stories bring the horror home," not only to witnesses, but often to the victims themselves. "They singularize suffering against the anonymity of evil."[28] I recall vividly the time that a counselee of mine interrupted her matter-of-fact recitation of the horrors of her life. "You're crying," she said to me. "Is it really that terrible?" It was. Later she told me, it suddenly hit her that "if you were crying for me, I must be worth crying for."

---

27. Ogden et al., *Trauma*, 237, 219.
28. Kearney, *On Stories*, 62.

The listener as witness becomes a companion sufferer, affirming, comforting, protesting, abiding. At the same time, the victim as story-teller also becomes a witness who testifies, eliciting response, questing affirmation and validation. Indeed, as happens so often through the deep sharing, the witness feels as connected, comforted, and encouraged as the trauma survivor. Remembering the trauma that shattered one's sense of self becomes a process of remembering that sense of self, with the victim emerging as survivor with restored agency, as one who has lived through, survived. This two-way movement of mutual witnessing—a suffering-with experience of suffering love—is what I am calling wit(h)nessing.

Wit(h)nessing is a process of restor(y)ing by giving voice to the hurt, by the baring of wounds, by letting pain be pain, by grieving, protesting, and integrating. Letting pain be pain is not a giving in to pain or a giving *up* of passive surrender on account of weakness, but a giving *over* from strength of spirit—a charting of the geography of pain so as to pass through it—and let it go. Grief is the healing emotion through which, by acknowledging the depth of the loss and hurt, the victim allows pain to be borne in new ways. In mourning a space opens through defenses to the heart and the victim owns the pain instead of the pain owning the victim. In following the pain where it leads, the suffering person learns a strength: when the mourning is a shared experience, the unbottled pain may break out in a shared lament and protest, with the pain ebbing away on the road to healing. Restor(y)ing empowers the wounded to bear the past in new ways—ways that open paths to the future. Victims become survivors, no longer living *in* the past, but living *out* of the past.

Letting healing happen is the goal. Staying-with, suffering-with is the healing gesture. When both victim as sufferer, and witness as sufferer-with, meet-in-the-middle, trust grows, defenses are let down, tears flow, hearts connect, a rhythm takes shape, and remarkably a new space opens for the streaming influx of God's healing love. Sites of trauma turning into surprises of grace. Tapping into love as the generative and regenerative energy of the universe, we experience a homecoming with ourselves, with each other, with creation, and with God. Then we are opening ourselves, letting the love of God well up and stream through us as the beat, pulse, and rhythm of our lives. "God is love" and who "dwells in love, dwells in God, and God dwells" in them (1 John 4:16). Even if the trauma has no good ending, even if it ends in death, we are enabled to live the dying together in respect and love, knowing that "our life is hidden with Christ in God" (Col 3:3).

Maybe, just maybe, hoping against hope, healed, we can continue on this road less travelled. Maybe, just maybe—without any guarantee except our trust in the God of love—we can participate in the flow of love in the world without succumbing to our fears and needing to exercise control. "The Biblical sign of salvation is not control (whether self-control, control of others, or being controlled)—it is celebration."[29]

The witness of suffering-with turns into a celebrating-with. When we are able to let go of the evils we have suffered (or committed), we enter the holy space of forgiveness, a release from the past which is a giving-forth to the future. It is our school of compassion, opening us to the pain of others. When a person's sufferings have been witnessed, and healing begins, that person, no longer dissociated and internally preoccupied with self, is enabled with open heart to suffer-with, empathize, and be witness of another person's suffering. Suffering witnessed, owned, and worked through in love is then transformed into the ability to suffer-with others in love. Despite trauma's undertow, love is made visible in the face of its absence. Whereas trauma in its contagion disconcerts and fragments, love in its outpouring attracts, connects, and heals. Suffering love gives us "a path back home."[30]

Political Witness and Trauma

The role of the witness's suffering-with in the healing of the wounds of trauma on individuals and intimate groupings is abundantly clear. However, a praxis of compassion on a global, national, and international scenes is a much more complicated and difficult undertaking. In this broken world where the suffering is so often overwhelming, disfiguring, and dismembering, it is crystal clear that compassion calls for us to stand in solidarity with and suffer with victims of cruelty, violence, and injustice of whatever kind: the homeless and refugees, the starving, the marginalized and disenfranchised, the abused, the victims of sexism, racism, war, and genocide, the very planet itself.

However, in a climate in which self-interest habitually trumps everything else, both individually and corporately, compassion is exiled. Each of us is considered an island of self-interest in competition with every other island, seeking to acquire as much as we can and giving away as little as possible. Greed, fear, lack of concern for others, and insensitivity to the ecology of creation numb us to human as well as ecological suffering and injustice. Freedom-from and power-over, rather than freedom-with and power-with, set the tone and tenor for socio-economic, political, and global relationships.

29. Fox, *A Spirituality*, 89.
30. Middleton and Walsh, *Truth*, 161.

As a result, practicing compassion on the broader national, international, and global stages is particularly sensitive, complex, and difficult. The witnessing of suffering-love, always an exercise in speaking the truth—the "way of faithful relationality in which we are called to walk and talk"[31]—becomes a more prophetic than priestly undertaking. Speaking truth to power calls for people of compassion to band together out of ardent, heartfelt distress about needless and useless suffering and raise voices of concern, protest and resistance. Such acts of wit(h)nessing, such speaking the truth in love, "truthing,"[32] (Eph 4:15) require a double focus.

On the one hand, it is important to let the afflicted know that we are chagrined, ashamed and embarrassed. "What you are going through is unacceptable and insufferable. We suffer-with you. Tell us how to support you." On the other hand, to the powers that be, the witness needs to be insistent. "This is not right. This is not the road to blessing. It is intolerable. For the sake of all the family of the earth's creatures, including the earth itself, we must find ways to do things differently. There is no other choice." Such witnessing can prove to be a tricky and sticky high-wire act. On the one front: How to join voices *with t*he oppressed without speaking *for* them? On the other front: How to suffer-with, as love demands, the very people, factions, and enemies responsible for the atrocities?[33]

Nevertheless, despite its challenges and responsibilities, protest wit(h)nessing—"whistle-blowing" par excellence—against the regimes, the systems, the forces, and the ideologies that produce hurt is an awesome privilege that is needed so often and in so many differing circumstances and places. Since each of us can only do so much, it is well to especially involve ourselves in supporting the specific prophetic movements that excite us the most, in this way channeling our anger at injustice and suffering into the energy for transformation.

But whatever choices we make, may they be impassioned with a daring and tender love, suffering-with those who suffer, weeping with those who weep, celebrating with those who celebrate. The world is waiting, the creation groans . . .

---

31. Keller, *On the Mystery*, 38. A wonderful description of truth!

32. Truthing as a gerund. Bouma-Prediger and Walsh underline the fact that the Greek text "could be translated 'truthing in love'" in *Beyond*, 277.

33. See Volf's *Exclusion and Embrace* for the struggle of suffering with not only victims of violence, but also perpetrators.

The Ambience of Love[34]	Isaiah 61:1–3
We all	The Spirit of the Lord God is upon me,
Sit in Her orchestra	because the Lord has anointed me,
Some play their	to bring good tidings to the afflicted;
Fiddles.	he has send me to bind up the brokenhearted,
Some wield their	to proclaim liberty to the captives,
Clubs.	and the opening of the prison to those who are
Tonight is worthy of music	bound: to proclaim the year of the Lord's
Let's get loose	favor, and the day of vengeance of our God;
With	to comfort all who mourn
Compassion,	to grant those who mourn in Zion—
Let's drown in the delicious	to give them a garland instead of ashes,
Ambience of	the oil of gladness instead of mourning,
Love.	the mantle of praise instead of a faint spirit.

Bibliography

Bouma-Prediger, Steven, and Brian Walsh. *Beyond Homelessness: Christian Faith in a Culture of Displacement*. Grand Rapids: Eerdmans, 2008.

Brueggemann, Walter. *The Prophetic Imagination*. 1st ed. Philadelphia: Fortress, 1978.

Caruth, Cathy. *Trauma: Explorations in Memory*. Baltimore: Johns Hopkins University Press, 1995.

Farley, Wendy. *Tragic Vision and Divine Compassion: A Contemporary Theodicy*. Louisville: Westminster John Knox, 1990.

Fox, Matthew. *A Spirituality Named Compassion and the Healing of the Global Village, Humpty Dumpty and Us*. Minneapolis: Winston, 1979.

Fretheim, Terence E. *The Suffering of God: An Old Testament Perspective*. Overtures to Biblical Theology. Philadelphia: Fortress, 1984.

---

34. Hafiz, *The Gift*, 186. Note: "His" is here "Her."

Hafiz. *The Gift*. Translated by Daniel Ladinsky. New York: Penguin Compass, 1999.
Herman, Judith Lewis. *Trauma and Recovery*. New York: Basic, 1992.
Heschel, Abraham. *The Prophets: An Introduction*. Philadelphia: Fortress, 1984.
Hoffman, Marie. *When the Roll Is Called: Trauma and the Soul in American Evangelicalism*. Eugene, OR: Cascade Books, 2016.
Johnson, Elizabeth. *She Who Is*. New York: Crossroad, 1992.
Jüngel, Eberhard. *God as the Mystery of the World*. Translated by Darrell Guder. Grand Rapids: Eerdmans, 1983.
Kearney, Richard. *On Stories*. London: Routledge, 2002.
Keller, Catherine. *On the Mystery: Discerning Divinity in Process*. Minneapolis: Fortress, 2008.
Middleton, J. Richard, and Brian J. Walsh. *Truth Is Stranger Than It Used to Be: Biblical Faith in a Postmodern Age*. Downers Grover, IL: InterVarsity, 1995.
Moltmann, Jürgen. *The Crucified God*. Translated by R.A. Wilson and John Bowden. New York: Harpert & Row, 1974.
Nouwen, Henri. *The Wounded Healer*. Garden City, NY: Doubleday, 1979.
Ogden, Pat, Kekuni Minton, and Clare Pain. *Trauma and the Body*. New York: W.W. Norton, 2006.
Olthuis, James. *The Beautiful Risk: A New Psychology of Loving and Being Loved*. 2001. Reprint, Eugene, OR: Wipf & Stock, 2006.
———. "Thinking God Otherwise: Sovereignty without Sovereignty." In *Dancing in the Wild Spaces of Love*, a theopoetics of risk (forthcoming).
Purves, Andrew. *The Search for Compassion: Spirituality and Ministry*. Louisville: Westminster John Knox, 1989.
Rambo, Shelly. *Spirit and Trauma: A Theology of Remaining*. Louisville: Westminster John Knox, 2010.
Soelle, Dorothy. *Suffering*. Translated by Everett Kahlin. Philadelphia: Fortress, 1975.
Volf, Miroslav. *Exclusion and Embrace: A Theological Exploration of Identity, Otherness, and Reconciliation*. Nashville: Abingdon, 1996.

13

The Reconciling Power of Public Art In a Broken Home[1]

Adrienne Dengerink Chaplin & Jonathan Chaplin

> *"A wound must be cleaned out and examined before it will heal; it is the unexamined wound that festers and eventually poisons. Our work shows the wounds."*
>
> —The Bogside Artists[2]

Can Art Heal a Broken Home?

A broken home cannot be restored unless the truth about the wounds that broke it begins to be acknowledged. This is why so many broken homes—familial, local, cultural, national— never experience reconciliation, or why, at best, they settle for little more than a fragile and resentful *modus vivendi*. In most situations of entrenched conflict, radically contending accounts of real-

---

1. This essay draws on Dengerink Chaplin et al., *Art, Conflict and Remembering: The Murals of the Bogside Artists*. This is the catalogue accompanying the travelling exhibition of the same name, first shown at Coventry Cathedral in June 2017.

2. The Bogside Artists are here paraphrasing the sentiments of Archbishop Desmond Tutu expressed in an interview with Ray Uarez on South Africa's *Newshour* in 1999: "And that is why our people have been committed to the reconciliation where we use restorative rather than retributive justice, which is a kind of justice, that says—we are looking to the healing of relationships, we are seeking to open wounds, yes, but to open them so that we can cleanse them and they don't fester; we cleanse them and then pour oil on them, and then we can move into the glorious future that God is opening up for us." See also Desmond Tutu, *No Future without Forgiveness*.

ity square up against each other in a paralyzed stand-off with little prospect of resolution. Embittered factions hurl rival narratives in each other's faces and, imprisoned in their own pain and jealous of their own threatened identities, remain deaf to the narratives of their perceived enemies. They only have the emotional bandwidth to nurse their own wounds.

Such rival narratives are typically asserted through the medium of words. But while well-meant, well-crafted words do have potential to heal when seasoned with truthfulness and generosity, words are all too easily deployed to inflame, to humiliate, to demarcate, and to exclude. Where words become pervasively weaponized in these ways, sometimes it is only art—an evocative image, a telling metaphor, a haunting melody, an allusive gesture—that can break through the dividing wall. Sometimes only art can insinuate itself into the heavily defended inner vaults of resentment, grievance, and fear that sustain conflicts and block off reconciliation. At its best, art has the potential to circumvent cognitive bravado and offer imaginative, affective, unsettling—and often fiercely resisted—glimpses of the aching wounds of the hated Other. Such art can release subversive, potent memes of honesty, humility, and empathy into broken communities, inviting estranged parties to take the first steps towards the terrifying but tantalizing prospect of healing.[3]

This capacity arises from the unique vocation of art as a created gift to human beings who, bearing the *Imago Dei*, are far more than "rational animals." Humans are embodied, relational, storied, situated creatures equipped with multiple capacities for creativity and goodness who are yet—or, rather, therefore—vulnerable to many kinds of hurts. In that fragile fabric of the human condition, art has the unique ability to articulate deeply felt human experiences—painful as well as exhilarating—that cannot adequately be captured, or captured at all, in discursive, verbal prose.[4] Art can surprise, seduce, entice, or shock people into looking at the world with different eyes, eyes opened to the shared vulnerabilities of all human beings and the universal longing for relational healing—and reconciled home.[5]

---

3. Brian Walsh has always had a deep appreciation for the disturbing, truth-telling, meaning-making, healing power of the arts—its indispensable role in the human tasks of home-making and home restoration. For him, contemporary music has been the preferred medium through which to explore that capacity and he has done so with an insight and flair that have spoken powerfully to many. See, e.g., Walsh, *Kicking at the Darkness*.

4. For accounts of this view of art, see Seerveld, *Rainbows for a Fallen World*, and Brand and Chaplin, *Art and Soul*.

5. In *Beyond Homelessness* Bouma-Prediger and Walsh offer a profound meditation on the themes of "home," "homemaking," "homelessness," "displacement," and "homecoming." Their nuanced account of "boundaries" in chapter 2 speaks especially to the

Reconciling Art in Unexpected Places

A series of public murals from Northern Ireland might not seem the most promising place to look for "reconciling art."[6] For many, the mention of Northern Ireland murals immediately conjures up intimidating images of masked gunman, raised rifles, threatening slogans, and a plethora of signs and symbols representing various para-military organizations. Over twenty years after a peace agreement, they are still pervasive and visible in Belfast and other cities in Northern Ireland. Murals like this are meant to convey political messages, mark a community's neighborhood boundaries, and demonstrate who was in control.[7] As Bouma-Prediger and Walsh argue, boundaries are "constitutive for life," yet they can easily become an "ideological legitimation of our geographies of exclusion. . . . Boundaries used to erect fortresses of self-protection . . . can never be refuges of hospitality. The walls are simply too thick, the barriers too impenetrable."[8]

This essay introduces the story of the unique work of the remarkable "Bogside Artists," composers of a radically different form of mural—an arresting example of "reconciling art." This is a striking array of large gable-end murals known as *The People's Gallery*. These murals testify to the deep wounds of a broken home, the city of Derry/Londonderry—one that cannot even agree on its name.[9] The conflicted story of this city is emblematic of the larger divisions of the broken homes of Northern Ireland, of the island of Ireland, and of the "United" Kingdom; and, indeed, of conflict situations well beyond the British Isles. The artistic testimony of the Bogside Artists recounts the story of the traumatic events experienced by the Bogside community—the most disadvantaged and discriminated-against part of the city of Derry—during the extended conflict known as the "Troubles." This narrative project isn't simply expressive: its overriding goal is to open up possibilities of dialogue, truthfulness, and reconciliation across the divisions

---

broken homes of Derry and Northern Ireland.

6. A fuller account of this series of public murals will appear in Dengerink Chaplin, "Art, Protest and Peace: The Murals of the Bogside Artists."

7. For a comprehensive account of such murals in Northern Ireland, see Rolston, *Drawing Support*.

8. Bouma-Prediger and Walsh, *Beyond Homelessness*, 53.

9. The dual name of the city reflects a longstanding naming dispute between nationalists and unionists, the first preferring Derry, the latter Londonderry. The oldest name for the city was "Doire," later anglicized to "Derry." This was changed by Royal Charter to "Londonderry" in 1613. In 1984 the city's local authority changed its name to "Derry City Council." After merging with nearby Strabane in 2015, this became "Derry and Strabane District Council." Since the name "Derry" is widely used informally, and almost always locally, we will use that name to refer to the city.

that have marred the city and the various surrounding nations with which its destiny has been inextricably bound up.

The People's Gallery stands as a poignant witness both to a suffering community's insistence on the public remembrance of its truth and against the resistance to that remembrance from establishments that want to suppress it. It has carved out a striking, unsettling visual memorial that invites all who pass by to enter into the story it tells and be confronted and transformed by that story—and, in turn, to tell their own.

The People's Gallery

Between 1994 and 2006, brothers William and Tom Kelly and their friend Kevin Hasson painted twelve large-scale murals on the three-storey gable walls of a group of apartments in the Bogside neighbourhood of Derry.[10] The Bogside was the epicenter of the Troubles, a violent, thirty-year conflict that began on 5 October 1968 with a non-sectarian civil rights march in Derry, and concluded on 10 April 1998 with the "Good Friday" peace agreement (the "Belfast Agreement").[11]

The conflict was complex, brutal, and involved many actors. Essentially, it involved three parties: (mainly) Catholic nationalists and Republicans;[12] (mainly) Protestant unionists and Loyalists;[13] and the British government

---

10. The name "Bogside" goes back to the time that this land was flooded by the nearby River Foyle. The area lies at the bottom of a wooded hill that provided Derry with its original name of Doire (or "oak grove").

11. For an account of the Troubles in the Bogside, see McClenagham, ed., *Spirit of '68*.

12. "Nationalists" are those who seek a united Ireland; "Republicans" are the radical wing of Irish nationalism, believing in the legitimacy of armed struggle to achieve that goal (as formerly prosecuted by the IRA and its various offshoots). Since the 1998 Belfast Agreement, most of the Republican movement in Northern Ireland has rejected armed struggle (without renouncing its past use) and now supports participation in the new power-sharing government created by the Agreement. The political party representing Republicanism is Sinn Féin, which entered into this government after 1998. "Constitutional nationalists" are those who aspire to a united Ireland exclusively by peaceful democratic means. Its main political representative is the Social Democratic and Labour Party (SDLP).

13. "Unionists" are those who defend the "union" of Britain and Northern Ireland (the settlement instituted by the "Partition" of 1921); "Loyalists" is the term now generally given to the radical wing of unionism, distinguished both by its willingness to endorse or prosecute armed resistance against Republicanism and its insistence on the Protestant character of Northern Ireland. There are two unionist political parties: the Ulster Unionists (UU), long the dominant party, but now eclipsed by the dominant Democratic Unionist Party (DUP) founded by radical Protestant minister Rev. Dr. Ian Paisley.

and armed forces. It dominated Northern Ireland for a generation, blighted innumerable lives and communities, damaged a great deal of infrastructure, and left a deep legacy of entrenched bitterness. The combined number of deaths during this period, inflicted by both Republican and Loyalist paramilitaries as well as by British security forces, exceeded 3,600. In addition, over 50,000 people were physically maimed or injured, with almost an entire generation suffering long-term psychological damage.[14]

All three artists were born and grew up in the Bogside during this turbulent period. Each lost family and friends. The murals depict key moments of the Troubles as they affected ordinary local residents living in extraordinary times.[15] They are located on Rossville Street which runs through the center of the Bogside and are collectively named *The People's Gallery*.[16]

Visitors to the Bogside find themselves immediately struck by the strong visual impact of the murals. Against the background of their mundane urban surroundings, the large murals create an unsettling juxtaposition of feelings of strangeness—the incongruity between the stark images and the ordinary road signs and traffic islands—and a sense of familiarity—the images of conflict that reach us daily through the media. Taken together, the twelve murals constitute a unique grassroots, site-specific work of commemorative public art.

The murals are in a profound sense owned by the community whose story they tell. Prior to painting their first mural in 1994, the artists presented a petition to paint on the walls, signed by over two thousand local residents, to the Northern Ireland Housing Executive (NIHE), which owns the buildings. The Housing Executive is an independent housing authority that was established in 1971 in response to the unfair distribution of housing at the time.[17] Their policy on murals is that they allow their walls to be used

---

14. For detailed statistics on many aspects of the Troubles see CAIN (Conflict Archive on the INternet) based at the University of Ulster.

15. For more information, see the exhibition website listed in the bibliography. For detailed commentaries on each of the twelve murals, setting them in their immediate context, see Dengerink Chaplin, *Art, Conflict and Remembering*.

16. For images of all murals, see "The Wall Murals: The People's Gallery" (website listed in bibliography). Some murals have since been repainted in different versions. For a book on the murals written by the artists under the name Anthony C. Joseph, see *The People's Gallery*. ('Anthony C. Joseph' is a pseudonym, combining the second names of the artists: Kevin *Anthony* Hasson, Thomas *Columba* Kelly, and William *Joseph* Kelly.)

17. The establishment of the Northern Ireland Housing Executive was the direct outcome of the calls for reforms by civil rights leader John Hume, who demanded that decisions on housing allocation be taken away from unionist-controlled local councils and the Derry Housing Corporation.

for mural paintings as long as the residents who live in the buildings agree.[18] Since, at the time, the walls were covered by graffiti and the area around it was an urban wasteland littered with debris following many decades of neglect and vandalism, the Housing Executive was all too happy to agree to a professionally painted mural. Having been shown the planned design in advance, they not only granted the artists permission to paint on the walls but even cleaned and rendered them with smooth cement to make it easier to work on. Once the first mural to be composed, *The Petrol Bomber* (discussed below), was finished, residents started to take increased pride in the area and small improvements followed. It was only a matter of time before the artists decided to do another mural and the idea was eventually born to take on the entire street. With every new mural they would first show their plans to the residents for their approval before proceeding. Throughout, they had the full support of local people whose small donations contributed to the purchasing of paint and the renting of scaffolding.

Despite this enthusiastic local support, some politicians consider the murals unwelcome reminders of a tortured past, one in which they themselves were often implicated.[19] So far any attempts to remove the murals have been rebuffed by local residents who are strongly supportive of maintaining them and who, since the artists do not receive any public funding, continue to contribute to their upkeep.[20] For them the murals tell a story that is still very much alive. They are a public recognition and reminder of their past suffering and resilience. By being able to see their past stories visually narrated on the walls, they are enabled to look to the future with integrity and courage.

Defending the murals against their various critics has always been an uphill struggle for the artists and their supporters. For example, since the 1998 Peace Agreement many efforts have been made to replace the combative tribal murals of both Republicanism and Loyalism with more socially-friendly and peace-promoting ones. Politicians from both the unionist and nationalist sides of the new power-sharing government (the Northern Ireland Executive)—were eager to re-brand the country as a safe and inclusive post-conflict society that was economically viable and forward-looking. They funded several "re-imaging" schemes that offered generous grants to local communities who would agree to replace their most aggressive

---

18. See Woods, *Seeing is Believing*.

19. See Kerr, ed., *Murals in Derry*, and McCormick, "Death of a Mural."

20. Only in 2018 did the new Derry and Strabane District Council agree to provide funds for the lighting of the murals. The artists have never been paid for their work on the murals.

murals with more peaceful images.[21] Popular replacements included images of famous historical figures, sports icons or celebrities who, it was hoped, could be embraced across different communities. While the Bogside Artists emphatically reject the aggressive tribalism of sectarian murals, they nevertheless stand against attempts to airbrush the suffering from their community's agonized history. Instead they offer a fundamentally different mode of remembering.

Ironically, the least enthusiasm for replacing the old sectarian murals came from the tourist industry. Glamorised by the media's fascination with violence, these murals have now become a major tourist attraction, providing lucrative business opportunities for local tour guides and cab drivers, who were often ex-paramilitaries and ex-prisoners struggling to find employment elsewhere. The Northern Ireland Tourist Board now advertizes these tours alongside the province's other attractions as an important part of its cultural heritage. A typical mural tour begins by showing tourists murals "from this side" (Loyalists) and then, usually after a break, those "from the other side" (Republicans). On some tours in Derry—those under the de facto control of Sinn Féin—*The People's Gallery* is frequently presented as "from the other side."

Such tribalism reflects the still-pervasive view of *all* political murals in Northern Ireland: that they can always be classified according to the two basic categories that divide the province's politics and culture: *either* Catholic/nationalist/Republican *or* Protestant/unionist/Loyalist; *either* "Green" *or* "Orange." Such misrepresentations are often inadvertently aided and abetted by the media which, when scrambling for a suitable backdrop to the latest "Republican" happening—such as the recent funeral of former Derry IRA commander and longstanding Sinn Féin leader Martin McGuinness—typically choose one of the more provocative murals from *The People's Gallery*.[22]

Thus, from the beginning, the Bogside Artists have had to struggle to maintain the distinctiveness of their reconciliatory art against an amnesiac "re-imaging" strategy that would sweep difficult memories under the carpet, an intentional co-option by Republican leaders, and an unintentional

---

21. See "Building Peace through the Arts."

22. McGuinness played a vital role in securing the 1998 Belfast Agreement. He later entered the new Northern Ireland Executive, serving as Education Minister, and then Deputy First Minister of Northern Ireland from May 2007 to January 2017 alongside Ian Paisley as First Minister. He died in March 2017. His funeral cortège passed by *The Petrol Bomber* in Derry, an image captured widely in the media. McGuinness was willing to be seen associating with *The People's Gallery* when it suited him, but the Derry Sinn Féin leadership consistently attempted to marginalize the Bogside Artists themselves as the artists resisted their attempts to control them.

assimilation to a Republican agenda by a media with an unacknowledged interest in sustaining sectarianism (it makes for good copy).

The restrictive and debilitating assumptions behind such tribalism are challenged head-on by the Bogside Artists. They fiercely oppose the binary lens through which Northern Ireland is viewed, oppose the incorporation of their work into its sectarian schema and reject the toxic identity politics that informs it. And they have paid the price for doing so. They are not only, and predictably, ignored or rejected by the unionist community, but also marginalised by a Republican leadership which deeply resents the existence of a popular work of public art it doesn't control.

Sources of Brokenness—Obstacles to Reconciliation

Unlike South Africa, Northern Ireland has not yet had, and never may have, a proper truth and reconciliation process.[23] Despite a peace agreement and a power-sharing Executive, "post-conflict" Northern Ireland remains deeply segregated across many sectors of society. This reflects, and in turn continues powerfully to mold, people's relationship to their past— the contending histories of their rival "homes." An abiding obstacle to reconciliation is that there is simply no shared agreement about the fundamental cause and nature of the conflict. Was it primarily a Republican struggle for a united Ireland, a Loyalist battle for a Protestant state, or a socialist uprising campaigning for internal reforms and basic democratic rights? Given these fiercely contested narratives, both sides are quick to encode history to their own advantage, and then claim credit for the peace.[24] What follows are just a few episodes from that history which may help give some context to the distinctive achievement of the Bogside Artists (but even this sketch would be fiercely contested by some).

An Invaded Community

The Bogside was once the site of a monastic settlement, thought to have been founded by Saint Columba before he sailed on to establish a monastery and missionary school on the Island of Iona in 563.[25] The Catholic Church of Saint

---

23. See Simpson, *Truth Recovery in Northern Ireland*; and McEvoy, *Making Peace with the Past*.

24. For different accounts on the Troubles see, e.g., Mallie and McKittrick, *Endgame in Ireland*; Kerr, *The Destructors*; McKittrick and McVea, *Making Sense of the Troubles*.

25. The word Columba in Irish means dove, and *Colm Cille* means "church dove." Derry's full name in Gaelic is *Doire Colmcille*, thus reflecting both the native oak trees

Columba's Long Tower stands near the spot of this original settlement. Built in 1784 to meet the needs of the expanding Catholic community in Derry, it is still considered the Catholic heart of the Bogside today. It was also the church that the artists' families used to attend when they were young.[26]

For centuries the Bogside and surrounding region were sparsely populated with monks and migrating Gaelic Irish famers. After the Norman invasion in the twelfth century, however, Ireland came under English rule. In 1600, Sir Henry Docwra occupied Derry and fortified the dilapidated settlement with strong walls—a massive "home invasion" with fateful consequences for centuries afterwards. (Despite many attacks from outside, including the Great Siege of 1689, the walls have remained intact and remain one of Derry's main visitor attractions.) English rule was further consolidated under King James I's controlled "Plantation of Ulster"—the effective colonization of Ulster by Protestant English and Scottish, including a large group of London merchants who, by Royal Charter, succeeded in establishing the town as the city of "Londonderry."

A Divided Community

Derry had developed a large port and a linen industry and was a global exporter of shirts. From the 1700s on, many Irish families from neighboring Donegal moved to the Bogside seeking work in the docks and linen industry. A large influx arrived during the Great Irish Famine in the mid-nineteenth century when the British government abjectly and culpably failed to provide relief for the starving poor. A million died and another million emigrated to America, Britain, and Australia. This fueled growing demands for Irish "Home Rule" which gained further momentum as the century progressed. These demands might have been satisfied in 1893 had the British House of Lords—dominated by aristocratic landowners many of whom owned extensive tracts of land in Ireland—not blocked British Liberal prime minister William Gladstone's Second Home Rule Bill, which

---

in the area and the city's association with Saint Columba who, until this day, is Derry's patron saint. The image of the dove and the oak leaf appear in *The Peace Mural*, the last of the twelve murals.

26. As William Kelly recalls: "As children, we would assemble around St. Columba's Well on certain feast days. The streets would be festooned with ribbons and prayers would be intoned. Church was part and parcel of our daily experience. It was the very heart of the community. With trepidation we would go there to have our confessions heard. In the evenings we would often attend benediction and on Sundays we never missed Mass. With the heightened awareness that is the gift of childhood these experiences impact the psyche profoundly." Bogside Artists, *Healing and Art*, 18–19.

had, after an extended struggle, passed in the House of Commons. Irish nationalist sentiment surged in the early twentieth century, compounded by World War I, energizing the famous (though failed) "Easter Rising," the 1916 Republican rebellion in Dublin. Two years later, moderate nationalism was swept aside by Sinn Féin, who won a landslide victory in the 1918 UK parliamentary elections, provocatively declaring Ireland an independent state. By 1920 the UK government was forced to take the unpalatable and fiercely contested decision to partition Ireland into two territories: an overwhelmingly Catholic southern part that became the Republic of Ireland, and a (majority Protestant) northern part—the six counties of the province of Ulster—that remained part of the United Kingdom. This fateful step has been the principal grievance of all Irish nationalists (both "Republican" and "Constitutional") since then and was the enduring backdrop to the resurgence of a violent Republican para-military campaign (and its Loyalist counterparts) in the 1970s.[27]

An Oppressed Community

With a unionist-dominated Northern Ireland government loyal to Britain and systematically biased in favor of the Protestant unionist community, the Catholic minority in Northern Ireland felt increasingly marginalized and dispossessed. This applied especially to the Catholic population of Derry. Catholics were denied housing in the city itself and were relegated to the slums of the Bogside outside the city walls.

Ethno-religious segregation was compounded by economic exploitation. The invention of the sewing machine and introduction of the assembly line in the mid-nineteenth century produced a massive increase in production and exports to the UK and other European countries as well as the British colonies. Most businesses in Derry were owned and managed by Protestants, but the grinding hard work in their factories was done almost exclusively by Catholic women and girls. They often became the main breadwinners, since Derry lacked the larger male-dominated industries such as shipbuilding and engineering. It was not uncommon for young "factory girls" to support whole families in which husbands and fathers were unable to find work.

In 1891 the women in Derry's factories became the first female workers in Ireland to be unionized when they were allowed to join the Derry Trades

---

27. Indeed, the border between Northern Ireland and the Irish Republic continues to be a principal cause of controversy in the Brexit debate. Britain's (specifically, England's) historical ignorance and neglect of Ireland again comes back to bite it.

Council. Tom and William's great aunt Julia Kelly was one of the first female factory Trade Union Leaders in the UK.[28] By 1930 the city had forty-four shirt factories providing work for over 8,000 employees, one of whom later was Tom and William's sister Rose.[29] An ever-growing population in the Bogside led to overcrowded, cramped, and damp dwellings. Tuberculosis, malnourishment and alcoholism were widespread.[30] Conditions like these, together with the ongoing discrimination of Catholics by the unionist-dominated government, led to increasing resentment and anger within the Bogside community. Invigorated by other Civil Rights movements globally, the community started to organize its own protest marches and petitions to the government.[31] The campaign is commemorated in mural one, *Civil*

28. In that role she got to meet and have tea with Eleanor Marx Aveling, the English-born youngest daughter of Karl Marx and socialist activist when she visited the female trade unionists in Derry in that same year of 1891. Private communication via Facebook page, September 2016.

29. Rose recalls her experience as follows: "We all worked in the shirt factories, I, my mother and my two sisters, my cousins and my aunts. I joined the City Factory in July, two weeks after my fifteenth birthday. I never wanted to work there because I was a good student and wanted my parents to send me to a college in London to be properly educated; but we were dirt poor and living in The Wells at the time and I no more dreamt of being a college student than my poor dad dreamt of owning a car. We had previously lived in Fox's Corner, the Skid Row of the Bogside, probably the worst street in it, and my parents needed the money. The Wells was just around the corner, ten of us including my two uncles sharing a tiny, cramped house. We did piece-work and were often timed at our job by stopwatch in what they called a 'time and motion study.' We were paid for what we produced, not by the hour. We worked from 8 AM to 6 PM, Monday to Friday. To get more money you had to do more work and so, although working Saturday mornings was an 'option,' it really wasn't an option at all. The work was boring in the extreme livened only by the music played over loud speakers and of course the girls you worked with and got to know. Nearly all of us smoked. The factory is where I learned to smoke. And we worked in twos so that, if your partner was slower than you, you tended to produce less and so earned less and vice versa. If you were a minute late in the morning you were locked out for fifteen minutes and your pay deducted by an amount I could never figure out . . . It was damn hard work is my final say about the City Shirt Factory, slave labour." Private communication via Facebook page, September 2016.

30. William Kelly recalls: "When I was six, I lived with my parents and three sisters in a two-room downstairs hovel at Fox's Corner that had a cement floor and a couple of gas lanterns. The front room with its low ceiling was so small that when the settee that my parents slept in was unfolded there was hardly room enough to walk around. The old tenement had no front door. Drunks would often sleep in the hallway and I would have to sneak past them on my way to school. Occasionally, one of them would be my uncle Midge or my grandfather James." Private communication, adapted from a longer account in Joseph, *Bogside Artists*, 20.

31. The Northern Ireland Civil Rights Association (NICRA) was founded in 1967 as a response to forty years of unionist discrimination against Catholics. It was non-sectarian and also supported by some Protestants. It had five demands: one man, one

Rights. It was the suppression of these legitimate protests that sparked the conflict known as the Troubles. The brutal and calamitous event known as "Bloody Sunday"—depicted in mural five, *Bloody Sunday*—in which British soldiers shot dead fourteen unarmed protestors (six of them aged seventeen), was one such protest. These protestors are commemorated in mural six, *Bloody Sunday Memorial*.

A Betrayed Community

The 1998 Peace Agreement brought about a ceasefire between the two rival paramilitary movements and a "power-sharing" pact between the leading political parties (by then Sinn Féin and the Democratic Unionist Party). It has been widely hailed as a hugely important step towards creating the conditions for a genuine peace in Northern Ireland, and no-one wants to see it undermined. Yet on the ground, not least in places like Derry, there has been a mounting sense of disillusionment with the subsequent "peace process." Deepening discontent has arisen especially among large sections of the working classes on both sides of the divide, largely due to a sense of betrayal on the part of their leaders. Not only have such leaders not achieved their original objectives—a united Ireland for Republicans or a Protestant state for Loyalists—neither have ordinary people experienced any sustained improvement in their economic circumstances or their sense of social inclusion. Many of them still feel "marginalized" (Catholics) or "under siege" (Protestants). A disturbing level of vigilante-style violence (such as "kneecapping") continues below the radar, much of it perpetrated by IRA sympathizers who claim to be "protecting" local communities that have been left to their own devices by absent security services. Some feel that the 1998 Agreement has been good for the perpetrators of para-military violence who benefitted from large-scale amnesties and sometimes large financial compensations, but not for the surviving victims. They see many of their leaders moving on to comfortable positions in Stormont (the seat of the Executive) or elsewhere, while they have paid the price for other people's political and economic gains. At street level, there is casual contempt for what has become known as "the peace industry," which is often seen as little more than a gravy train for cynical careerists.

---

vote; ending gerrymandering; anti-discrimination measures; fair allocation of public housing; repeal of the Special Powers act and the disbanding of the B-Specials, a quasi-military police unit set up in 1921 and known for its rough methods (it was disbanded in 1970). It was inspired by the non-violent civil disobedience campaigns of Martin Luther King.

In the Bogside, many Republican politicians and community leaders are writing their own histories. In particular, they now try to claim ownership of the non-violent Civil Rights movement that emerged in the late 1960s. This, however, is not how many local residents remember it. They remember the Republican cause as a united Ireland, by whatever means. For those who lost their sons and brothers through the Hunger Strikes, that is not something easily forgotten. With the goal of a united Ireland still no closer they feel their loved ones were sacrificed in vain. For so-called "dissident" Republicans, for example, the Peace Agreement was an act of gross betrayal by their leaders, who are now shifting ground by aligning themselves with the memory of the Civil Rights movement. The tragic shooting of widely-admired twenty-nine-year-old journalist Lyra McKee in Derry on Maundy Thursday 2019 by one such dissident group (the "New IRA") —she was struck by a bullet aimed at the police as she stood yards away while reporting on a police raid—is only the latest manifestation of this particular (and twisted) narrative of betrayal.[32]

For most ordinary Bogsiders, however, the Republican cause was never at the top of their agenda, nor did they condone the violence that achieving it might involve. They worried less about territories and borders than about housing, work, and food. For them the real heroes of the time were Civil Rights campaigners John Hume and Ivan Cooper. Co-founders of the Social Democratic and Labour Party, they fought tirelessly for the same rights in housing, voting and employment for Catholics as were enjoyed by Protestants. As Hume's father used to say: "You can't eat a flag."[33] Hume is celebrated in mural ten, *John Hume*, alongside Martin Luther King, Mother Teresa, and Nelson Mandela. Whilst still advocating a united Ireland via constitutional means ("constitutional nationalism"), the primary goal of their campaign was, ironically, for Catholics to be treated as equal British citizens.

The British government, meanwhile, remains in deep denial about its own role in the conflict and unwilling to acknowledge that, far from being merely a peace-keeping force, it in effect constituted a third party in the conflict. With the single major exception of the large-scale Saville inquiry into the Bloody Sunday killings, it is only recently that inquests have been opened into various incidents involving the security forces.[34] One example

32. O'Shea, "The Tragic Killing."
33. Hume, interview.
34. Families of the protestors who were killed on Bloody Sunday were devastated when, in March 2019 after a protracted investigation, the Northern Ireland Director of Public Prosecutions announced that only one of the several soldiers suspected of shooting them would be prosecuted, due to lack of "admissible evidence." See Bowcott, "Prosecutors."

is the killing of fifteen-year old Manus Deery who features in mural eight, *The Runner*.[35] A close friend of Tom Kelly, Manus was killed by a bullet fired by a British sniper from the old city walls.

Incidents like that went largely unreported in the British media. Mainstream national news focused almost exclusively on the chaotic riots, showing stone-throwing youth and burnt-out cars, thereby serving to legitimate the ongoing presence of British "peace-keeping" troops in Northern Ireland. This merely enforced the popular image of the province as an unruly, combative society consumed by an ancient tribal dispute between Catholics and Protestants. The fact that unarmed civil rights demonstrators were being treated like insurgents, and that young children were being fired upon by British troops, is still not widely known. The common tendency is to downplay this long traumatic episode in recent British history as an unfortunate blip, rather than the logical culmination of centuries of colonial oppression and discrimination.

Given these rival narratives, suppressed memories and ongoing hostilities, it is hardly surprising that there is a lack of political will to initiate a meaningful truth and reconciliation process. Instead, ordinary citizens are urged to "draw a line under the past" and "move on." They should not stay "locked in the past" but "get on" with their lives. In such a climate, survivors of the Troubles such as the Bogside residents are not only left without public recognition of their plight or granted due justice, but are also deprived of the means to voice their experience of the past and to remember it in any meaningful way. They are being silenced once again as a means to keep the peace for others.

An Uneasy Space for Reconciliation

It is for people such as these that the murals of *The People's Gallery* provide a space of safety and open conversation to deal with the past. The murals facilitate the kind of open-ended dialogues necessary for the proper processing of complex and confused traumatic memories. They enable people to share their stories without them being annexed to others' master narratives or hijacked for the purposes of political propaganda. The painfully evocative story told by the murals of Bogside Artists strikingly exemplifies James Olthuis' proposal that "narratives are possible, not as grand control devices, but as tales of (broken) love co-authored in community."[36] The

---

35. BBC, "Magnus Deery: Inquest."

36. Olthuis, "Crossing the Threshold", 37, quoted in Steven Bouma-Prediger and Brian Walsh, *Beyond Homelessness*, 279.

murals help them keep alive the memories of those they lost and sustain their fragile hope for a different, reconciled future. The Bogside Artists are courageous examples of what Brian Walsh and Steven Bouma-Prediger call "aching visionaries."[37]

Because of their location and subject matter, the murals are often lazily classified as "Republican." Yet anyone who cares to look at them more closely quickly discovers that they are fundamentally different in content, style and tone. It is true, of course, that they tell the story from the standpoint of the Catholic working-class Bogside community; the artists don't presume to speak for Protestants and unionists, who they think must articulate their own stories. But unlike Republican murals, they bear no flags or symbols linking them to any para-military or political organization. They do not carry any threats or slogans promoting a Republican cause. There are no shamrocks, harps or Gaelic writings appealing to Irish history or identity. Many of them are based on photographs of actual people and events. They do not romanticize historical heroes or some distant mythological past. They do not demonize the enemy or glorify violence.

One mural in particular illustrates this point forcefully: *The Petrol Bomber* (mural two)—not least because it is often singled out for its supposed aggressiveness.

---

37. Bouma-Prediger and Walsh, *Beyond Homelessness*, 227. They take the term from Wolterstorff, *Lament for a Son*, 85–86.

All photographs are by Kevin Hasson and are used with his permission.

In fact, this image does not convey a threat but a defense. It does not show a gunman firing in our direction. The mural is based on what was to become a famous photograph by British press photographer Clive Limpkin during the "Battle of the Bogside" in August 1969. It shows a young boy with a gas mask holding a home-made petrol bomb made out of an empty milk bottle. These DIY Molotov cocktails were made collectively by the Bogside community as a defense against attacks from the police, and they were quite often thrown from rooftops. The boy in the photo is, in fact, fourteen-year old Paddy Coyle, a cousin of Tom and William Kelly.[38] Here he is as an adult, standing with the artists in front of the mural.

---

38. Paddy's face is visible on another photo, taken by French press photographer Gilles Caron, which appeared on the front cover of *Paris Match* that same month.

The Bogside Artists C

The image on the photograph and the mural is, like all good art, deeply ambiguous, recording, on the one hand, combative youthful bravura, and, on the other, defensive vulnerability. The old and defunct World War II gas mask was worn more for show than for protection against the teargas used by the police. Among the many disturbing questions this image raises are: What is a boy that age doing with a petrol bomb that can cause lethal damage? Who sanctioned and encouraged an entire community to produce these dangerous missiles? What desperate times and circumstances can drive sensible families to put themselves and their children at such risk?

Just how lethal these bombs could be is highlighted by *The Runner*, commemorating seventeen-year old Brian Coyle, another friend of Tom Kelly. Brian was killed in Tom's own backyard when the petrol bomb he had meant to throw over the wall at a passing British foot patrol exploded prematurely. Tom still has vivid memories of witnessing the agony in which his friend died. On a remembrance plaque installed by Brian's parents it is written that he died on "Active Service," a reference to the fact that he would have been a youth "volunteer" of the IRA. Two other friends of Tom who died are also commemorated in the murals: sixteen-year old Charles Love, who was killed by a piece of debris from an IRA bomb that exploded while he was watching a parade, and (as noted) Manus Deery, who was killed by a British bullet fired from the old city walls. Mural four, *Annette*, shows Kevin Hasson's fourteen-year old cousin Annette McGavigan, who was also shot and killed by a British sniper shooting from the city walls.

These murals do not glorify violence. They are laments. And they are penetrating critiques of the foolishness and futility of violence, from whatever hand. The people pictured on these murals are not generic cardboard figures but the sons and daughters, brothers and sisters, aunts and uncles, of local residents. The Troubles affected and will affect not just the generation of those caught up in it but their children and grandchildren. The twelve murals culminate, spatially and symbolically, in *The Peace Mural*, standing at the end of Rossville Street as an invitation to a different future.

In contrast to the monochrome greys of most of the other murals, this one displays an explosion of color. Based on ideas from local children from both Catholic and Protestant communities, the mural depicts a peace dove, referring to Derry's patron saint, St. Columba, superimposed on an oak leaf—a reference to the city's original name "Doire," or "oak grove."

The murals are not sectarian but they are inevitably political, and they speak far beyond their immediate context. As always, there are lessons to be learned from history, not just by Northern Ireland or by Britain, but by any divided society. The fact that many visitors from abroad, especially those from other conflict zones, are deeply moved when viewing *The People's Gallery* is testimony to the murals' universal appeal.[39]

To remember the past truthfully means to be able to listen to other's stories—to see and feel their wounds. The artists urge that only when the two sides have confronted the wounds they have inflicted on each other, and on themselves, can there be the possibility of healing and forgiveness. They fully endorse the words of Stanley Hauerwas: "Reconciliation happens when my enemy tells me my story and I am able to say: 'That is my story.'"[40] The artists often say: "This is our story—what is yours?"

39. The murals and the Bogside Artists have featured in a number of films and documentaries, most recently the Italian documentary *Bogside Story* which was premiered in Rome in 2018. See Forte and Laino, *Bogside Story*.

40. In private communication, Stanley Hauerwas has told Adrienne that he can't recall exactly where he might have said that, but it is certainly his view!

In situations of conflict crying out for authentic remembering, art can speak more powerfully than words. In a context of shattered hopes and broken promises, invocations of "peace," "truth," and "reconciliation" easily sound hollow and tired. In such situations, art can bring a new medium of communication to the conversation. As visual documents of human lived experience, the murals of *The People's Gallery* offer the possibility of articulating unspoken, nuanced feelings that cannot easily be put into words. As a television correspondent observed of the murals: "The desire to create art reflects the need to tell a story no matter how difficult, painful or controversial that may be. Only in this case, the entire street is the artists' canvas."[41]

The People's Gallery is the only major public work of art in Northern Ireland that tells the story of the Troubles through the eyes of those who lived through it. It is the story of a very visibly broken home that cannot begin to be restored unless its truth be told, in public. As such, the murals speak for those who are often silenced or ignored, or who as yet have no voice: the children of Derry yet to be born. The powerful visual impact of the murals means that they cannot easily be ignored. They invite all who are prepared to confront—and be confronted by—them, allowing them to penetrate into the inner recesses of their own being where hurt, grief, anger, resentment, and alienation may continue to lurk, in order that their own wounds may be "cleaned out" and thus made open to the possibility of healing.

Bibliography

"Art, Conflict, and Remembering: The Murals of the Bogside Artists." https://www.bogsideartistsexhibition.org.

Bogside Artists, The. *Healing and Art*. Derry, NI: printed by the authors, 2005.

Bouma-Prediger, Steven, and Brian J. Walsh. *Beyond Homelessness: Christian Faith in a Culture of Displacement*. Grand Rapids: Eerdmans, 2008.

Bowcott, Owen. "Prosecutors Explain Bloody Sunday Murder Charges against 'Soldier F'." *The Guardian*. March 14, 2019. https://www.theguardian.com/uk-news/2019/mar/14/prosecutors-explain-bloody-sunday-charges-against-soldier-f.

Brand, Hilary, and Adrienne Chaplin. *Art and Soul: Signposts for Christians in the Arts*. Downers Grove, IL: InterVarsity, 2001.

"Building Peace through the Arts: Re-Imaging Communities." Arts Council of Northern Ireland. Accessed May 12, 2019. http://artscouncil-ni.org/the-arts/visual-arts1/re-imaging-communities.

Dengerink Chaplin, Adrienne, "Art, Protest and Peace: The Murals of the Bogside Artists." In *Peacebuilding and the Arts*, edited by Jolyon Mitchell et al. New York: Palgrave Macmillan, forthcoming 2020.

---

41. UTV's North West Correspondent Mark McFadden, reporting from the Bogside, *Evening News*, 8 April 2015.

Dengerink Chaplin, Adrienne, with William Kelly, Tom Kelly, and Kevin Hasson. *Art, Conflict and Remembering: The Murals of the Bogside Artists*. Self-published, 2017. Published in conjunction with a travelling exhibition of the same name, first shown at Coventry Cathedral in June 2017. www.bogsideartistsexhibition.org.

Forte, Rocco, and Pietro Laino, dir. *Bogside Story*. Megapixell, 2017. https://www.lulifilm.net/bogside-story.

Hume, John. Interview by Marika Griehsel. *The Nobel Prize*. August 31, 2006. https://www.nobelprize.org/prizes/peace/1998/hume/26092-interview-transcript-1998-4.

Joseph, Anthony C. *The People's Gallery*. Derry, NI: a joint production by The Bogside Artists, 2007.

Kerr, Adrian, ed. *Murals in Derry*. Derry, NI: Guildhall, 2016.

Kerr, Michael. *The Destructors: The Story of Northern Ireland's Lost Peace Process*. Dublin: Irish Academic, 2011.

"Manus Deery: Inquest Names Soldier Who Shot Londonderry Teenager." *BBC*. October 17, 2016. http://www.bbc.co.uk/news/uk-northern-ireland-foyle-west-37676316.

Mallie, Eamonn, and David McKittrick. *Endgame in Ireland*. London: Hodder & Stoughton, 2001.

McClenagham, Pauline, ed. *Spirit of '68: Beyond the Barricades*. Derry, NI: Guildhall, 2009.

McCormick, Jonathan. "Death of a Mural." *Journal of Material Culture* 10.1 (2005) 49–71.

McEvoy, Kieran. *Making Peace with the Past: Options for Truth Recovery in Northern Ireland*. Report commissioned by Healing Through Remembering, 2006.

McFadden, Mark. *Evening News*. April 8, 2015. Television, news report.

McKittrick, David, and David McVea. *Making Sense of the Troubles: A History of the Northern Ireland Conflict*. London: Viking, 2012.

O'Shea, Sinead. "The Tragic Killing of Lyra McKee in Derry Shows How Hard It Is for Wars to End." *The Guardian*. April 21, 2019. https://www.theguardian.com/commentisfree/2019/apr/21/killing-lyra-mckee-derry-shows-how-hard-it-is-for-wars-to-end-sinead-oshea.

Olthius, James H. "Crossing the Threshold: Sojourning Together in the Wild Spaces of Love." In *The Hermeneutics of Charity*, edited by James K. A. Smith and Henry I. Venema, 23–40. Grand Rapids: Brazos, 2004.

Rolston, Bill. *Drawing Support*. 4 vols. Belfast: Beyond the Pale, 1992–2013.

Seerveld, Calvin. *Rainbows for a Fallen World*. Toronto: Toronto Tuppence, 1980.

Simpson, Kirk. *Truth Recovery in Northern Ireland: Critically Interpreting the Past*. Manchester: Manchester University Press, 2009.

Tutu, Desmond. Interview by Ray Uarez. *Newshour*, 1999, https://www.sahistory.org.za/archive/bishop-tutus-1999-interview-newshour.

Tutu, Desmond. *No Future without Forgiveness*. London: Rider, 1999.

Ulster University. "CAIN: Conflict Archive on the INternet." https://cain.ulster.ac.uk.

———. "The Wall Murals: The People's Gallery." CAIN. https://cain.ulster.ac.uk/bogsideartists/murals.htm.

Walsh, Brian J. *Kicking at the Darkness: Bruce Cockburn and the Christian Imagination*. Grand Rapids: Baker, 2011.

Wolterstorff, Nicholas. *Lament for a Son*. Grand Rapids: Eerdmans, 1987.

Woods, Oona. *Seeing Is Believing: Murals in Derry*. Derry, NI: Guildhall, 1995.

14

Of Tents and Temples

A Sermon for the Wine Before Breakfast Community[1]

1 Corinthians 3

Beth Carlson-Malena

Hello, friends. It's good to see you again.
  I bring you greetings from Open Way, my little church in Vancouver. The idea for Open Way started as a seed, planted inside me while I lived here in Toronto. It began to germinate when you commissioned and blessed me at my last Wine Before Breakfast (WBB) service in April 2017, and I carried it with me back to Vancouver. Thanks in part to the inspiration and influence of the Wine Before Breakfast community, this seedling is now growing into something beautiful.
  In this sermon, I want to draw together several threads, including seeds, plants, tents, temples, wildernesses, the LGBTQ+ community, family, and how we build home. In ambitious hope of weaving some of these threads together, I will pull them through two looms: chapter 3 of Paul's first letter to the Corinthian church, and Brian Walsh's work at Wine Before Breakfast.

---

1. Because Beth knows Brian in the context of the Wine Before Breakfast community, she decided to write her contribution as a sermon she would preach in one of their weekly services. While her audience is specific, her words are broadly applicable, and she invites all readers to listen in.

When I think of Brian and some of the shelter-related threads I've mentioned, I think of him as a "big tent" kind of guy. He goes out of his way to welcome people like me, who might not automatically feel included.

He also literally owns a big tent.

The first time I saw Brian's big tent was at his home, at Russet House Farm, in August 2015. A few of us from the Generous Space community helped him set it up as a shelter for forty of our friends. They were mostly queer Christians like me, with some straight/cisgender family and friends in the mix. It would be our first annual Generous Space Camp-OUT.

We spent the weekend soaking up the midsummer sun; cooking, eating, and playing cards under the big tent; sleeping in our little tents; learning about permaculture; and listening to Brian and Sylvia share wisdom from the commentary they'd been writing on the book of Romans.

We had anticipated more games and singing on our final evening together, but at sundown, we watched in dismay as menacing storm clouds tumbled toward our campsite. As the wind began to pick up, Brian tightened the straps of the big tent and pounded the stakes deeper into the soil. We huddled closer around our picnic tables and steeled ourselves for a rough night.

And then, just as the first heavy raindrops began to strike the canvas, word spread through the tent that Brian and Sylvia were inviting all of us into their farmhouse, which had been off-limits to campers up until that point.

We gladly gathered up our bags of chips and piled into their house, leaving a stack of 80 muddy shoes on the porch with the dogs. Circles of cross-legged card-players filled the floor of two side rooms. Sylvia led an impromptu bread-making workshop around the long kitchen table while another crowd filled the couches in the living room and talked music and politics with Brian. A guitar drifted around; songs were shared. When it got late, Sylvia put foam mattresses on the floor and welcomed anyone whose tent had flooded to spend the night indoors.

Most of the folks who squeezed into Brian and Sylvia's home that night had been strangers to them at the start of the weekend, building trust with the understandable slowness of LGBTQ+ folks who are encountering straight Christian theologians for the first time. But that evening, when these theologians invited our sweaty, soggy selves into the shelter of their warm home, into their private space, any hint of tentativeness vanished. We had become family.

This is one of my favorite stories about hospitality. It also reminds me that while big tents can be useful, sometimes what you really need is a home.

And if there's any group that needs homes, it's queer people. A study by the Williams Institute found that approximately forty percent of homeless youth in America identify as LGBTQ+, and the most common reason they gave for being homeless was familial rejection.[2]

As distressing as that statistic should be, I also want to highlight an additional, though less tangible kind of homelessness. In my work with Generous Space I've met hundreds of queer Christians, and I have yet to meet one who hasn't endured rejection in some form, whether inflicted by members of their family, Christian friends, churches, ministries, or camps. Some of these shunned ones seek healing and belonging in the wider queer community, but they often find their Christian faith unwelcome there, considering its homophobic baggage. This can leave them feeling displaced, insecure, compartmentalized, censored, unsure if there is any place where they belong. They are wilderness wanderers.

When the Israelites wandered in the wilderness, God gave them detailed instructions to construct a big tent: the tabernacle. In Exodus 31, God chose Bezalel and Oholiab and a team of skilled workers to fashion this tent, made to measure. The tabernacle would carry God's presence with them while they were homeless in the desert.

Over a millennium later, another Jewish tentmaker, another man on the move, the apostle Paul, wandered into the Greek city of Corinth. He found some fellow tentmakers, Priscilla and Aquila, and they became friends and coworkers, making tents together (Acts 18:1–3). They gathered a band of misfits and planted a church, staying there a couple of years before traveling on to Ephesus.

Fast forward another couple millennia. My wife and I wandered our way from Toronto to Vancouver in search of home. I found a friend named Mark to help me plant a church there. With our own band of misfits at Open Way, many of them queer wilderness wanderers, we've been studying the first letter that Paul wrote to his congregation in Corinth.

This letter got me thinking about belonging, and welcome, and big tents . . . and Brian.

Brian came to mind especially when we reached 1 Corinthians 3. Maybe it was the way Paul mixed his metaphors in this chapter, swerving from image to image, reminding me of Brian's multi-faceted, multi-vocational, multi-site way of life.

Paul begins by comparing the church to a nursing infant. They're spiritually immature, not yet ready for solid food, as demonstrated by their tendency to divide into factions based on which leader they prefer: Paul, Cephas, or Apollos. (It's a good reminder not to idolize anyone, not even Brian!) By verse 6, the church has become a seed. We've transitioned to the world

---

2. Durso and Gates, "Serving Our Youth," 3.

of gardening, the household/economy of creation, in which Paul plants the church, Apollos waters it, and God brings growth.

In verse 9, we watch Paul switch mid-verse from farming to construction: "For we are God's servants, working together; you are God's field, God's building" (1 Cor 3:9).[3] And after discussing foundations and materials, the image crystallizes; we learn this is not just any old building, but the very temple of God. What a huge honor for this motley crew in Corinth, surrounded by the lavish temples of Poseidon, Isis, and Aphrodite, to be collectively called a sanctuary of the Living God! Paul, the tentmaker, refuses tent imagery, and imparts them instead the permanence of a temple. He uses this image not once, but twice in this letter (1 Cor 3:10; 6:19), and again in his second letter to them (2 Cor 6:16).

This is even more surprising when we consider that the temple in Jerusalem was still standing when Paul wrote this letter. When someone with Paul's Jewish pedigree equates a ragtag bunch of (mostly) Gentiles with the Holy of Holies, it would seem to minimize the Jerusalem temple's importance, to put it mildly.

Yet by de-emphasizing the temple, Paul is in good company. Jesus, who was well acquainted with the way power and greed had poisoned the temple system, pointed to a day when the temple would be destroyed, when the Spirit would rush to the corners of the world, inhabiting people of all nations, all ages and genders: a fluid, human house of prayer. He referred to himself as the stone rejected by the builders, which would become the cornerstone of this new community (Mark 12:10).[4]

It's likely Paul is picking up on that oral tradition when he references Jesus as the foundation already laid. Paul writes about having begun the temple construction project in Corinth, building wisely on the foundation of Christ, and he exhorts their leaders to continue building sustainably, using quality materials.

They may be tempted to follow the so-called "wisdom of the world," the capitalist, colonial wisdom that throws up cheap walls of wood, hay, and straw, whatever sounds or feels good, to quickly claim ground, cover over vulnerabilities and lull people into a false sense of security. But this is a slapdash, hollow safety; this easy plaster will only be a fire hazard in the end, when the work is tested.

Paul urges them instead to build community in the slow, difficult, two-steps-forward-one-step-backward ways that are foolish in the eyes of the world. Today, Paul might call it "permaculture temple-building." (He did love

---

3. All scripture references are from the NRSV.
4. Sweeney, "Jesus, Paul," 622.

to mix his metaphors!) Permaculture temple-building uses the long, painful alchemy of love, taking no shortcuts, no herbicides or pesticides, no easy ways out, waiting patiently for the durable silver and gold to emerge. This is what produces a sustainable community with a diamond-sharp prophetic edge. This was the work that would survive the test, work to be rewarded.

I honor Brian for following Paul's advice in his nurturing, farming, and temple-building work. For almost twenty years at Wine Before Breakfast, Brian has been making room, welcoming wanderers like us under the big tent, and slowly crafting us into living stones, sealed with the mortar of sacred story: "Jubilee, Exodus, Creation, Sabbath—embedded in these we find a narrative that is worth living in. Here is a story that engenders a way of living that can make a home amid the ruins."[5]

The rhythm of Tuesday morning services with the Wine Before Breakfast community quickly became integral to my own sense of home when I lived in Toronto. Queer folks, retired people, slightly-jaded non-profit workers, students drifting through the fog of higher education . . . we all arrived clinging to the scraps of our tabernacles, our half-deconstructed wilderness faith. Through the songs, the prayers, the homily, the crumble of gluten-free bread, the wine goblet passed from friend to friend, and the delicious breakfast cheeses, impossibly, we became a haven, a chosen family, the very temple of God.

And yet we have been a transient temple, with a steady flow of people in and out. We come, we contribute, and all too soon, we are commissioned, and we leave. In theory, this is good, as the community only continues to expand and spread, sprouting up in new places like Open Way. Still, I imagine these constant hellos and goodbyes cannot have been easy for Brian.

A couple of days before I finished this sermon, Brian made hopeful reference to this reality in an email to the Wine Before Breakfast list: "While home is always placed, always requires some sense of 'geographical proximity,' there is also a spiritual sense of home that perseveres even in geographical distance. I know one person who has a sense of spiritual home with WBB who only actually attended one service a long time ago. But we became home, and through our weekly emails that sense of home is sustained."[6]

My friend Becca Sawyer, a fellow queer Christian who has also worked closely with Brian, wrote her master's thesis about refugees and their sense of home. Her studies led her to define "home" not as a place, but as a constellation

---

5. Bouma-Prediger and Walsh, *Beyond Homelessness*, 157.
6. Brian Walsh, email message to Wine Before Breakfast email list, March 29, 2019.

of memories, experiences, ideas, and associations. She tells me that home is a process, and that process isn't always easy.

Her words about home also remind me a lot of my queer community, of people who come out of the closet. "Coming out" is a phrase that carries the illusion of finality, but in reality, we never arrive at this elusive destination called "out." There will always be strangers we meet who do not yet know this aspect of our personhood; we will always be revealing ourselves anew.

And so whether we're coming out or coming home, we will always be a people in process, a pilgrim people. Even when we taste the blessing of reconstructed faith, of rebuilt homes, of shoulders unburdened in the shelter of chosen family, we will still remain somewhat restless until we finally enter God's rest (Heb 3). We only tabernacle here for a time, journeying onward until we reach the house with many dwellings, the generously spacious place Jesus is preparing for us (John 14:1–3).

In that place, there will be no temple, because our homemaking God is so beautifully present in every corner of the new heavens and earth (Rev 21:22). Our friend Paul will be there, perhaps a bit startled at the presence of queer bodies like mine in this holy people of God, yet pleased to see the tent pegs stretched wider than he expected.

Brian will be there too, wearing his reward, a crown that he will, no doubt, be all too eager to lay again at Jesus' feet.

As we await that day with hope, friends, and as we walk on together here at Wine Before Breakfast, and in all the places the seed has scattered, may you continue to find shelter and rest in one another.

Bibliography

Bouma-Prediger, Steven, and Brian J. Walsh. *Beyond Homelessness: Christian Faith in a Culture of Displacement*. Grand Rapids: Eerdmans, 2008.

Durso, L. E., and G. J. Gates. "Serving Our Youth: Findings from a National Survey of Service Providers Working with Lesbian, Gay, Bisexual, and Transgender Youth Who are Homeless or At Risk of Becoming Homeless." *The Williams Institute with True Colors Fund and The Palette Fund* (2012). http://williamsinstitute.law.ucla.edu/wp-content/uploads/Durso-Gates-LGBT-Homeless-Youth-Survey-July-2012.pdf.

Sweeney, James. "Jesus, Paul, and the Temple: An Exploration of Some Patterns of Continuity." *JETS* 46 (2003) 605–31. https://www.etsjets.org/files/JETS-PDFs/46/46-4/46-4-pp605-631_JETS.pdf.

15

Revillaging the City

How One Congregation Transformed Its Charitable Food Ministry to an Agent of Shalom

ANDREW STEPHENS-RENNIE

My church finds itself at a crossroads, and a busy one at that. Christ Church Cathedral sits on the northeast corner of Georgia and Burrard streets in the downtown financial district of the city colonially known as Vancouver, on the traditional, ancestral, and unceded lands of the Musqueam, Squamish and Tsleil-Waututh nations. Although it didn't start this way, the Cathedral now finds itself at the intersection of luxury hotels, office towers, high-end retailers, and many of our neighbors who live close to the street.

This neighborhood swells by 145,000 people each day as commuters come to work. It is an area where most encounters are transactional—whether at the bank, in the retail space, with young non-profit contractors seeking to secure a donation, or religious communities handing out literature to prospective converts. With all of this seemingly anonymous activity, the under-reported stories are those of the downtown's residents who do not leave, who do not live in the high-rise towers that surround us, but who, instead, take shelter in the alleyways and loading docks hidden from view. We might see them, but rarely do we know them by name.

One Friday, I biked—as I always do—up Hornby Street from Dunsmuir before jetting across a few lanes of traffic to duck into the laneway behind the church. Turning the corner, heading uphill past couriers huddled together before early-morning deliveries, it became clear that something was amiss. The pallet and tarp structure that had housed a regular at the

Cathedral's Maundy Café—our five day a week food ministry—was gone. He had been connected to the Cathedral for longer than I had. A decade, I'm told. That morning, the only remaining evidence of his existence was the pattern in the dirt where his makeshift residence once stood. By Sunday, that too, was gone.

The Spirit of Homelessness

In their expansive theological treatment of homelessness, Steven Bouma-Prediger and Brian J. Walsh observe:

> Ours is a culture of displacement, exile, and homelessness. Socioeconomic homelessness is growing, with many people seeking adequate housing. Ecological homelessness is increasing, with its sense of alienation from a degraded and defiled earth.[1]

Displacement is not limited to the kind of homelessness experienced by our neighbors who live in the alleyways, parks, empty lots, and loading docks of the downtown core. It takes little effort to think of the ways in which this sense of displacement pervades peoples' experiences of the region's housing crisis and the world's climate emergency. The problem is becoming more acute year after year. In *Divisions and Disparities in Lotus Land*, David Ley and Nicholas Lynch observe that neighborhoods throughout Greater Vancouver have seen increasing income stratification for over 40 years. In their words, "the middle-income city of the 1970s has become the polarized city of the 2000s."[2] Through relationships developed over shared meals in the Cathedral's Maundy Café, I have come to see some of the ways in which this culture of displacement affects a broad cross-section of people in my city.

The Crying of the Times

Since becoming involved with the Cathedral's food ministries in 2015, three interrelated themes have dominated conversation: social isolation, food insecurity, and a lack of affordable housing. These themes have demanded our attentive response as we have sought to live faithfully alongside the neighbours we meet in our downtown parish. These problems are not new, of course, and they are not aberrations. As Paul Taylor, Executive Director of FoodShare put it in his address to the Maple Leaf Center for

---

1. Bouma-Prediger and Walsh. *Beyond Homelessness*, 40.
2. Ley and Lynch, *Divisions*, 35.

Action on Food Security's symposium in April 2019, "Let's never forget that our food and political systems aren't broken—they are working just the way they were designed to."[3]

The poverty we see isn't an aberration, but rather the result of our current political system in which "colonialism, patriarchy, white supremacy and racism all shape who gets to eat. They shape where we live. Or who gets to work. And who gets to lead the solution finding."[4]

When I started with the Café, our program saw fifty people each weekday. Over the last three years, these numbers have multiplied. I'm not convinced this is a good thing, even though it provides more of a chance to connect with our neighbours. Today, an average week sees between six and seven hundred people through the Café. Where previously the folks who visited the Café were limited to street-involved men in their 50s and 60s, these same folks have now been joined by many women and seniors living in rental apartments in the city's West End—a neighborhood on whose edge we sit. In addition to my experience, and that of many of my peers, it has become apparent through conversations with members of the Café community that the disparity between the cost of living and access to resources in this city is increasing. The number of people we see each week continues to rapidly increase.

With all of this as background, how then is a church to respond?

The Fruit of the Spirit

Like many churches throughout the region, Christ Church Cathedral has operated a charity food program for many years. The Cathedral's foray into charitable food work began in the early 1980s when, in response to the economic tumult of that time, it opened its doors to the hungry, becoming the first site of the Greater Vancouver Food Bank. In the decades following, the Cathedral began to offer free takeaway and sit-down meals for those who needed them. The evolution is complex and messy.

From its beginnings, the Cathedral's approach to food ministry was rooted in a sense of Christian duty offered with a charitable spirit. What ought we to do, parishioners wondered, for "those less fortunate?" In response to the need for food, members of the congregation stepped forward to provide out of personal excess. In the early days, sandwiches were prepared at home and brought to church where they were frozen until needed. After the local health authority (rightly) ended this practice due to safety concerns, food

3. Taylor, "Food, A Sort of Right."
4. Taylor, "Food, A Sort of Right."

preparation was moved in-house. Over time, the congregation added two sit-down meals to complement sandwiches handed out the other three days of the week. As the food ministry expanded, so too did the number of residential fridges shoehorned into back corners of the building.

The ministry grew and sprawled in response to need. The initiative, driven by parishioners, operated largely outside of the Cathedral's official governance and authority structures. Over time it became part of the regular Cathedral budget, and flows of power and authority over the ministry were informally cobbled together. Change emerged organically in the absence of a far more regulated and organized system. The freedom to act responsively came with a shadow side. Dedicated lay volunteers who had invested time, physical labor, and emotional energy in the ministry did not feel empowered or supported to initiate significant changes to the larger church structure that were required to properly respond to the needs before them. Like the residential fridges tucked into any remaining available space, the ministry grew piece by piece without an integrated, overarching vision.

Transforming Vision

The Cathedral's approach was called into question in 2015, when, prompted by a significant fundraising campaign to replace the roof, raise a bell spire, and to renovate the kitchen, a prospective donor asked Dean Peter Elliott what the Cathedral would do differently with its additional space. While that exploration began with an assumed need to increase capacity (more meals, more of the time), it ended up in a startling, transformative question:

> *"How might we transform our food ministries in ways that honor the agency, creativity, dignity, intellect, and worth of all who come to share food at the table?"*

Since 2016, Christ Church Cathedral has centered this question as a means of embedding a transforming kingdom vision in the Maundy Café. At its core, this question seeks to involve all who encounter it in discerning the way forward together. It also got us a walk-in fridge/freezer.

This vision, as with any social innovation, has transformed the Cathedral's approach by challenging "the defining routines, resource and authority flows, and beliefs" at play within the Café and the larger Cathedral community.[5] Perhaps one day these shifts will be experienced and even embraced within the broader faith-based and region-wide charitable food system. Where we had previously served food to people who were poor out

---

5. Westley and Antadze. "Making A Difference," 2.

of charitable impulse, we have now harnessed our way of sharing food as a means of cultivating connection, holistic health, and community resiliency. Put in other words, we are seeking the peace of the neighborhood and city to which God continues to send us. In a city plagued by loneliness, this is a table of connection across dividing lines. In short, this transformation has allowed us to bear witness to and to hear the good news in a more holistic way. On a more personal level, it has become a place where I regularly encounter God through conversations with, and the embodied presence of, those who welcome me to the table.

Months before my work with the Maundy Café began, in one of my long, rambling conversations with the late Bishop Jim Cruickshank, we found ourselves reflecting on God's reconciling mission and the church's participation therein. I clearly remember Jim sharing his contention that we can be certain that God's kingdom is near when people who appear to have no business eating together are found joyfully sharing food at the same table. For him, this was a picture of God's shalom. For me, it seemed a vision worth participating in.

The Kingdom of God is Like...

As the Cathedral sought to receive, respond to, and live in light of this kingdom vision, we began to name the biblical traditions of sabbath, shalom, jubilee, and eucharist as core to the Cathedral's philosophy of sharing food. More than that, rather than centering a food bank lineup or a soup kitchen as our starting point, we have begun to ask members of our community, including guests, volunteers, and staff, to reflect on their favorite experience of a shared meal. When they think of their favorite meal, what do they see, hear, smell, and taste? Who is there? What conversations did they have? How did it change them? Most importantly, how did it feel? This act of imagination is helping us to develop—not as individuals, but as a community—a more holistic vision that points us towards tables of love, hope, belonging, and enough.[6]

Put into conversation with people within and people beyond Cathedral walls, this vision has continually evolved with the help of multiple providential conversations and the experiences of local and national organizations whose approaches to sharing food were already challenging the status quo. There were conversations with the likely suspects: leading food security practitioners, church leaders, and social service providers. When several key

---

6. Christ Church Cathedral's Food Philosophy is fully articulated on its website (link in bibliography).

Cathedral volunteers visited the Oasis Café at Tenth Church in Mount Pleasant, new questions were seeded. Over time, we were led into conversations with artists, business owners, people of other faiths, and most importantly, the people who called the Maundy Café community home.

These were the people whose stories helped illuminate the challenges faced when people are seen as clients rather than as community members, a common challenge in food programs elsewhere in the city. Through these conversations, we became more deeply aware of the uneven contours and power dynamics of the faith-based charitable food system in the region. Members of the Café community know a great deal about the city, not least of which, where to find the best meals and which places they are treated with the most dignity. As those of us in leadership began to shift our understanding through the centering of previously marginalized voices, we learned a lot about the state of the faith-based food system in Vancouver, and were challenged to further shift our approach to sharing food. It took building relationships with and learning at the feet of the diverse individuals who call the cafe home to expand our understanding of God's kingdom and imagine how the Cathedral might participate more fully in such a grand reconciling vision.

To do this required change at multiple levels:

- Initially, we reflected on every step of the journey between entering our building, receiving and eating food, cleaning up and leaving, and asked "how do each of these typical interactions reinforce isolation or connection?"
- In light of these responses, we moved the Café into a brighter, more inviting space, eliminating the sandwich lineup, and offering sit-down service at all meals
- Musicians are regularly brought in to play popular classics and familiar hymns, creating a more celebratory atmosphere
- We began to prepare fresher, healthier food from scratch. We eliminated processed foods, and foods high in sodium and sugar
- We extended food service times from thirty minutes to two hours, creating the opportunity for people to relax and connect with one another free from the pressure to move along
- Volunteer shifts began to include time eating at the table with those who had come to share food, slowly shifting our understanding of who needs food (hint: we all do)

- We made space for a four-week contemplative art practice culminating in "The Beautiful Table," an art exhibition focused on themes of love, hope, belonging, and enough that was displayed upstairs in the church sanctuary for three weeks
- We hosted a four-week sermon series in October 2018 focused on the intersection of food justice and Christian faith
- This year, we have begun the process of developing an approach to advocacy alongside those who are underhoused, and to pay attention to what connections Holy Spirit might be revealing to us next

Renewed Imagination for an Urban Village

In response to this evolution, we've heard a significant change in community members' experiences. People now talk about acceptance, of the ability to open up, and to be heard. There is talk about the Café as a place of calm and beauty. It's a place where folks now celebrate the quality and freshness of the food, where you can hear an entire table taking time to reflect on the flavors in the homemade salad dressing. More often than not, I'll end up in a conversation where someone says, "that's all fine and good, but that's not why I come here—I come here for the people." It's becoming (or perhaps re-embracing its role as) the center of a modest village in the midst of the city. Or, as one person put it, "a place where everybody knows your name."

And that's true too. When a member of the community recently announced a cancer diagnosis, she did so with fear and stress in her voice. She wasn't sure how it was going to go, or how she would get to her first appointment alone. That's when a long-term volunteer stepped forward to share her own story of treatment, and offered, without skipping a beat, to accompany her to the hospital. Three years ago, that kind of response would have been unthinkable. All of which say that this is just a start.

As a church, we required a renewed imagination, one that imaged God's inbreaking kingdom as a giant feast, with all of the family drama that can bring. Watching this transformation take place, I'm starting to ask the question that guided our exploration in other places, too. It's a question that I'm finding can generate a great deal of energy and imagination:

> How might we nourish our communities in ways that honor the agency, creativity, dignity, and worth of all who come to the table?

It's a question I grapple with daily. It's a question in which I find great hope. It's a question meant to get us thinking and exploring together. I don't know where the question ultimately leads, but there have definitely been signposts along the way.

A few days after our neighbor's disappearance, I found that he—after a decade's worth of homelessness—has been relocated to one of the city's new temporary modular housing units. Speaking to a colleague of mine later that week, he said with a glint in his eye, "I haven't said these words in a long time, but I'm going home. I'm going home, but don't worry, I'll see you soon."

Bibliography

Bouma-Prediger, Steven, and Brian J. Walsh. *Beyond Homelessness: Christian Faith in an Age of Displacement*. Grand Rapids: Eerdmans, 2005.

Christ Church Cathedral. "Food Philosophy." https://www.thecathedral.ca/food-philosophy.

Ley, David, and Nicholas Lynch. *Divisions and Disparities in Lotus Land: Socio-Spatial Polarization in Greater Vancouver, 1970–2005*. Cities Centre, University of Toronto, 2012. http://neighbourhoodchange.ca/documents/2012/10/divisions-and-disparities-in-lotus-land-socio-spatial-income-polarization-in-greater-vancouver-1970-2005-by-david-ley-nicholas-lynch.pdf.

Taylor, Paul M. "Food, A Sort of Right." *Medium*. April 29, 2019. https://medium.com/@FoodShareTO/food-a-sort-of-right-bb58805e20df.

Westley, Frances, and Nino Antadze. "Making A Difference: Strategies for Scaling Social Innovation for Greater Impact". *The Innovation Journal: The Public Sector Innovation Journal* 15.2 (2010) Article 2.

16

Setting Another Place at the Table

Matt Bonzo

Wherever you find yourself in this world, you will not have to look too hard to find a celebration centered on the sharing of a meal. I remember being both humbled and amazed at a small township church in South Africa where church members prepared their version of a potluck for their visitors. Laid out before us was a sacrificial feast of various and ample offerings. Surrounded by poverty, we ate as honored guests. The meal was sacrificial because those who had prepared the various dishes had shared with us from their stock for the coming week. While we walked away well-fed, our satisfaction meant there would be less food in the coming week for the generous households who had offered the meal to us. Sometimes in this wounded world, the margin between feast and famine is razor thin. Not all feasts are celebrated in places that flow with milk and honey.

Finding oneself in the difficult juxtaposition of feast and famine makes you utterly aware of the tenuous nature of being at home in a world where violence, strife, selfishness, and injustice are not just remotely present, but where they threaten your reception of the incredible gift of a meal placed before you. Knowing what the meal cost your host, you are moved to say, "please take your food first," or "we will eat later." However, your hosts rightly resist any hesitancy on your part to partake; this is their gift to you. The meal as gift, prepared in gratitude and offered in hospitality, especially in places where material resources are not abundant, is one of the deepest expressions of love, a love that welcomes both members and strangers home. Few homemaking practices create a sense of belonging like that of meal making and sharing.

Receiving the gift of such an offering reveals that a meal is much more than merely facilitating the consumption of food. There is a basic difference between eating as a way to provide ourselves with enough calories to exist and gathering together to share a meal. The difference is more than pausing long enough to sit down to eat using silverware in the presence of another person. Especially as the practices associated with eating change, we should not take for granted the difference between the mere consumption of food and the partaking of a meal. According to a report by the Food Marketing Institute, nearly half of all meals in the U.S. are eaten alone.[1] All of this eating alone is noteworthy if for no other reason than both physicians and psychologists are beginning to understand loneliness as a serious health issue.[2] Food and drink often facilitate companionship, literally the sharing of bread. There is no surprise to find that eating alone and feelings of loneliness are both on the rise. These trends are even more understandable given the reality that more of us are living alone. Individualism is not an abstract foundation from which we make rational choices. Rather, it is how we live. Sometimes chosen, many times not.

Yet, consuming food does not become a meal by adding more consumers. Furthermore, just as a person can be alone without being lonely, a person can enjoy a meal by herself. The transformation of food into a meal happens through an array of rituals that culminate in setting a place at the table. Not that there must be a literal table; whether it is a blanket, benches pulled together, or the tailgate of a pick-up truck, any place or setting can create the space where longing and belonging can meet.

The qualities that distinguish a meal become more apparent when we examine the reality behind the statistic regarding the number of meals that are eaten alone. We have also changed where and what we eat. In our hypermodern lives, we often eat on the run. Whether that is at your desk, in a car as you commute, or in class as my students often do, the consumption of food no longer has its own time and place. Eating is viewed as a necessary intrusion into our supposed autonomous existence, an existence that finds us too busy to leave our work, too stressed to shop and cook, and too tired to do more than open a box or order take out. Rather than recognizing a given time and place to commune, for example, in the dining room at 5:30, eating is often layered onto our already full plate of other activities. In abandoning the shared preparation and partaking of a meal, we lose the opportunity to work together, talk together, and find rest together.

1. Ferdman, "The Most American Thing."
2. Ali, "What You Need to Know." For instance, see the widespread concern shared among healthcare workers as discussed in this article.

Most of the food we eat on the run is a combination of highly processed vegetables, fruits, and meats with chemicals that enhance taste and preserve the product to give it an unnaturally long shelf life. These natural ingredients are industrially transformed in order to provide the calories we need, to have an acceptable taste, and to make them consumable as we are doing other activities. With the various additives and rearranging of nutrients, the food obtains a certain appeal. However, it is often difficult to produce a mixture that can balance the goal of creating a healthy food, the goal of creating a food that tastes good, and the goal of doing so at an affordable price. The result is industrially processed food that supplies extra sugar, extra fat, and extra salt, more than we require to live.

Because of how and what we eat, it is not easy to eat healthily on the run. Changing our diet by replacing industrially produced food with raw foods presents its own problems. The number of calories that a typical human requires is difficult to obtain by simply picking fruit from a tree or vegetables from a plant and consuming it raw.[3] Much of our waking time would be spent hunting and gathering simply to supply ourselves with enough calories to live. Not that raw food is unhealthy, but uncooked vegetables and fruits are not as easy to digest as cooked food. More work is required by the body to acquire the calories. The added use of calories to obtain calories is one of the reasons consuming raw foods is helpful in attempting to lose weight. However, sustaining health on such a diet over a long term would be challenging given the rhythm of modern life.

The increased efficiency of obtaining calories by cooking our food is of biological importance. Richard Wrangham argues that food preparation, particularly cooking, made food more digestible and calories more easily accessible, both of which allowed the brain to develop.[4] There seems to be a fundamental link between preparing food for consumption and becoming human. According to Wrangham, as human ancestors mastered fire and cooking, they were able to transform raw fibrous plants and tough tubers into a digestible food whose nutrition was more easily absorbed. The energy that was once used to consume food was made available for other purposes. Instead of a constant search and consumption of food, eating could be limited to a few times a day. With this free time, the activities and levels of intelligence associated with human beings became possible.

Wrangham's theory has its skeptics, and the theory taken by itself offers a too reductionistic understanding of being human. No one is

---

3. Pollan, *Cooked*, 4–10. For example, see Pollan's argument where he discusses the idea that cooking is central to human identity, biology, and culture.

4. Wragham's research is explored in Moeller Gorman's article "Cooking Up."

suggesting that brain size alone is sufficient to identify us as human beings. Nevertheless, the link between cooking and being human is significant. The cooking of food to ease digestion is not cooking's sole aim. At some point, the art of cooking developed as eating moved beyond a purely utilitarian act. Cooking became concerned with an aesthetic appeal. The meal emerged as a palette where creative combinations could be sampled. Spices were added, new combinations of ingredients were tried, and methods other than direct cooking over fire were established. These developments were historically significant; global exploration and trade were encouraged by the quest for new foods and drinks.

Beyond the search for new ingredients and new methods of preparation, the presentation of the food began to matter. An aesthetics of how the food looked accompanied the concern for taste. Alongside the look of the food, protocols emerged for dining. Human creativity did not end with learning to prepare and present the food. Expectations regarding how a person should conduct oneself were attached to eating a meal.

Patrick Deneen argues for the connection between having good manners while eating and the development of western civilization.[5] The creation of eating utensils such as forks and knives in the west mark a different relationship to food. Instead of simply using hands to handle food efficiently, we began to use tools that could cut smaller pieces and slow the delivery of that food to the mouth. A certain etiquette began to define the rituals of a meal, both in its formal and informal versions. From the abiding questions regarding which fork to use for what at a banquet, to your mom telling you to keep your elbows off the table at dinner, a set of expectations has come to surround the meal.

Meeting these expectations requires work. The work is multi-faceted: coming up with a menu for a week of meals, buying the groceries, cleaning, cutting, and measuring the ingredients, preparing and cooking the food, setting the table, presenting the food, and cleaning up afterward. When children are part of the household, the work increases with the added task of teaching them how to participate in preparing and enjoying the meal. Given the many concerns competing for our attention in a hyperactive world and the increase in time spent away from home, it is understandable that the meal shifts to festive occasions. The result, however, is and that the daily consumption of food loses significance.

Food on the run may require fewer forks, knives, and expectations for us; however, the one thing it does not require is less work. Even if we cut up

---

5. Deneen, "Manners and Morals," 98–101. This article discusses the need for virtue as part of becoming civilized.

the carrots and celery that go into our lunch container, from which we eat from at out desk, we rely upon the hard work of farmers, truckers, and the workers at grocery stores to make our food easily accessible. Moreover, if our grab and grow food is processed, the number of hands involved increases greatly. While such an approach to food may have freed us from work, it usually does so by making the work of homemaking invisible to us.

In doing the work of acquiring the ingredients and preparing the food, the meal is an example of what Enrique Dussel describes as the subjective response to the material. Dussel explains that the making of bread is a form of labor whereby the resources of nature are transformed into a "*pro-duct*, it is that which comes forward (*pro-*) to our view as a phenomenon in the world."[6] In this way, the bread is an unleashing of the potential of creation's goodness. For Dussel, bread is a "human creation; it is an extension of divine creation."[7] Creation is a gift that calls us to responsible action. The particular act of creation in making bread can be generalized to apply to the very art of meal making. Transcending Wranghem's biological understanding of the role that cooking contributes to becoming human, and even more than the patterns of behavior that become associated with the meal as noted by Deneen, the preparation and offering of the meal is a way in which we image the divine. As we have noted, food is present throughout nature in its simplest and most direct form, a life-giving gift that only needs to be eaten. To say that we create food is not to say we create *ex nihilo*. Human creativity begins with the given-ness of creation. The first true response to this gift is gratitude, a giving of thanks. The materiality of creation is full of potentiality and the work of image bearing is to open up all this potential in ways that are loving and life affirming. The preparation of a meal is a fundamentally human work. Without this work, the food given by God may sustain us, even delight us, but fails to "objectivize human dignity in nature."[8]

The hidden work that allows for much of our food consumption today clouds us from seeing the injustices of our food system. Dussel's argument about the production of bread is part of a larger argument he makes about the stealing of bread from the poor. Bread is stolen when an adequate wage is not paid to the laborer who makes our daily bread. Without an adequate wage, the laborer goes hungry while the rich dine in excess. Beyond the injustice of a system that permits the production for only one class of people, Dussel describes the scandal that occurs when the bread is that is used within the Eucharist comes from the labor of the poor: "So those who offer God

---

6. Dussel, *Beyond Philosophy*, 43.
7. Dussel, *Beyond Philosophy*, 43.
8. Dussel, *Beyond Philosophy*, 43.

bread stolen from the poor give the life of the poor as their offering."[9] The preparation of food elicits a recognition of the gift which food preparation begins and the responsibility intrinsic to that gift. Food as gift resists the human attempts to turn it into a weapon, a purely economic object, or a source of death. Food is a gift of life, the very imagery Christ himself invokes when he calls himself "the bread of life" (John 6:35).[10]

As suggested earlier, the work of the meal is not finished with the preparation of the food, but extends to the place setting. By place setting, I do not mean just laying out the table, providing plates and silverware, and arranging seating. Rather, life and love are not only present in the substance of the meal, but also in how we gather for the meal. The way we commune while eating embodies an important part of being human. The sustenance provided by meals comes both in partaking of the food offered and by partaking as a member or guest of a household. The meal is an important part of the practice of homemaking. The work of preparing and then sharing a meal helps to establish the rhythm of the daily life of a home. Meals bring an order to each member's life, an order that places each individual's schedule under the household schedule. By establishing a shared time and place, the meal provides the opportunity for regular interactions between members. In the security of mutual recognition, the table is a place, maybe *the* place, where laughter and tears flow, hard decisions are worked through, and the seemingly mundane accounts of one's day become important. This description of the meal and table are too good, but not too good to be true. While eating together guarantees nothing of which I have described, and having a place *set* for you can be a means of control, a table of love can become a place that affirms both the individual and the membership of a household. The dreadful meals, full of tension, strife, and silence often portrayed in movies and television shows are not the norm. Every day around the world people gather together to eat, and the dinner table affords the occasion to relax, to converse, to take delight, and to receive, as well as to give, love.

While a good host often makes a meal seem effortless and the best kind of fellowship around the table flows with ease, neither happens without what Dussel calls human creation.[11] Place setting requires the work of hospitality, the extending of a place at the table to those who gather often, as well as to those strangers who are welcomed home. Christine Pohl describes this type of hospitality as biblical.[12] The effort to create a fine meal and to set a proper

---

9. Dussel, *Beyond Philosophy*, 48.
10. All scripture quotations are from NASB.
11. Dussel, *Beyond Philosophy*, 49.
12. Pohl, *Living into Communities*, 159–78.

table are important. However, without the creation of a place to be at the table, which is the work of hospitality, the meal and setting can ring hollow. Such hospitality is a virtue of the household. As a virtue, it appears more often than for the rare formal meal. This sort of hospitality is what in part energizes the household. Hospitality of the household anticipates the unexpected, always ready to set another place at the table. Out of the gratitude for the very gift of food, for their daily bread, the hospitable household has learned to live with an open hand, ready to pull up another chair.

Wendell Berry's short story "The Solemn Boy" offers insight into this type of hospitality.[13] Set in the Depression, the story describes the offering of a seat at the table given to an un-named, homeless father and son who happen to be walking down the road that passes by the farm of Tol and Minnie Proudfoot. Maybe it would be better to say wandering rather than walking down the road, as it is clear the two are headed nowhere in particular. The poverty that drives them onward is as cold as the wind that penetrates their worn out clothes. Their journey is not a walk home. They belong nowhere. Tol extends to them the unexpected grace of a warm lunch, in a warm home. Miss Minnie has prepared the meal for the small lunch. The work of turning lard and flour into biscuits repeats an oft-shared ritual. A simple farmer's lunch made in anticipation that only the two members of the household would be present transforms into a sort of feast by adding the guests. As Berry describes the interactions between Tol and Minnie, one comes to understand that there is always more than enough love undergirding their practices of homemaking. Enough love that it naturally overflows to the guests. There is no sense of resentment or inconvenience present in the couple. Rather, it is as if they had been preparing for lunch guests all along.

Hospitality is not given because there is an excess of food. The "miracle" here is not the multiplication of five fish and two loaves into enough food to serve a crowd. This is an ordinary act of grace found in a household that knows the only way to receive the gifts of life is to give the gifts of life. In particular, the actions of Tol force the issue of hospitality at the table. As the title of the story suggests, the boy appears much too solemn for his age. His seriousness is caused by the traumas of lacking food, shelter, and belonging. In response to the boy's solemnity, Tol goes to great lengths to try to lighten the moment for the boy. However, lighthearted conversation does little to penetrate the boy's shell. Tol's silliness climaxes in his "accidently" pouring a glass of buttermilk down the front of his shirt. This wasteful act finally coaxes laughter from the boy and everyone else. A long

---

13. Berry, "The Solemn Boy," 181–95.

buried sense of delight in both father and son emerges with the ease of belonging. The welcome dissipates the formal stiffness of being an outsider. Tol and Miss Minnie had offered a place at the table that gave sustenance to both body and soul.

As Christine Pohl explains, hospitality is much more than "planned dinner parties" or "donuts at church."[14] The hospitality offered in "The Solemn Boy" is an example of a more "substantive and significant"[15] hospitality that considers the other as worthy of love and treats her accordingly. The other often arrives at unexpected times and in unexpected ways so that hospitality often comes "in the form of interruption."[16] The exceptional feast can turn a meal into a notable occasion and can function as a way to remember significant events from the past, to honor a person, or to mark the achieving of a goal. For example, the work and hospitability needed to prepare a Thanksgiving feast, especially to make all members of an extended family feel at home even when there may be deep-rooted tensions and hurts, is a minor miracle. However, the everyday grace of extending an ordinary meal to include the unexpected other requires an open hospitality that cannot be planned ahead.[17] On the other hand, maybe it is better to say that an open hospitality always looks to the future. An orientation to the future that requires the practices of home to not be viewed as an end unto themselves, but to be lived out in such a way that the boundary between home and world remains porous, for the gift of the other never arrives through a locked door.

Another Berry story reminds us that the unexpected other is not always the unknown stranger. Berry capture the intensity of the returning to home of a household member in a memorable scene. "Making it Home," tells of a son and brother whose absence is both unique and common. Art Rowanberry had left his home and community to join the army during World War II. He belonged to the community that felt his absence along with so many other young men, some whose return would never be celebrated. The household members who remained on the farm from which he was absent sensed acutely the particulars of his being gone. The description in the story of Art's time at war is brief. He had seen those around him die; he had killed and wondered why. The day when a shell hit and injured him was the beginning of the long trip home. Much of the

---

14. Pohl, *Living*, 160.
15. Pohl, *Living*, 160.
16. Pohl, *Living*, 165.
17. See Derrida and Dufourmantelle, *On Hospitality*, 3–23, for the extended discussion regarding the limits of hospitality.

story is Art reflecting as he walks from the not-too-distant town where he had arrived by bus to his home. The long walk home for Art marks the slow transition back to his place.

In Art's absence, his father and his brother continued the work of the farm, but the work itself was a reminder of what was missing. The members of the household, in a way even the farm itself, longingly expected Art's return but neither knew when, or if, for sure he would return. Therefore, the daily habits of the farm continued in anticipation. On this particular morning, father and brother are plowing the field with their mules when Art's journey home ends. Art's simple "howdy" is greeted by his father's handshake, but he is welcomed home by his father's tears. The homecoming continues when Art's brother, maybe not so playfully, asks him, "You reckon your foot'll still fit in a furrow?"[18] The question helps set the place for Art. He belongs behind a mule and not behind some instrument of death.

However, the return to the work of the farm does not complete his arrival. The fulfillment of the welcome home is declared by his father who tells his grandson (who happens to be in the field with them that day), "Honey, run yonder to the house. Tell your granny to set on another plate. For we have our own that was gone and has come again."[19] There is no reason to think that the Rowanberry meal would be a grand feast that day—maybe bigger celebrations would happen later—but Art's place would be set at the table. His place being set did not merely mean a plate and silverware. The household knew the space where Art sat would again be filled. No one anticipated that it would be on that day, but that place was always already being offered by a love that waits for, that expects, the arrival of the other.

There is no possibility of homecoming without the prior work of homemaking. To craft a home is more than dwelling in a particular space. Homemaking is to indwell a place through shared stories, through embodying habits, and through practiced virtues. Eating is a physical necessity; however, the sharing of a meal is a vital ritual in making a home that affirms us as whole beings. Setting a table of love establishes a place for each of us to be and a place for each of us to be celebrated. A meal can offer hospitality to both the stranger and the household member. While the activities of homemaking, such as preparing a meal, often rely on the necessary distinguishing between host and guest, these distinctions fade in the sharing of the meal as "the wild space of love"[20] surrounds the well-set table.

18. Berry, "The Solemn Boy," 235.
19. Berry, "The Solemn Boy," 236.
20. Olthuis, "Withing," 66–77. This phrase comes from James Olthuis' many works, including "Withing." In Olthuis, *The Beautiful Risk*, 230, he also uses the phrase "the amazing ways of love" to describe the inviting nature of love.

The table of love is set in the townships of South Africa, on a farm in Ontario, and in the neighborhoods of Mexico City. These meals echo the table of love that was set in an upper room just outside old Jerusalem where Christ invited his followers to remember him through the sharing of a meal. This re-enacting of the last supper invites us to "taste and see the Lord is good" (Ps 34:8). Through the work of Christ, the table of love offers a seat where we find a place among brothers and sisters.

In a world where famine is all too common and hunger haunts millions of people, many of them children, tasting the goodness of a meal may seem a luxury. Yet, gathered around a table we find each other, we come home, and we hope for the "Feast of Eternal Joy" where the delights set before us in love heal all the pains of hunger.[21]

Bibliography

Ali, Shainna. "What You Need to Know about the Loneliness Epidemic." *Psychology Today*, July 12, 2018, https://www.psychologytoday.com/us/blog/modern-mentality/201807/what-you-need-know-about-the-loneliness-epidemic.

Berry, Wendell. "The Solemn Boy." In *That Distant land*, 181–95. Washington, DC: Shoemaker & Hoard, 2004.

Deneen, Patrick. "Manners and Morals: Or, Why You Should not Eat the Person Sitting Next to You." In *Conserving America? Essays on Present Discontents*, 98–101. South Bend, IN: St. Augustine, 2016.

Derrida, Jacques, and Anne Dufourmantelle. *On Hospitality*. Palo Alto, CA: Stanford University Press, 2000.

Dussel, Enrique. *Beyond Philosophy: Ethics, History, Marxism, and Liberation Theology*. Lanham, MD: Rowman & Littlefield, 2003.

Ferdman, Roberto. "The Most American Thing There Is: Eating Alone." *The Washington Post*, August 18, 2015. https://www.washingtonpost.com/news/wonk/wp/2015/08/18/eating-alone-is-a-fact-of-modern-american-life.

Moeller Gorman, Rachel. "Cooking Up Bigger Brains." *Scientific American*, January 1, 2008, https://www.scientificamerican.com/article/cooking-up-bigger-brains.

Moltmann, Jürgen. *The Coming of God*. Translated by Margaret Kohl. Minneapolis: Fortress, 1996.

Olthuis, James. *The Beautiful Risk: A New Psychology of Loving and Being Loved*. 2001. Reprint, Eugene, OR: Wipf & Stock, 2006.

———. "Withing: A Psychotherapy of Love, " *Journal of Psychology and Theology* 34.1 (2006) 66–77.

Pohl, Christine. *Living into Communities: Cultivating Practices that Sustain Us*. Grand Rapids: Eerdmans, 2012.

Pollan, Michael. *Cooked: A Natural History of Transformation*. New York: Penguin, 2013.

---

21. Moltmann, *The Coming of God*, 336. This is the phrase used to describe the fulfillment of creation by the coming of God.

17

Reconciling the World?

Theology and Exegesis in 2 Corinthians 5

N. T. Wright

Introduction

"God was in Christ reconciling the world to himself." The King James translation of 2 Cor 5:19 has become famous in debates about the origins of Christology, not least because of the use of its first four words as a book title by the former St Andrews professor Donald M. Baillie (1887–1954).[1] Baillie's book, exploring the paradox of grace and applying that to incarnational theology, is rightly prized. It has been, for many, a kind of way-marker by which to steer Christological reflection. That is important, and I shall return to it; but my focus is on the other half of 2 Cor 5:19, which has often been either overlooked or taken for granted. God, declares Paul, was "reconciling the world to himself." What does he mean here by "the world," and what does it mean that the world was thus "reconciled"?

This seems an appropriate subject to offer in gratitude and congratulations to Brian Walsh, who was instrumental in helping me shed my previous implicit dualism when we got to know one another at McGill in the early 1980s. We spent many happy hours wrestling together with Colossians, where such questions are of course central (and which, as I shall suggest, has a good deal in common with 2 Corinthians). For me, this issued in the Tyndale Commentary, and in various articles and sections of my later works. For Brian—once he had teamed up with my former research student Sylvia Keesmaat!—it paved the way for one of the most spectacularly innovatory commentaries of

---

1. See Baillie, *God Was In Christ*.

recent times. It was also through Brian that I got to know Richard Middleton, whose work has been so fruitful for me as for many, not least in relation to my present topic. For this and for much more, deep thanks.[2]

"Reconciling the world to himself" appears, in fact, to be the proper emphasis of 2 Cor 5:19. The famous translation, and its modern use, has tended to take the first four words (the opening words in Greek as well as in the King James) as the primary thrust, as though Paul's first thought was to state a "doctrine of incarnation" and only secondarily to explain *why* God came to be "in Christ," that is, what purpose this incarnation was serving. Within theologically orthodox circles it might even be thought that any attempt to read the Greek slightly differently might be a covert way of undermining what had seemed to be a central Pauline statement of incarnational theology. Thus a modern rendering like that of the New English Bible might be supposed to be following a liberal protestant agenda when translating "In Christ, God was reconciling the world," thus carefully *not* saying the magic words "God was in Christ."[3] But in fact this seems to be one of those cases where the word-for-word rendering of Greek into English may lead us astray. When Paul writes *theos ēn en Christō kosmon katallassōn heauton* the ēn goes so naturally with *katallassōn*, and so awkwardly if taken by itself as the primary verb, that most translations come out more or less as I have in my own version: God was reconciling the world to himself in the Messiah.[4] It is worth stressing, for the avoidance of doubt, that Paul held a robust view of Jesus' embodiment of Israel's God; to criticize the proof-texting which has taken place with 5:19 is in no way to undermine the truth which that verse has sometimes been held to teach.[5]

The immediate context provides a strong argument in the same direction. "Reconciliation" is the main theme of verses 18 to 20, highlighting God's primary work of reconciliation and explaining that the apostolic ministry of reconciliation—which I, like many others, have argued was central to Paul's perception of his own vocation—belongs within, and as the outflowing of, that primary divine work. But this then raises the question, on which I shall focus here: what does Paul mean here by "the world," and what

---

2. See chapter 5 of Wright, *The Climax of the Covenant*; Wright, *The Epistle of Paul to the Colossians*; Walsh and Keesmaat, *Colossians Remixed*; Middleton, *The Liberating Image*; Middleton, *A New Heaven and a New Earth*.

3. Bultmann saw the idea of "God" being "in Christ" as being "inconceivable" for Paul. See Bultmann, *The Second Letter to the Corinthians*, 161–62.

4. See Wright, *The New Testament for Everyone*. Quotations from the New Testament are from this version unless otherwise specified.

5. See chapter 9 of Wright, *Paul and the Faithfulness of God*. On the danger of proof-texting at this point see Young and Ford, *Meaning and Truth*, 255.

did he mean by saying that in the Messiah the world has been "reconciled"? I offered a brief discussion of this matter in *Paul and the Faithfulness of God*, but since the discussion in question is found at pages 1489–94 it is just possible that some readers may have lost concentration by that point. In any case, I want here to amplify somewhat the points I made there. I shall argue that by "world" here Paul is gesturing towards a theme he explores in other places, in which the obvious application to individual humans is simply one manifestation of the larger reality of an entire new creation; and that he himself seems to have contextualized this within a theological perspective in which the created order of heaven and earth was seen as the ultimate temple for the Creator God, the temple in which the Messiah is the true image, the temple which is then extended by the spirit to include all the Messiah's people. The coming together of heaven and earth (one might be tempted to say, the fusion in a single vocation of theology and farming?) is an important Pauline theme, and it is arguably in Paul's mind here even if the specific thrust of the passage, within that larger context, is more specifically on the reconciliation of humans.

"World" and "New Creation": Only Human or Also Cosmic?

First things first. Paul's emphasis here is obviously on his apostolic ministry, as it has been since the end of chapter 2 and will continue to be until the middle of chapter 6. He is writing a kind of apostolic *apologia*, or at least one part of it, with more to come in chapters 10 to 12. He has, it seems, been fiercely criticized by some in the Corinthian church, and he is explaining what it is that he has been called to do and why that work takes the shape it does. The immediate focus of this work, which he highlights here, is on sinful human beings who need to be reconciled to the Creator God, and who can indeed be thus reconciled because of the work of Jesus the Messiah. Verse 19 sets this out in three stages:

a. God was reconciling the world to himself in the Messiah,
b. Not counting their transgressions against them,
c. And entrusting us with the message of reconciliation.

For some, the explanatory statement in 5:19b—not counting *their* transgressions against *them*—is sufficient evidence that here Paul has individuals, and only individuals, in view. The "their" and "them" in clause

(b) can only refer back, however uncomfortably, to the "world" (*kosmos*) in clause (a). But is that the end of the matter?

It certainly was for Rudolf Bultmann. He insists in his commentary that *kosmos* here "denotes persons."[6] He cites two parallels for this supposed usage. The first, Rom 1:8, is not so clear, since when Paul says there that the faith of the Roman church is proclaimed in all the world this seems to have a geographical, not just a personal, reference. And when, in 1 Cor 4:9, Paul says that he and the other apostles have been displayed as "a public show for the world" he specifies angels as well as humans, and once again these seem to be specific viewers of the spectacle, not necessarily exhausting the category "world." Margaret Thrall agrees, insisting in her large-scale commentary that the referent is "exclusively personal."[7] So too Edward Adams states, without noting alternative views, that in this passage *kosmos* "clearly bears the sense 'humanity.'"[8]

There is, however, a counter-tradition in the commentaries. C. K. Barrett allows that "world" here might denote more than simply humans, citing Colossians 1 to which we shall return.[9] Jean Héring points this way too.[10] A fuller case is offered by Victor Furnish.[11] He cites Romans 8, where, granted Paul speaks of the whole creation (*ktisis*) rather than the "world" (*kosmos*) as here, he clearly indicates that the entire created order will be liberated. (Significantly, Bultmann could see no point in that passage in Romans, regarding it as an extraneous bit of Jewish apocalyptic.) And then there are other equally obvious parallels such as Col 1:19. Perhaps, says Furnish, Paul here refers to the whole "universe of creation."[12] He suggests that in Romans 8 the "freedom" for which the whole creation longs is equivalent to the "reconciliation" of which Paul speaks here. Another advocate for this view is J.-F. Collange, who speaks of the reconciliation not only of humanity but of "l'ensemble de l'univers créé."[13] Both Furnish and Collange, however, make this point by means of a hypothetical tradition-historical proposal: that in the first two lines of verse 19 Paul is quoting a phrase from early Christian tradition, stressing the universal import of the Christian faith, and then

---

6. Bultmann, *The Second Letter to the Corinthians*, 161–62.

7. Thrall, *Second Epistle to the Corinthians*, 434–35.

8. Adams, *Constructing the World*, 235.

9. Barrett, *The Second Epistle to the Corinthians*, 177.

10. Héring, *St. Paul to the Corinthians*, 44. He cites in support Bachmann, *Der zweite Brief des Paulus*, 267.

11. Furnish, *II Corinthians*, 317–20, 333–37.

12. Furnish, *II Corinthians*, 318.

13. Translation: "the entirety of the created universe." Collange, *Enigmes de la Deuxieme Epître*, 272.

relating this tradition (which, by implication, Paul himself may not fully have shared) to the specific targets of his own reconciling work, in other words, individual human beings.

The suggestion of a pre-Pauline tradition of "cosmic" reconciliation, quoted and then perhaps modified by Paul here, resulting in subtly different theological emphases joggling together at this point, was made by Ernst Käsemann.[14] Furnish lists the admittedly slight linguistic clues that might point in this direction.[15] For Käsemann these, and more importantly a supposed theological divergence, were tell-tale signs of different sources: Paul, he hypothesized, was picking up an older tradition, perhaps from Hellenistic ideas of the reconciliation of heaven and earth, and bringing it into fresh and more specifically Christian (or at any rate Pauline!) expression in terms of individual human beings who still face temptation and the call to humble service. Käsemann coupled this distinction (a quasi-pagan "enthusiasm" over against a vision of Christian life in terms of the concrete daily struggle) with his familiar antithesis, as in his exegesis of Rom 3:24–26, of an essentially non-Pauline stress on *guilt* and the truly Pauline emphasis on the *power* of sin. Thus he discerned, underneath the surface of Paul's text, quite different, and perhaps incompatible, emphases.

This complex tradition-historical and theological analysis, however, seems to me in danger of collapsing under the weight of its own unproveable and actually unlikely multiple elements. I think Käsemann was right to see that a larger-than-human referent is present here, but wrong to suppose that this was a foreign body which Paul was somehow taming. Besides, the suggestion that the reconciliation of heaven and earth was a pagan or Hellenistic idea strikes me as fanciful, for all Käsemann's invocation of Vergil's Fourth Eclogue and the idea of the *pax Romana*. Käsemann, as ever, was wary of an "unbridled enthusiasm" in which the Christian might try to live in the fairy-tale dream of imagining that "cosmic peace" had already settled over the world.[16] He imagined a pre-Pauline stage (later retrieved in Ephesians and Colossians) in which Jesus would be hailed as Cosmocrator (a combination, he thinks, of pagan dreams and apocalyptic fantasy), with Paul then correcting it through his emphasis on the Crucified One. This dense, complex theory strikes me as the projection of Käsemann's own theological and ecclesial anxieties on to the fictive screen of hypothetical

---

14. Käsemann, "Some Thoughts on the Theme," 49–64. See too Stuhlmacher, *Gerechtigkeit*, 77–78. On the use of hypothetical tradition-history as a means of critically distancing Paul from some of the apparent implications of his actual words see Wright, *Paul and his Recent Interpreters*, 52–56.

15. Furnish, *II Corinthians*, 334.

16. Käsemann, "Some Thoughts on the Theme," 56.

tradition-history.[17] Paul's vision of the cosmos renewed in Romans 8, or indeed 1 Cor 15:20–28, was not an attempt to copy Vergil or other imperial apologists. It grew directly out of the prophetic visions of new creation in Israel's scriptures, brought into fresh focus by the resurrection of Jesus. I suspect that, here as elsewhere, what we are seeing is an ancient Jewish theme which Paul is not denying, but rather developing. Indeed, Romans 8 and Colossians 1, not to mention Ephesians 1, indicate that he was thoroughly at home with this concept and did indeed see it as the larger context for human salvation. It is of course quite possible that, again here as elsewhere, Paul was reworking formulae and even quasi-liturgical sayings—though to guess at such things, within the first thirty years of the church, does rather strain the imagination. This might be one explanation for any apparent changes of subjects or grammatical awkwardnesses—though 2 Corinthians is the letter above all where Paul's style becomes jerky and uncomfortable, for reasons about which I have speculated elsewhere.[18]

This brings us back to the placing of 2 Cor 5:19 within the larger world of Pauline sayings. For a start, the other parallels in Romans need to be factored in. In Rom 11:12 Paul speaks of the "riches for the world" which have come about through the strange unbelief of ethnic Israel. In 11:15 he indicates that there is almost an instrumentality about this: their "casting away" has meant "the reconciliation of the world," *katallagē kosmou*. This is in fact the closest Pauline parallel to our present passage. It clearly refers to the burgeoning Gentile mission, and while Paul obviously has actual humans in mind, believing Gentiles to be precise, it shows that he can use the word *kosmos* in various senses, particularly to throw the net quite wide. I have argued elsewhere that Paul's theological understanding of the Gentile mission flows directly from his belief (held in common with other early Christians, notably John) that on the cross Jesus won the decisive victory over the pagan idols that had kept the nations captive, so that the actual evangelization of specific Gentile communities took place within a context where the dark oppressive powers had already been conquered and their former captives had nothing to lose but their chains.[19]

This would indicate that the cosmic reach of Colossians and Ephesians, so often cited as a reason for regarding them as non-Pauline, is in fact a reason to include them. Indeed, not only does Romans serve as a middle term between 2 Corinthians and those two frequently-doubted letters, there

---

17. On Käsemann see chapter 4 of Wright, *Pauline Perspectives* and *Paul and his Recent Interpreters*, 50–56.

18. See chapters 10 and 12 of Wright, *Paul: A Biography*.

19. See particularly Wright, *The Day the Revolution Began*.

are several points at which 2 Corinthians and Colossians are in close parallel with one another though not with any other Pauline letters; and the idea of cosmic reconciliation is one of those. Immediately after the poem in which that theme is clearly stated (1:19) Paul explains the nature of his own apostleship, as he is doing in 2 Corinthians 5, and states remarkably that the gospel *was already preached* to every creature under heaven (*pasē hē ktisei hypo ton ouranon*) and that Paul became its servant, its *diakonos*. This would fit very well with a reading of 2 Cor 5:19 in which Paul's specific ministry, focused on urging human beings to be reconciled to the Creator God, is set by implication, and perhaps by explicit statement, within a larger context of the renewal of all creation, the reconciliation of heaven and earth; or, as one might say, the reconciliation of "the world" to God.

The final intra-Pauline parallel is Galatians 6. There, summing up the message of the whole letter, Paul declares that through the cross of the Messiah "the world has been crucified to me and I to the world" (6:14). This, admittedly, does not speak of the *reconciliation* of the world, but rather, in line with Gal 1:4, of the dramatic effect of the Messiah's crucifixion, through which (he says) we are "rescued from the present evil age." This gives the wider meaning to the phrase which then sends us back to 2 Corinthians 5: neither circumcision nor uncircumcision matters, he says, since "what matters is new creation," *kainē ktisis*. That then sets the standard for the Galatian church. God has launched his new creation in Messiah Jesus and by the spirit; both the gospel itself and the formation and maintenance of the single Jew-plus-Gentile family depend on, and implement, that decisive achievement. I believe we are right to see the same larger claim under Paul's apostolic apologia in 2 Corinthians 2–6, and not least in the climax to chapter 5.

Coming back to 2 Corinthians, then, we find the same phrase as in Gal 6:15. "If anyone is in the Messiah," writes Paul in 5:17, "there is a new creation!" This translation is naturally controversial; the older readings regularly personalised it, reading "he is" for "there is," but actually there is no equivalent phrase in Greek, where Paul simply wrote *ei tis en Christō, kainē ktisis*, "if anyone in Messiah, new creation!" This is the sharp edge of the larger claim in verses 16 to 18. Again, it might be possible to read these verses as referring simply to human beings. But taking into account Galatians, Romans, and especially Colossians it seems more natural to take the reference to humans as indicating the focal point of a larger, cosmic vision. Thus we read in 2 Cor 5:15–18:

> From this moment on, therefore, we don't regard anybody from a merely human point of view. Even if we once regarded the

Messiah that way, we don't do so any longer. Thus, if anyone is in the Messiah, there is a new creation! Old things have gone, and look—everything has become new! It all comes from God . . .

This final emphasis there—at the start of verse 18—may indeed explain the otherwise strange anarthrous *theos* at the start of verse 19, or rather after the introductory *hōs hoti*. The Greek phrase *Theos ēn en Christō* slips so easily into word-for-word English that we readily forget that normally, if *theos* is the subject of the sentence, it would carry the definite article. That inclines me to Barrett's view that the tell-tale phrase should read, "It was God who, in the Messiah, was reconciling the world to himself," reading (in other words) *theos* as the complement of *ēn* rather than the subject: "The one reconciling the world to himself was—none other than God!"[20]

So why might Paul have wanted to put it like that? Well, he does almost exactly the same thing in 5:5: "It is God who has been at work in us, the God who has given us the spirit as the first instalment and guarantee." Perhaps he emphasizes this, both there and here, because, as throughout the passage, he is looking to the Creator God as the one who is also responsible for the work of reconciliation, avoiding any suggestion that reconciliation might be simply a human work, or, worse, that the gospel might be offering some alternative divinity, a god other than the world's creator. We find a very similar construction in Phil 2:13: *theos gar estin ho energōn en hymin*, "it is *God* [emphatic] who is at work in you." The point being stressed there is that what is happening "among you" is not just some strange, self-driving spiritual process; it is none other than the presence and power of the living God.[21] That again would emphasize that here in 2 Corinthians Paul is thinking of a "new creation" that was not simply confined to humans, as though the work of grace and the gospel were to take someone away from the created world. Rather, that human new creation was a sign and foretaste of the entire new creation which was launched in Jesus the Messiah, through his death and resurrection, and was now grasping and transforming human beings so that they became living models or exemplars of that same *kainē ktisis*.

This sends us back once more to the sequence of thought in Romans 5–8, where Paul first sketches the rescue of humanity in chapter 5 and then applies it to the whole created order in chapter 8. Redeemed humans in this picture are not simply signs and foretastes of that new creation, but actually its agents. The "freedom" for which the whole creation is longing will come when the renewed humans are themselves glorified (8:21).[22]

20. Barrett, *The Second Epistle to the Corinthians*, 176–77.
21. On this point see particularly Young and Ford, *Meaning and Truth*, 171–72.
22. See Goranson Jacob, *Conformed to the Image*, 233–51.

I think this argument would stand up on its own. It would not, I suppose, convince the determined Bultmannian, or indeed the evangelical individualist. It would still be possible to insist that *kainē ktisis* in 5:17 and "reconciling the world" in 5:19 were simply somewhat grandiose expressions for the transformation of humans through the gospel. But there is another whole argument, not usually advanced at this point, which I think needs to be brought into the equation. When we do this, we not only strengthen the reading I am proposing. We shed light on the larger theological cast of Paul's whole mind. I refer to what we may call the implicit Temple-theology throughout the passage.

The New Temple

When we suggested a moment ago that what Paul says about the renewal of human beings might be a pointer towards the larger theme of a renewed cosmos, an actual "new creation," a reconciled "world," those who have followed recent discussions of what can loosely be called "Temple-theology" may have pricked up their ears. Following many scholars from different backgrounds, I like others have argued that in the Jewish world of Paul's day many would have seen the Temple in Jerusalem not only as the place where heaven and earth overlapped and interlocked, but as the foretaste of the eschatological promise that one day that overlap would be complete, with all things in heaven and on earth brought together—reconciled, in fact. This theme has been observed in the Pentateuch itself, where the original creation of heaven and earth, and the fracturing of their intended close harmony by human sin, was answered in principle by the construction of the Tabernacle in Exodus, with the divine glory coming to dwell in the tent (Exodus 40) to constitute it as a small working model of the ultimately intended new creation.[23] Some Jews in the second Temple period retrieved this theme, seeing either the Temple itself or their substitute community as the heaven-and-earth place, the sign of new creation. There are strong signs that the early Christians understood the events concerning Jesus and the spirit in this way: he was the Temple-in-person, and by the spirit they were themselves constituted as a new-Temple community. Within the implicit cosmic and eschatological meaning of the Temple, Jesus himself, and by the spirit they themselves, were to be seen as advance working models of the ultimate new creation, of the reconciliation of heaven and earth.

---

23. All this is spelled out in detail, with copious annotation, in chapter 5 of my forthcoming Gifford Lectures, *History and Eschatology: Jesus and the Promise of Natural Theology*.

The easiest text from which to make this case would be Ephesians—and I take it that this is part of the reason why, in the still-lingering liberal protestant atmosphere of much New Testament scholarship, that letter continues to be regarded with suspicion. In Eph 1:10 Paul sets out the ultimate eschatological goal, namely, God's plan to unite all things in the Messiah, things in heaven and things on earth. If the Messiah is the means and the ultimate foretaste of that goal, the church will embody it as Jew and Gentile come together, creating a single "new human" through their reconciliation and constituting the new Temple where the one God lives through the spirit (2:15–22). This is then to be worked out both in the unity and holiness of the church (chapter 4) and in the mutual submission and mysterious unity of husband and wife (chapter 5). This in turn points back to the creation story where that same union is a reflection of the heaven-and-earth creation.

What, then, about 2 Corinthians? There is so much going on in this letter that it has been easy to miss the many sub-texts and implicit themes that run through it. But a strong case can be made for seeing a reworking of Temple-theology throughout chapters 3, 4 and 5 at least—and emerging into an explicit statement in 6:14–7:1. This can easily be missed for the usual reason, namely, that scholarship has regarded allusions to the Tabernacle or Temple as purely metaphorical, a bit of Jewish decoration around the edge of Paul's thought rather than constituting an organic theological theme. I suggest, on the contrary, that Paul is thinking in Temple-terms all through.

Thus in chapter 3, when he contrasts his hearers with Moses' hearers, he is referring specifically to the last ten or so chapters of Exodus, when the project to construct the Tabernacle is nearly aborted because of the sin of the Golden Calf. Moses, however, is allowed to go into the tent and speak with God face-to-face, then veiling his shining face when coming out so as not to alarm the Israelites. Paul by contrast has no need to use a veil, since he and his hearers all have the spirit and thus "gaze at the glory of the Lord as in a mirror, and so are being changed into the same image." They are, in fact, becoming genuine humans, renewed image-bearers (as he says in Col 3:10); and the idea of the "image" belongs, as we might expect, within a theology both of new creation and of new Tabernacle. The humans are the image-bearers within the original creation; they stand, like the "image" in a pagan temple, at the heart of the cosmic Temple. Thus in 4:1–6 Paul declares that the Messiah himself is the true divine image, in whose face one can see the glorious reflection of the Creator God: "the God who said 'let light shine out of darkness' has shone in our hearts, to produce the light of the knowledge of the glory of God in the face of Jesus the Messiah" (4:6).

This is the vision that sustains Paul in his apostolic sufferings (4:7–18). He is sharing, and indeed displaying, the sufferings of the Messiah, and the coming resurrection will reveal the glorious life that is at present hidden. At this point many scholars have taken a wrong turning, assuming that Paul is looking to Plato rather than to the Hebrew Scriptures when he speaks of the outer and inner humanity (4:16) and then of being "away from the body and at home with the Lord" (5:6–8). But this is a misapprehension.[24] Once again, as he says explicitly, this is Temple-theology:

> We know that if our earthly house, our present "tent," is destroyed, we have a building from God, a house no human hands have built: it is everlasting, in the heavenly places. (5:1)

Here the common mistake is to assume the normal western idea that the goal of the Christian life is an ultimate "going to heaven." But that is not how this language works. As we should know from Revelation 21, it is "new Jerusalem" language. And the point of the New Jerusalem is that, although it is presently in heaven, it will come down *from heaven to earth*, so that the twin halves of God's good creation can be united for ever. Paul is here personalizing that expectation. Each believer, as a small working Temple-model in himself or herself, needs the "new Temple" which is already prepared and waiting and will one day be revealed:

> At the present moment . . . we are groaning, as we long to put on our heavenly building, in the belief that by putting it on we won't turn out to be naked. Yes: in the present "tent," we groan under a great weight. But we don't want to put it off; we want to put on something else on top, so that what is doomed to die may be swallowed up with life. (5:2–4)

The resurrection body is thus to be seen as the personal, individually tailored version of the New Jerusalem, the great cosmic temple in which heaven and earth are joined at last. And the theme of "groaning" here goes so closely with the identical theme in Rom 8:18–30—where we also find, in verse 29, the climactic notion of being "conformed to the image of the Son"—that we would be correct to interpret each passage in the light of the other. Paul, then, is talking here precisely of the larger "new creation" and drawing that theme down on to the personal expectation of each believer, and particularly himself as the suffering apostle.

This resurrection hope entails, as it is bound to, a hope for the interim, for the meantime between bodily death and bodily resurrection. We would rather, he says, be away from the body and at home with the Lord—much as he says in Phil 1:23 that his desire is to depart and be with the Messiah, which would be far better. But in neither case is this the final destination.

---

24. See full discussion in Wright, *The Resurrection*, 364–70.

In the end comes the judgment (5:10), and with that the resurrection. And Paul clearly sees this resurrection as the moment when heaven and earth come together, when the new body, prepared in heaven, is "put on" over the present humanity. Thus, as arguably in Romans 8, we have once more a Temple-theme. The spirit indwells God's people in the present as the sign and foretaste of what is to come, exactly as the wilderness Tabernacle, and then the Jerusalem Temple, were genuine signs and foretastes of the eventual complete joining of heaven and earth. That would be the time when the divine glory would fill all creation, as in Numbers 14, Psalm 72 or the famous passages in Isaiah 11 and Habakkuk 2. The idea of the spirit as the "first instalment and guarantee" (5:5) belongs precisely here.

All this means, I suggest, that we should read 2 Cor 5:11—6:2—the climax of the whole passage—in the implicit context set up by the Tabernacle-language of chapters 3 and 4 and the New Temple theme at the start of chapter 5. (This makes it far more natural, of course, to read 6:14–7:1, the explicit "new Temple" passage, not as a sudden change of subject but as a natural implication and outflowing from what has gone before.) I believe that this substantially strengthens the case for seeing "new creation" in 5:17 as meaning what it says, with the transformed individual being both a living microcosm of the large-scale new creation already launched in the gospel and a pointer to its ultimate fulfilment. And I believe that this therefore further strengthens the case of Furnish and others for seeing the reconciliation of the world itself in 5:19 as meaning what it says, that is, the whole renewed cosmos, heaven and earth brought back together at last. I know that is shocking to Platonists and others but it is profoundly biblical. It is not, *pace* Käsemann, a pagan idea which has crept into a tradition to which Paul is alluding but which he is then modifying with his own rather different theology. When Paul announces the gospel to individuals and urges them to be reconciled to God, as he says in 5:20, he believes that he is thereby establishing both individuals and nascent Christian communities as small working models of the new creation, of the reconciliation of heaven and earth. There is no distinction: the spirit's work to transform hearts and minds through the gospel is, he believes, the genuinely heavenly transforming of the genuinely and appropriately earthly. The good creation, though now heading for death because of sin, may be rescued and transformed not only in the ultimate resurrection but in the penultimate life of faith, hope, suffering, and love.

Theological Results

There are many "results" that might flow from this exegesis. Since space is limited, I simply name two.

First, there has been a recent push-back among some systematic theologians against the idea of the reconciliation of heaven and earth. In his recent book *Grounded in Heaven*, Michael Allen has argued that the thesis of myself and Richard Middleton, among others, represents what he calls "eschatological naturalism," and constitutes a capitulation to the secular mood of our times.[25] He wants to resist the idea of a "new earth," joined to a "new heaven," and repeatedly offers as an alternative the notion of being "spiritual" or "heavenly minded," and of "recentering" Christian life on God. This reflects multiple misunderstandings, and simply caricatures what I and others have argued. (I have been informed that the caricature comes about partly at least because of some contemporary teachers who are indeed peddling a kind of Christian materialism. But even a cursory reading of my work, or that of Richard Middleton who is also named as a culprit, ought to make it clear that our new-creational eschatology is indeed both biblical and "centred upon God.") Allen uses the rhetoric of "spiritual" or "heavenly" to avoid even facing the strong biblical points that I and others have advanced; and his case can in principle be countered by actual biblical exegesis on every front. It is telling that despite making a general polemical case (mostly on the grounds that the enemy of the gospel is the "secular" world as described by Charles Taylor,[26] which he sees exemplified in the theology of the "new earth") he never mentions, let alone discusses, all the many passages that tell in the other direction—despite his stated adherence to *sola scriptura*.[27] His charge of "eschatological thinness" is bizarre when the people he is attacking are stressing the prophetic vision of the earth being full of the glory of the Lord, or the Pauline theme of God in the end being "all in all" (1 Cor 15:28—another passage not mentioned). Allen's work seems in particular to lack an awareness of what the whole Bible, and particularly Jesus himself, mean by the kingdom of God, and what it might mean for God to answer the prayer that this kingdom would indeed come "on earth as in heaven," not "in heaven as in heaven," and not with "earth" as simply a temporary stage. It is no surprise when Allen reveals that his real hope is for a new synthesis of Christianity and Platonism. I, and the others he critiques, totally agree on the priority

---

25. See Allen, *Grounded in Heaven*.
26. See Taylor, *A Secular Age*.
27. Allen, *Grounded in Heaven*, 134.

of being centered on God, in faith and ethical life. But the question remains as to which God we are talking about.

The answer to that must focus on Jesus, and the second theological theme which naturally grows out of what I have said is thus Christology itself. Without revisiting Baillie's famous book, and without wishing to suggest that the traditional King James translation of 5:19 is right after all, I think the perspective I have been exploring does circle back to a point which on other grounds I am sure that Paul would affirm. Paul's Christology and Pneumatology together, I have argued elsewhere, foreground the Temple-focused theme of the return of Yhwh to Zion: the long-awaited coming back of the divine glory to rescue and redeem, to dwell in the midst of God's people. Messiah and spirit bring this into historical and practical reality as a foretaste of the ultimate heaven-and-earth new creation.[28] Jesus is thus the ultimate "image of God," as in 2 Cor 4:4, which turns out to be the deeply biblical and Jewish way of saying *both* that he is the ultimate human being *and* that he is the one who not only reveals but fully embodies the living presence of the Creator God. Paul, in fact, as the first Christian theologian, gives us rich and multi-layered Jewish categories within which to say what needs to be said about Jesus, about the spirit, and not least about the reconciliation of heaven and earth which then contextualises all other reconciliation. It would be good for theologians to step back from time to time from the cumbersome thought-patterns of later centuries, and to pay more attention to the *scriptura* which is so often, and so emptily, claimed as *sola*.

Bibliography

Adams, Edward. *Constructing the World: A Study in Paul's Cosmological Language.* Studies of the New Testament and Its World. Edinburgh: T. & T. Clark, 2000.

Allen, Michael. *Grounded in Heaven: Recentering Christian Hope and Life on God.* Grand Rapids: Eerdmans, 2018.

Bachmann, Philipp. *Der zweite Brief des Paulus an die Korinther.* Kommentar zum Neuen Testament 8. 4th ed. Leipzig: Deichert, 1922.

Baillie, D. M. *God Was in Christ: An Essay in Incarnation and Atonement.* London: Faber, 1948.

Barrett, C. K. *The Second Epistle to the Corinthians.* Black's New Testament Commentaries. 1973. Reprint, Peabody, MA: Hendrickson, 1993.

Bultmann, Rudolf. *The Second Letter to the Corinthians.* Translated by Roy A. Harrisville. Minneapolis: Augsburg, 1985.

---

28. For a recent statement of this Christology, see chapter 9 of Wright, *Paul and the Faithfulness of God*.

Collange, Jean-François. *Enigmes de la Deuxieme Epître de Paul aux Corinthiens: Etude Exégètique de 2 Cor. 2,14—7,4*. SNTS Monograph Series 18. Cambridge: Cambridge Uni-versity Press, 1972.

Furnish, Victor Paul. *II Corinthians: Translated with Introduction, Notes, and Commentary*. Garden City, New York: Doubleday, 1984.

Goranson Jacob, Haley. *Conformed to the Image of His Son: Reconsidering Paul's Theology of Glory in Romans*. Downers Grove, IL: InterVarsity, 2018.

Héring, Jean. *The Second Epistle of Saint Paul to the Corinthians*. London: Epworth, 1967.

Käsemann, Ernst. "Some Thoughts on the Theme 'The Doctrine of Reconciliation in the New Testament.'" In *The Future of Our Religious Past*, edited by James M. Robinson, 49–64. New York: Harper & Row, 1971.

Middleton, J. Richard. *The Liberating Image: The Imago Dei in Genesis 1*. Grand Rapids: Brazos, 2005.

———. *A New Heaven and a New Earth: Reclaiming Biblical Eschatology*. Grand Rapids: Baker Academic, 2014.

Stuhlmacher, Peter. *Gerechtigkeit Gottes bei Paulus*. Göttingen: Vandenhoek und Ruprecht, 1965.

Taylor, Charles. *A Secular Age*. Cambridge: Harvard University Press, 2007.

Thrall, Margaret Eleanor. *A Critical and Exegetical Commentary on the Second Epistle to the Corinthians*. Vol. 1. International Critical Commentary. Edinburgh: T. & T. Clark, 1994.

Walsh, Brian, and Sylvia Keesmaat. *Colossians Remixed: Subverting the Empire*. Downers Grove, IL: InterVarsity, 2004.

Wright, N. T. *The Climax of the Covenant: Christ and the Law in Pauline Theology*. Edinburgh: T. & T. Clark, 1991.

———. *The Day the Revolution Began*. San Francisco: HarperOne, 2016.

———. *The Epistle of Paul to the Colossians and to Philemon*. Leicester, UK: Tyndale, 1987.

———. *History and Eschatology: Jesus and the Promise of Natural Theology*. Waco, TX: Baylor University Press, 2019.

———. *The New Testament for Everyone*. San Francisco: HarperOne, 2011.

———. *Paul: A Biography*. San Francisco: HarperOne, 2018.

———. *Paul and the Faithfulness of God*. Christian Origins and the Question of God 4. Minneapolis: Fortress, 2013.

———. *Paul and His Recent Interpreters: Some Contemporary Debates*. London: SPCK, 2015.

———. *Pauline Perspectives: Essays on Paul, 1978-2013*. London: SPCK, 2013.

———. *The Resurrection of the Son of God*. Minneapolis: Fortress, 2003.

Young, Frances M., and David F. Ford. *Meaning and Truth in 2 Corinthians*. 1967. Reprint, Eugene, OR: Wipf & Stock, 2008.

18

Holiness and Homemaking

The Christian Doctrine of Creation Performed

—— STEVEN BOUMA-PREDIGER ——

Worrisome Signs of the Times

In his book *Landmarks*, which is about the connections between landscapes and words, Robert Mcfarlane observes that the most recent *Oxford Junior Dictionary* has dropped certain words that the editors think are less relevant for children today, e.g., acorn, fern, nectar, otter, pasture, willow. In their place, the dictionary has added certain other words: blog, broadband, MP3 player, voice-mail.[1] As Thomas Friedman put it in a September 2016 editorial in the *New York Times*: "Who can blame the Oxford editors for dumping Amazon words for Amazon.com words? Our natural world is rapidly disappearing."[2]

In his book *Voices of the Wild: Animal Songs, Human Din, and the Call to Save Natural Soundscapes*, eco-acoustic researcher Bernie Krause writes about the soundscapes of more than 2,000 different habitat types, marine and terrestrial. With powerful illustrations Krause provides a manifesto for the appreciation and protection of natural soundscapes. In this book and his previous book, *The Great Animal Orchestra,* Krause also draws our attention, in the words of Jane Goodall in her endorsement for the book, to "the harmonies of nature . . . [that are being] one by one by one, snuffed out by

---

1. Macfarlane, *Landmarks*, 3–4.
2. Friedman, "Editorial", A23.

human actions."[3] The acoustic symphony is being decimated by our behavior. The symphony of creation, so richly described in Psalm 104, is literally languishing because of the havoc we humans are causing.

Plenty of scientific evidence could be presented to verify these (and other) claims. Deforestation and desertification, water pollution and acid rain, species extinction and climate change—such is just the tip of the proverbial iceberg on the long litany of ecological woe. In some cases the natural world is indeed disappearing; in other cases it is becoming degraded and abused. In my neck of the woods, the lake that bisects my hometown into north and south, Lake Macatawa, is in the process of being cleaned up, but is still too eutrophic or nutrient rich for its own good. While not all the news is bad, many expert earth-watchers agree that the state of our home planet is not good.[4]

In her scholarly paper "The Earth Our Home," to which I was a respondent at a recent conference, Cambridge University biblical scholar Hilary Marlowe notes that "in the Bible the land mourns and languishes because of human sin." The Bible testifies, in her words, to "a close and causal connection between human activity and the well-being of the earth."[5] She goes on to speak of the earth as groaning, to use the words of the Apostle Paul from Romans 8, because of our ecological sins of commission and omission.

Dumping Amazon words for Amazon.com words. The acoustic harmonies of nature being snuffed out by human actions. The earth groaning and the land languishing. Three snapshots of our world today.

This is not the place to review the long litany of ecological woe. My central concern here is that we are aiding and abetting the pillage and plunder of the earth and its plethora of creatures, all too often without realizing it. The languishing of the land goes largely unnoticed because we do not act responsibly as earthkeepers and thus perpetuate a kind of homelessness on our home planet. We are failing to cultivate the knowledge, skills, and character required for us to fulfill our common calling to care for our common home, to use the words of Pope Francis in his encyclical *Laudato Si': On Care for Our Common Home*.[6] In short, we are not living in such a way that our planet and all its creatures will flourish.

This concern is powerfully summarized when, speaking about our disconnectedness from the land, contemporary novelist Barbara Kingsolver

---

3. Jane Goodall endorsement on book cover, Krause, *Voices of the Wild*.

4. For example, Hertsgaard, *Earth Odyssey*; Speth, *Red Sky at Morning*; Pearce, *When the Rivers Run Dry*; Brown, *Plan B*; and, Hansen, *Storms of My Grandchildren*.

5. Marlowe, "The Earth Our Home," 7.

6. Pope Francis, *Laudato Si'*, 3, 133.

writes: "I think of the children who will never know, intuitively, that a flower is a plant's way of making love, or what silence sounds like, or that trees breathe out what we breathe in . . . I wonder how they will imagine the infinite when they have never seen how the stars fill a dark night sky. I wonder how I can explain why a wood-thrush song makes my chest hurt to a populace for whom wood is a construction material and thrush is a tongue disease."[7]

Where We Are and Who We Are

In his essay "Christianity and the Survival of Creation" Kentucky farmer, essayist, and poet Wendell Berry argues that the indictment by anti-Christian conservationists that Christianity is culpable in the destruction of the natural world "is in many respects just." He writes that "Christian organizations, to this day, remain largely indifferent to the rape and plunder of the world and its traditional cultures. It is hardly too much to say that most Christian organizations are as happily indifferent to the ecological, cultural, and religious implications of industrial economics as are most industrial organizations."[8] In the very next breath, however, Berry insists that "however just it may be, it [the indictment of Christianity by anti-Christian conservationists] does not come from an adequate understanding of the Bible and the cultural traditions that descend from the Bible." Critics too often dismiss the Bible, usually without ever reading it, Berry observes. He thus concludes: "Our predicament now, I believe, requires us to learn to read and understand the Bible in light of the present fact of Creation."[9]

Berry is quick to note that the "us" includes Christians as well as non-Christians. Indeed, Berry turns a scathing spotlight on the church when he observes: "I see some virtually catastrophic discrepancies between biblical instruction and Christian behavior. I don't mean disreputable Christian behavior, either. The discrepancies I see are between biblical instruction and allegedly respectable Christian behavior."[10] If there are such inconsistencies between what Scripture teaches and what we think is acceptable behavior, then what? What does it mean to understand the Bible in light of the present fact of Creation?

Never reticent to speak his mind, Berry offers his own short list of basic understandings. First, in the Bible we discover "that we humans do not own the world or any part of it." We are always guests and stewards of

7. Kingsolver, *Small Wonder*, 38–39.
8. Berry, *Sex, Economy*, 94.
9. Berry, *Sex, Economy*, 94–95.
10. Berry, *Sex, Economy*, 95.

God. Second, we find that "God made not only the parts of Creation that we humans understand and approve but all of it," including stinging insects, poisonous weeds, and dangerous beasts. Third, we discover that "God found the world, as He made it, to be good, and that He made it for his pleasure, and that He continues to love it and find it worthy, despite its reduction and corruption by us." Fourth, we find that "Creation is not in any sense independent of the Creator, the result of a primal creative act long over and done with, but is the continuous, constant participation of all creatures in the being of God."[11] And so we discover, Berry concludes, if we read the Bible with an eye to the survival of both Christianity and creation, that "Our destruction of nature is not just bad stewardship, or stupid economics, or a betrayal of family responsibility; it is the most horrid blasphemy. It is flinging God's gifts into his face as if they were of no worth beyond that assigned to them by our destruction of them." In his reading of Scripture Berry strenuously insists "we have no entitlement from the Bible to exterminate or permanently destroy or hold in contempt anything on the earth or in the heavens above it or in the waters beneath it. We have the right to use the gifts of nature but not to ruin or waste them."[12]

In stark contrast to a reading of Scripture that underwrites the exploitation of the earth, Berry argues:

> The Bible leaves no doubt at all about the sanctity of the act of world-making, or of the world that was made, or of creaturely or bodily life in this world. We are holy creatures living among other holy creatures in a world that is holy. Some people know this, and some do not. Nobody, of course, knows it all the time. But what keeps it from being far better known than it is? Why is it apparently unknown to millions of professed students of the Bible? How can modern Christianity have so solemnly folded its hands while so much of the work of God was and is being destroyed?[13]

So where are we and who are we? We are holy creatures living among other holy creatures in a world that is holy. If this is true, then Berry's questions bear repeating. What keeps this biblical understanding from being far better known than it is? Why is it apparently unknown to millions of professed students of the Bible? How can modern Christianity have so solemnly folded its hands while so much of the work of God was and is being destroyed?

---

11. Berry, *Sex, Economy*, 96–98.
12. Berry, *Sex, Economy*, 98.
13. Berry, *Sex, Economy*, 99.

The Christian Doctrine of Creation

Among the many factors at work here, allowing our hand folding while the work of God is destroyed, is a grave misunderstanding about what the doctrine of creation is and how it should work. "Any error about creation also leads to an error about God," wisely advises Thomas Aquinas in *Summa Contra Gentiles* II.3.[14] We must get our doctrine of creation right if we are to get our doctrine of God right. But what does it mean to "get our doctrine of creation right"? What exactly constitutes an error about our understanding of creation?

In my own reflections I have followed a typical path on this matter. For example, I have spelled out the Christian doctrine of creation in terms of what I call "The Seven D's."[15] Following my former teacher Bernard McGinn—who presents "four basic constituents of the idea of creation" found in Christian theology in what he calls "The Four D's"[16]—I enlarge McGinn's list (*dependence, distinction, decision,* and *duration*) to include three more ideas: *design, defect,* and *delight.* For each theme I propose several affirmations and several denials concerning both creation and God.

First, *distinction*. A central belief of the Christian faith is that there is a fundamental ontological distinction.[17] God is ontologically different from creation. Creation is other than God in being and God is transcendent to creation. Creation is, for example, finite while God is infinite. These affirmations are meant to repudiate a number of other views. For example, disavowed is any pantheism or ontological monism in which God and creation are fundamentally identical in being. Creation is not divine or quasi-divine and God is not the same as or part of creation. Creation is God's, but not God.[18]

Second, *dependence*. Equally central to the Christian tradition is the conviction that creation depends on God for its very existence. Creation is ontologically dependent on God for its being, while God, in contrast, is self-existent.[19] As Creator and sustainer God is immanent in, with, and under creation. These affirmations seek to rule out another set of alternative viewpoints. For example, an ontological dualism in which matter is

---

14. Aquinas, *Summa Contra Gentiles*, II, 3.

15. Bouma-Prediger, "Creation as the Home of God", 72–90.

16. Bernard McGinn, "Do Christian Platonists", 208–209. McGinn states that the list is not exhaustive, but rather, "a heuristic device for raising some of the right questions" concerning the adequacy of a given doctrine of creation.

17. See, e.g., Hart, *Understanding Our World*, 334–38.

18. Sittler, "Ecological Commitment", 178.

19. Morris, *Our Idea of God*, 157.

seen as ultimate with or independent of God is rejected.[20] Creation is not self-originating, self-perpetuating, or self-explanatory. So also deism is unacceptable. God is not aloof or on holiday. Any God-of-the-gaps theology must be rejected. While creation is not God, it is God's.[21]

Third, *decision*. Another basic conviction of the Christian faith is that God did not have to create. Creation is both ontologically and existentially contingent.[22] That is, God did not have to create any world at all, and God was not obligated or forced to create this particular world. Creation need not be. It is, rather, a gracious act of a loving God. Thus God is an agent able to freely intend and effect action, unconstrained by anything except the divine nature itself and characterized by grace and love. These affirmations rebut certain historically prevalent perspectives, for example, both a Platonic cosmogeny in which the Creator is externally limited by recalcitrant matter and a neo-Platonic cosmogeny in which a principle of plenitude necessitates that God create.[23] Creation could not have been. It exists only because of God's gracious decision.

Fourth, *duration*. Following Boethuis and the mainstream of the tradition, the fourth theme affirms that creation is temporal while God is eternal. Creation comes to be in or with time. God the Creator, in contrast, stands outside of time altogether.[24] What is denied with these affirmations are the claims that creation is eternal (except perhaps for ontologically dependent but necessary and eternal things, e.g., ideas in the mind of God or abstract objects like numbers) and that God is temporal. Even those who argue that God is best viewed as everlasting rather than eternal still insist that, however God is in time, God is temporal in a quite different way than creatures.[25] While able to act in time, God is also the master of time. God's relationship to time is unique—unlike that of any creature.

Fifth, *design*. Another central conviction of the Christian faith is that creation is both orderly and purposive. Creation is a cosmos—a universe of patterned regularity—and hence intelligible.[26] Creation is, furthermore, an intentionally ordered cosmos. It exhibits the order it does for a reason, namely, because God the Creator made it so. As Psalm 104 declares, creation is fashioned in wisdom to manifest the glory of a creating and sustaining

20. Gilkey, *Maker of Heaven and Earth*, chapter 3.
21. Sittler, "Ecological Commitment," 178.
22. Russell, *Cosmos as Creation*, 195.
23. Morris, *Our Idea of God*, 148–149.
24. See, e.g., Stump and Kretzmann, "Eternity," 219–52.
25. Wolterstorff, "God Everlasting," 181–203.
26. Gilkey, *Maker*, chapter 5.

God. These affirmations constitute rejections of any position that views the world as ultimately chaotic or which understands the order of the world as entirely arbitrary or random. Also rejected is any position in which God is construed as non-personal or capricious. Creation is the ordered system it is because God made it that way.

Sixth, *defect*. One of the distinguishing features of Christian theology is the belief that creation is essentially good.[27] Evil is real, but a perversion of God's intentions for creation—an adventitious quality rather than an essential property. The fall, in other words, is contingent, not necessary. God is, correspondingly, omnibeneficent. These affirmations are intended to repudiate a variety of commonly held beliefs, e.g., that finitude is evil and hence something to be escaped. Evil is not intrinsic or essential to creation—contra Manicheanism or certain forms of Gnosticism. Evil is all too real, but it is an alien intruder which has no legitimate place in God's good creation. God does not have a split personality—part good, part evil. God is not morally imperfect. God is, rather, the summit of moral goodness.

Seventh and last, *delight*. An often overlooked aspect of the Christian doctrine of creation is the conviction that creation is a place of beauty and enjoyment—of value simply because God made it. In the effusiveness of divine grace, God has created and continues to create and sustain a profusion of beings whose existence provokes wonder and whose value extends beyond their usefulness to humans. Instrumental value to humans is only one of several values non-human creatures have.[28] So God is not only a faithful supplier of things needful, but also a generous giver of that which evokes joy.[29] Repudiated by these claims is any utilitarianism that finds creation valuable only insofar as it serves human needs and wants. In contrast, this last D insists that creation is valuable irrespective of its utility for humans and that God is generous in creating a world both bountiful and beautiful.

A Performative Understanding of the Doctrine of Creation

Such is one fairly standard approach to understanding the Christian doctrine of creation. But now back to my questions. What does it mean to get our doctrine of creation right? What exactly constitutes an error about our understanding of creation? In answering this question most people have assumed that understanding the doctrine of creation means giving intellectual

---

27. Gilkey, *Maker*, chapter 7.
28. Rolston, *Environmental Ethics*, chapter 1.
29. Wolterstorff, *Until Justice and Peace Embrace*, chapter 7.

assent to propositions such as those above. Getting the doctrine of creation right means adequately understanding The Seven D's. But my attempt at stating the doctrine, like most such articulations, is too abstract. While perhaps helpful in certain ways, it is bloodless and lifeless—a living, breathing, Holy Spirit-inspired world away from warblers and waxwings and woodpeckers. Because we assume that assent to such formulations constitutes understanding of the doctrine, we have, to use Berry's words, solemnly folded our hands while much of God's work has been and is being destroyed. Our construal of what a proper understanding of this doctrine means has contributed to the pillage and plunder of our planetary home.

But what if an adequate understanding of the doctrine means performing the actions implicit in the claims? What if it means doing what the propositions behaviorally entail? What if rightly understanding the doctrine of creation means knowing in our bones, and thus living in our everyday behavior, that we are holy creatures living among other holy creatures in a world that is holy?

Nicholas Lash, in his insightful essay "Performing the Scriptures," argues that different kinds of texts call for different kinds of readings.[30] In his words, "for different kinds of texts, different kinds of activity count as the fundamental form of their interpretation."[31] Lash uses two analogies to help us understand what he means. For a Beethoven string quartet, the academic skills of the text critics who make the score available and the historical research of musicologists who contribute to the on-going history of Beethoven interpretation are important, but to properly interpret a Beethoven score, four skilled musicians must actually perform the music. As Lash puts it: "The fundamental form of the interpretation of Beethoven consists in the performance of his texts."[32] So also with Shakespeare's plays. As Lash states, *King Lear* is "another example of a text the fundamental form of the interpretation of which consists in its performance." As with the musical analogy, with a Shakespeare play "the expertise required by actors and producer in order to perform well is of a different order from that required of the indispensable but subordinate academic interpreters: the textual critics, historians of Elizabethan drama, literary critics and philosophers."[33] Lash's point with these analogies is simply this: "There are at least some texts that only begin to deliver their meaning in so far as they

---

30. Lash, *Theology*, chapter 3.
31. Lash, *Theology*, 40.
32. Lash, *Theology*, 41.
33. Lash, *Theology*, 41.

are 'brought into play' through interpretive performance."[34] To understand the text is to perform it.

Lash proceeds to argue that "although the texts of the New Testament may be read, and read with profit, by anyone interested in Western culture and concerned for the human predicament, the fundamental form of the *Christian* interpretation of scripture is the life, activity, and organization of the believing community." This Christian practice, furthermore, "consists in the performance of texts which are construed as 'rendering,' bearing witness to, one whose words and deeds, discourse and suffering, 'rendered' the truth of God in human history."[35] In other words, insofar as we Christians live out the story we claim we believe and embrace, we represent the life and teachings of Christ in the life of the church. This approach, Lash suggests, has the merit of reminding us "that the poles of Christian interpretation are not, in the last analysis, written texts . . . but patterns of human action: what was said, done, and suffered, then, by Jesus and his disciples, and what is said, done, and suffered, now, by those who seek to share his obedience and his hope."[36] Could not the same be said for the doctrine of creation, namely, that its "truth" ultimately is a set of practices, a way of being in the world that reproduces the way of Christ? If so, then "getting the doctrine of creation right" means *enacting particular patterns of human action*.

In his book *The Moral Vision of the New Testament*, Richard Hays makes a very similar argument. The last of his ten "proposed guidelines for New Testament ethics" is that "right reading of the New Testament occurs only where the Word is embodied."[37] As Hays continues: "The hermeneutical enterprise is not completed by the work of analysis and commentary; to interpret a text rightly is to put it to work, to perform it in a way that is self-involving so that our interpretations become acts of 'commitment at risk.'" By way of support Hays explicitly seconds Lash's claim that "the fundamental form of the *Christian* interpretation of scripture is the life, activity, and organization of the believing community."[38] Hence in his "diagnostic checklist" Hays emphasizes what he calls "the fruits test." In other words, one crucial question to ask of any interpretation is "How is this vision embodied in a living community? Does the community manifest the fruit of the Spirit?"[39] Could not the same be asked of the doctrine of creation? Paraphrasing Hays'

---

34. Lash, *Theology*, 41–42.
35. Lash, *Theology*, 42.
36. Lash, *Theology*, 42.
37. Hays, *The Moral Vision*, 310.
38. Hays, *The Moral Vision*, 305.
39. Hays, *The Moral Vision*, 213.

key question: what sort of communities result from putting this understanding of the doctrine of creation into practice?[40]

Let me be brutally honest. I agree with Berry's observation that many Christian organizations are indifferent to the despoliation of the earth. All too often we are so busy debating the origins of the universe ("creationism versus evolutionism") to notice either the degradation of our watershed or the beauty of the night sky. We sing the doxology ("Praise God all creatures here below") while ignorant of or indifferent to the fact that we are causing the largest mass extinction since the dinosaurs disappeared 65 million years ago. Church parking lots on Sunday morning, with their gas-guzzling SUVs, look no different than corporate parking lots on Monday morning. Christian college and university campuses appear to be no different than their secular counterparts.

And I share Berry's frustration that however just the indictment of Christianity by anti-Christian conservationists may be, it does not come from an adequate understanding of the Bible. The Bible begins and ends with rivers and trees. The Bible speaks of Christ as the One for whom all things were created, the One in whom all things hang together, and the One through whom all things will be reconciled. The Bible portrays God's glorious good future as earthly and earthy. Alas, we Christians—and perhaps especially we Christian theologians, called to be teachers of the church—have not done near enough to help people understand the full meaning of the doctrine of creation as enacted, performed, and lived. A performative understanding of the doctrine of creation would help us to realize that knowing the doctrine means living it. As Joseph Sittler presciently put it, in a 1973 essay entitled "Evangelism and Care of the Earth":

> If *in piety* the Church says, "The earth is the Lord's and the fullness thereof" (Psalm 24:1), and *in fact* is no different in thought and action from the general community, who will be drawn to her word and worship to "come and see" that her work or salvation has any meaning? Witness in saying is irony and bitterness if there be no witness in doing.[41]

The Doctrine of Creation Performed

Kent runs a church camp in upstate New York. In the summer, he trains staff, deals with emergencies, and pays the bills. He also tells bedtime stories

40. Hays, *The Moral Vision*, 212.
41. Sittler, "Evangelism," 206.

to the many kids who flock to camp, and when he gets a chance joins in the evening music by playing his mandolin. The rest of the year he runs retreats, raises money, and promotes the camp among neighbors near and far. In his spare time he puts up bat houses, cleans composting toilets, and cultivates an organic garden in unforgiving Adirondack soil. The work is seemingly endless, the job never done.

You sense things are different the moment you arrive at Camp Fowler. Whether it's the sign by the parking area that reads "Future world and local leaders in training here," the bicycles the maintenance workers use to haul their gear around camp, or log buildings that properly fit their northwoods setting, you sense that this camp has been carefully thought through. Your first impressions are confirmed at the first meal: the menu includes organic and vegetarian items seldom found among typical camp fare, prepared by a woman who got a master's degree in home economics so she could more knowledgably align the kitchen practices with the core values of the camp. After the meal the campers have a competition to determine which cabin has the least amount of non-compostable food left over, with all the compostable leftovers going into the bear-proof compost bins near the garden.

This is no ordinary Christian camp. There are certainly many of the usual staples of church camp: morning worship before breakfast, time each day devoted to learning the stories of the Bible, chapel time at night with enthusiastic singing. Much of this is led by a local minister who volunteers as chaplain for the week. There are wilderness trips for fishing, sailing, canoeing, and backpacking. Indeed, the Camp Fowler philosophy is similar to many Christian camps: to glorify God, to foster growth in Jesus Christ as Lord, to experience life in a Christian community, to encourage people to live as disciples of Christ. But what is striking at Camp Fowler is that all of it is suffused with a spirit of shalom. Among the camp's core values are simplicity, hospitality, and community. In recent years its summer-long themes have been peace and justice. And woven through everything is the theme of earthkeeping.

Kent has been at Fowler since 1986, and his imprint more than two decades later is now considerable. Through the years he has intentionally and creatively shaped the place and its practices to reflect the core values of the gospel, not least of which is the commitment to caring for the earth. But that care is always specific to a particular place. So Kent knows the history of his camp, and while he has learned much from its past he is not slavishly bound by it. Kent also knows his home place well, the nonhuman as well as human inhabitants. He knows the pileated woodpeckers and barred owls, the tamarack and the golden birch, as well as the director of the library in the local village and the owner of the local paddle shop down the road. Because of his extensive local knowledge, Kent is able to discern the possibilities and the limits of his place. He knows when enough is enough, and thus resists the pressures to think bigger is better. Consequently, the camp remains relatively small—of a human and humane scale. In short, Camp Fowler incarnates a kind of wisdom, and this wisdom joins arms with an infectious joy, such that all who come to Fowler—campers, volunteers, staff—catch the spirit of Kent's joyful wisdom and wisdom-filled joy. Kent Busman not only intellectually understands the Christian doctrine of creation, he performs it every day at Camp Fowler. Each summer he and his staff attempt to live out "The earth is the Lord's and the fullness thereof" with their witness in doing.

Kicking at the Darkness

Brian Walsh has been a gift to many people for many years. In this essay I have tried to honor the work of my long-time friend by focusing on two of the basic worldview questions that Brian and co-author Richard Middleton made famous in their early work together: where are we and who are we?[42] The thought-provoking writings of Wendell Berry, whom Brian has also found to be inspiring, provide answers to those two questions by reminding us that we are holy creatures living with other holy creatures in a world that is holy. Creation in its broadest sense—not only how we understand the natural world but also what it means to be human—has been a central theme of Brian's writing as far back as one can go: in his graduate studies at ICS, in his doctoral dissertation on Langdon Gilkey, in the many more recent writings arising from his innovative teaching and creative campus ministry at the University of Toronto. Indeed, it is striking, when re-reading Brian's books, essays, sermons, and book reviews, to see how pervasive and pivotal the theme of creation (along with fall and redemption) is. I am also (again) struck by the insightful biblical exegeses and perceptive cultural analyses that consistently mark Brian's scholarship.

For Brian, however, the doctrine of creation was never a tenet happily shelved on the closest bookcase. In keeping with the language of performative understanding, Brian knows that all right doctrine (orthodoxy) is to be rightly practiced (orthopraxis)—enacted, lived out, rooted in the soil.[43] My attention to the performative nature of the doctrine of creation, to the witness of living out "The earth is the Lord's and the fullness thereof," is simply a friendly Walshian reminder to us all of the calling to practice our faith on God's good earth.

Brian's typical way of reminding us of this calling is to creatively combine readings of Scripture with readings of culture. One theme emphasized

---

42. Walsh and Middleton, *The Transforming Vision*.
43. Middleton and Walsh, *Truth Is Stranger*, 181.

by Brian is the need to know our place. On the topic of place, in the late 1990s Brian and I discovered that we were, without knowing it, both doing research on the themes of home, homelessness, and homecoming. So we decided to collaborate, the fruit being our book *Beyond Homelessness: Christian Faith in a Culture of Displacement*.[44] It is no surprise that the themes of home, homelessness, and homecoming are woven like a common thread through so much of Brian's academic work and his personal life, especially evident in the generous hospitality that he and Sylvia provide at their home, Russet House Farm.

Finally, in what Brian has written I am struck by the all-pervading theme of hope. In Wine Before Breakfast homilies—"Homemaking in the Ruins." In reviews of contemporary music—"Walk On: Biblical Hope and U2." In books—"Waiting for a Miracle," the last chapter of the Cockburn book. No matter how gloomy the cultural analysis, hope never fails to show up. And this hope is genuine hope, not one of the counterfeits masquerading as hope these days. Brian insists that we must kick at the darkness until it bleeds daylight while also knowing that God's good future of shalom is in God's good (crucified and risen) hands.

Thank you, Brian, for embodying and conveying so much faith and hope and love to so many, not least me.

Bibliography

Berry, Wendell. *Sex, Economy, Freedom, and Community*. New York: Pantheon, 1993.
Bouma-Prediger, Steven. "Creation as the Home of God: The Doctrine of Creation in the Theology of Juergen Moltmann." *Calvin Theological Journal* 31.1 (April 1997) 72–90.
Bouma-Prediger, Steven, and Brian Walsh. *Beyond Homelessness: Christian Faith in a Culture of Displacement*. Grand Rapids: Eerdmans, 2008.
Brown, Lester. *Plan B 3.0: Mobilizing to Save Civilization*. New York: Norton, 2008.
Francis, Pope. *Laudato Si': On Care for Our Common Home*. Brooklyn, NY: Melville, 2015.
Friedman, Thomas. Editorial, *New York Times*, September 7, 2016, sec. A23.
Gilkey, Langdon. *Maker of Heaven and Earth: A Study of the Christian Doctrine of Creation*. New York: Doubleday, 1959.
Hansen, James. *Storms of My Grandchildren: The Truth about the Coming Climate Catastrophe and Our Last Chance to Save Humanity*. New York: Bloomsbury, 2010.
Hart, Hendrick. *Understanding Our World*. Lanham, MD: University Press of America, 1984.

---

44. Bouma-Prediger and Walsh, *Beyond Homelessness*. A decade-long incubation, but what a labor of love this book was—long conversations, visits to our respective homes, and a memorable canoe trip in northern Ontario with our daughters Sophia and Madeleine.

Hays, Richard B. *The Moral Vision of the New Testament: A Contemporary Introduction to New Testament Ethics*. San Francisco: HarperSanFrancisco, 1996.

Hertsgaard, Mark. *Earth Odyssey: Around the World in Search of Our Environmental Future*. New York: Broadway, 1998.

Holmes, Rolston. *Environmental Ethics: Duties to and Values in the Natural World*. Philadelphia: Temple University Press, 1988.

Kingsolver, Barbara. *Small Wonder*. New York: HarperCollins, 2002.

Krause, Bernie. *Voices of the Wild: Animal Songs, Human Din, and the Call to Save Natural Soundscapes*. New Haven: Yale University Press, 2015.

Lash, Nicholas. *Theology on the Way to Emmaus*. 1986. Reprint, Eugene, OR: Wipf & Stock, 2005.

Macfarlane, Robert. *Landmarks*. New York: Penguin, 2016.

Marlowe, Hilary. "The Earth Our Home." Paper for the Institute for Biblical Research, the Society of Biblical Literature annual meeting, San Antonio, TX, November 18, 2016.

McGinn, Bernard. "Do Christian Platonists Really Believe in Creation?" In *God and Creation: An Ecumenical Symposium*, edited by David Burrell and Bernard McGinn, 197–219. Notre Dame, IN: Notre Dame University Press, 1991.

Middleton, Richard J., and Brian Walsh. *Truth Is Stranger Than It Used To Be: Biblical Faith in a Postmodern Age*. Downers Grove, IL: Intervarsity, 1995.

Morris, Thomas V. *Our Idea of God: An Introduction to Philosophical Theology*. Downers Grove, IL: Intervarsity, 1991.

Pearce, Fred. *When the Rivers Run Dry: Water—The Defining Crisis of the Twenty-First Century*. Boston: Beacon, 2006.

Russell, Robert. "Cosmology, Creation, and Contingency." In *Cosmos as Creation: Theology and Science in Consonance*, edited by Ted Peters, 177–209. Nashville: Abingdon, 1989.

Sittler, Joseph. "Ecological Commitment as Theological Responsibility." *Zygon* 5 (1970) 172–81.

———. "Evangelism and Care of the Earth." In *Evocations of Grace: Writings of Joseph Sittler on Ecology, Theology, and Ethics*, edited by Steven Bouma-Prediger and Peter Bakken, 202–6. Grand Rapids: Eerdmans, 2000.

Speth, James Gustave. *Red Sky at Morning: America and the Crisis of the Global Environmental Movement*. New Haven: Yale University Press, 2004.

Stump, Eleonore, and Norman Kretzmann. "Eternity." In *The Concept of God*, edited by Thomas V. Morris, 219–252. Oxford Readings in Philosophy. Oxford: Oxford University Press, 1989.

Walsh, Brian. "Homemaking in the Ruins." Sermon on Isaiah 58 given at Wine Before Breakfast, Toronto, ON, February 8, 2005.

———. *Kicking at the Darkness: Bruce Cockburn and the Christian Imagination*. Grand Rapids: Brazos, 2011.

———. "Walk On: Biblical Hope and U2." Lecture, early 2000s.

Walsh, Brian, and J. Richard Middleton. *The Transforming Vision: Shaping a Christian Worldview*. Downers Grove, IL: InterVarsity, 1984.

Wolterstorff, Nicholas. "God Everlasting." In *God and The Good*, edited by Clifton Orlebeke and Lewis Smedes, 181–203. Grand Rapids: Eerdmans, 1975.

———. *Until Justice and Peace Embrace: The Kuyper Lectures for 1981 Delivered at the Free University of Amsterdam*. Grand Rapids: Eerdmans, 1983.

19

Animism Reconsidered

Coming Home in a More-Than-Human World

Rodney Clapp

Theologian and farmer Brian Walsh wants us humans to wake up to the lively expressiveness of the creation that contains, sustains, and suffuses us—of which we are intricately a part. In modernity we suppose that rocks and trees, dogs and bees, are mute and dumb. They have nothing to say to us. They do not truly interact with us. Utterly objectifying them, we heedlessly lord over them. True enough, we may occasionally employ agential verbs to refer to the more-than-human creation. We say that thunder roars and rocks hit us. But this is figurative, "merely poetic" language. In fact, creation possesses no voice or volition.

Walsh, however, subverts the relegation of all such language to the "merely poetic" (as if there were such a thing), by turning to the eminently modern practice and substance of science. Writing alongside a trained forester, Walsh shows that trees are "responsive creatures." Cooperating with neighboring fungus, trees actively enhance their own and the fungi's existence. Fungus assists trees by absorbing nitrogen and phosphorous, and in return receives the trees' surplus carbohydrates. Furthermore, trees communicate with one another through the vast underground "train systems" of the fungus. For instance, a tree may warn nearby trees that an endangering pest has invaded it and may soon invade them. It is time to ramp up chemical systems that may repel or eliminate the pest.

No less fascinatingly, Walsh and his coauthors write,

> trees display qualities totally inexplicable if considered solely from a mechanistic, nonresponsive viewpoint. For example, a

mechanical model could lead us to reasonably expect that tree growth could be predicted accurately and that foresters could create an "ideotype" or model tree. The fact that foresters cannot do this and that trees of the same species growing in the same soil, climate, and spacing conditions seem to respond individually to the same stimuli suggests that there is something else in trees—a selfhood, or subjectivity, or a factor "x"—contributing to their infinite variety.[1]

Thus Walsh attributes individuality, "selfhood," and "subjectivity" to trees. In the same spirit, he and his coauthors cite the Nobel prizewinning work of botanical geneticist Barbara McClintock. McClintock scrutinized the corn plant as "a unique individual," "a mysterious other," and "a kindred subject." "This 'kindred subjectivity' is a 'special kind of attention that most of us experience only in relation to other persons'; as J. B. McDaniel explains, corn plants to McClintock 'are distant, perhaps very distant cousins: strange but lovable kin.'"[2]

Of course, Walsh is a theologian. So his ultimate aim is to argue that Christians especially should recover a sense of the more-than-human creation as truly alive, responsive, and subjective. The biblical witness entails nothing less. In a particularly sweeping and pregnant passage, Walsh, with coauthor Sylvia Keesmaat, proclaims:

> [I]n stark contrast to the anthropocentric preoccupations of both modernity and postmodernity, biblical faith affirms that creation is an eloquent gift of extravagant love. This is not a world of objects that sit mutely waiting for the human subject to master them. Rather, this is a world of created fellow subjects, all called into being by the same Creator, all born of the Creator's love, all included in the Creator's covenant of creational restoration, and all responsive agents in the kingdom of the beloved Son . . . . A creation called into being by the Word of God, created in, through and for Christ in whom all creation coheres, is not a mechanistic system but a dynamic, personal, living creation that has a voice.[3]

This is exactly, and thoroughly, right. In what follows, then, I unpack Walsh's pregnant assertions. The more-than-human creation, theologically

---

1. Walsh, et al., "Trees, Forestry, and the Responsiveness of Creation." For an engrossing novelistic exploration of trees' subjectivity and agency, see Powers, *The Overstory*.

2. Walsh, et al., "Trees, Forestry, and the Responsiveness of Creation."

3. Keesmaat and Walsh, *Colossians Remixed*, 123.

considered, is "eloquent." It is "a world of created fellow subjects." All creatures are "responsive agents." Creation is "dynamic, personal, living," and it "has a voice." Indeed, and though Walsh does not use this language, I will press further and argue that we should embrace nothing less than a Christian animism.

Redemption and Ecology

Obviously the biblical witness provides grounds for a doctrine of creation that includes the more-than-human creation, from Genesis 1 onward. So we may here best begin with the themes of soteriology and eschatology. It has been assumed that salvation is simply and solely for human beings. But this is obtuse and shortchanges the biblical testimony.[4]

In Jesus' life, death, and resurrection, the kingdom of God has come. Through the cross, the saints have "been set free from the present evil age" (Gal 1:4).[5] Because the Messiah has died and risen from the dead, "the end of the ages has come" (1 Cor 10:11). Everything old has passed away and there is a new creation (2 Cor 5:17).

With Jesus the kingdom has been inaugurated, but it has not yet been manifested in its fullness. We look ahead to Jesus' parousia, when God will raise the dead into transformed, new bodies (1 Corinthians 15). More than this, we look ahead to a new heavens and a new earth. The Apostle Peter anticipates Jesus' return, which will effect the "*universal restoration that God announced long ago through the prophets*" (Acts 3:21). Second Peter 3:13 similarly declares that, "in accordance with [God's] promise, we wait for new heavens and a new earth, where righteousness is at home." Revelation likewise expects "a new heaven and a new earth" (21:1) and the New Jerusalem, the city of God that descends to earth, to include a rolling river that nourishes trees of life (22:2). At the fullness of time, the Letter to the Ephesians says, God "will gather up all things in [Christ], things in heaven and on earth" (1:10).

At more length, the Apostle Paul writes:

> For the creation waits with eager longing for the revealing of the children of God; for the creation was subjected to futility, not of its own will but by the will of the one who subjected it, in hope that the creation itself will be set free from its bondage to decay

---

4. For a more detailed consideration of the following, see Clapp, *New Creation*. Do not neglect the seminal works of Middleton, *A New Heaven and a New Earth*, and Wright, *Surprised by Hope*.

5. All scripture quotations are from the NRSV.

and will obtain the freedom of the glory of the children of God. We know that the whole creation has been groaning in labor pains until now; and not only the creation, but we ourselves, who have the first fruits of the Spirit, groan inwardly while we wait for adoption, the redemption of our bodies. (Rom 8:19–23)

In their hope for a new heavens and a new earth, the New Testament writers draw on a rich trove of Old Testament traditions. Isaiah 11 foresees the famous peaceable kingdom, with animals in harmony with one another and humans. Jeremiah 31:37 declares, "The days are surely coming, says the LORD, when I will sow the house of Israel and the house of Judah with the seed of humans *and the seed of animals.*" Hosea 2:18 understands God's covenant to encompass the more-than-human animals: "I will make a covenant on that day with wild animals, the birds of the air, and the creeping things on the ground; and I will abolish the bow, the sword, and war from your land; and I will make you lie down in safety." Accordingly, Ps 36:5–6 exults:

> Your steadfast love, O LORD, extends to the heavens,
> your faithfulness to the clouds.
> Your righteousness is like the mighty mountains,
> your judgments are like the great deep;
> you save humans *and animals* alike.

We need not look far for the origins of this biblical sensitivity to the whole of creation. The ancient Israelites were a people of the land. And their land was steep, rock, and semiarid. Droughts came to pass every three years out of ten. There was little room for error—and no margin for oblivious waste—in their gardening and farming. They knew they depended on the earth and its bounty for their welfare; if it suffered, so did they. Thus the Israelites were necessarily, and deeply, ecologically sensitive.

For the health of soil, they let the land lie fallow at regular intervals (Exod 23:11). They took care for their own livestock (Deut 25:4) and that of their neighbors (Deut 22:4). And they were solicitous of wildlife, which sometimes also provided sustenance. "If you come upon the bird's nest, in any tree or on the ground, with fledglings or eggs, you shall not take the mother of the young. Let the mother go, taking only the young for yourself, in order that it may go well with you and you may live long" (Deut 22:6).

At the same time, the Israelites were capable of considering the more-than-human creation's welfare in distinction from their own. Their creation story imagined that God created flora and fauna and declared it good *before* the existence of humanity (Genesis 1). They saw God's beneficent creation and provision extending to "every wild animal," "creeping things," wild goats, coneys, and lions (Psalm 104)—aspects of creation quite apart from providing any human resource or use. In addition, as I will elaborate, creation by its very being is understood to offer praise to God. In other words, God would not lack praise and honor even if creation included no human beings. In the biblical vision the more-than-human creation is neither mute nor ungrateful.[6]

Jesus inherits the ecological heritage of Israel. He manifestly had an ecological, agrarian sensibility of humanity's place within a larger, undergirding and surrounding creation. His teachings drip with creaturely resonances. His parables draw often from the farmer's world: seeds and growth in different qualities of soil, planting and harvest, wheat infested with weeds. He allays human anxiety with an appeal to the demeanor and behavior of other creatures, alluding to the cheapest of birds, the sparrows, not one of whom is "forgotten in God's sight" (Luke 12:6-7). Likewise he is sensitive to the lilies of the field, which "neither toil nor spin," but are clothed in stupendous beauty (Matt 6:25-30).

Nor should we neglect, in these regards, a key event in Jesus' life, the temptation in the wilderness. For the biblical cultures, the wilderness (among its more benign properties) was dangerous to humans, and seen as the haunt of demons (Isa 13:21-22; 34:1-5; Rev 18:2). This is crucial background to Mark's brief account of the temptation, which, in our translation (NRSV), comprises a single sentence: "He was in the wilderness forty days, tempted by Satan; *and he was with the wild beasts;* and the angels waited on him" (1:13).[7] At Jesus' baptism, he is anointed with the Spirit and identified as God's Son, thus embedding him in the lineage of King David not only genealogically (Matt 1:1) but spiritually and politically (see Ps 2:7-8). Now he goes to confront Satan directly on his own territory.

Mark's account is terse but extremely suggestive. It breaks Jesus' sojourn in the wilderness into three encounters. First, with Satan. Second, "he was with the wild beasts." Third, "the angels waited on him." Satan is Jesus' implacable foe. The angels are his friends. In between, he is with the wild beasts. Jesus does not tame or domesticate them. He is merely "with" them. Such beasts, in the Palestinian desert of Jesus' time, would have included bears, leopards, wolves, cobras, desert vipers, scorpions, hyenas, jackals, desert lynx, foxes, wild boars, wild asses, antelopes, gazelles, wild goats, porcupines, and rabbits. In the Greek translated "he was with," we have the sense of a close, benign presence. Again, Jesus does not leash the

---

6. Nor necessarily sinful or fallen, though clearly "subjected," as Paul writes in Rom 8:20. See Garvey, *God's Good Earth*.

7. For the following exegesis, I am indebted to Bauckham, *Living with Other Creatures*, 111-32.

leopard or cuddle the jackal. But in a way he befriends them, letting them be what they are.

So Jesus confronts Satan and makes peace with the wild animals (as in Isaiah 11) before he proclaims and enacts the kingdom of God among humans. It is as if he establishes his messianic and eschatological bona fides with the more-than-human creation, only then entering the human arena as the Anointed One. His peaceful sojourn among the wild animals may be likened to his later healing ministry. He does not, with a mass gesture, heal every sick person in Israel. Inaugurating the kingdom of God, he heals some and so signals the later healing of all in the eschaton. Likewise, Jesus' presence among the wild beasts for forty days does not once and for all make the wilderness safe for any and all subsequent wanderers. But it too is a sign of the inauguration of the kingdom awaiting its fullness, to arrive with the eschaton. How marvelous that it includes the animal kingdom as well as human and demonic kingdoms.

Finally, in this blitz through the biblical ecological story, we should not forget that God on occasion embodies or acts through the more-than-human creation. God engages Moses in the form of a burning bush (Exod 3:5–6). Supremely, the Holy Spirit descends on the baptized Jesus "in bodily form like a dove" (Luke 3:21–22). In the Old Testament, the dove is a symbol of God's compassion, a "divine emissary and guardian of sacred order," a "living embodiment of God's protection, healing, and love" (Gen 8:6–12; 15; Song 2:14; 4:1; 5:2; 6:9; Ezek 7:16; Jer 48:28).[8] As the ecotheologian Mark Wallace astutely notes, "Gently alighting on Jesus' person, just like the creation bird hovering over the deep in Genesis, the Gospels' heaven-sent dovey pigeon is God enfleshing Godself in carnal form, but now not only in human flesh in the person of Jesus (God's Son) but also in animal flesh in the person of the Spirit (God's Spirit)."[9]

All told, then, the more-human-creation is very much included in the biblical story. Considered doctrinally, this is true in terms of creation (all is created good), of soteriology and eschatology (all of creation is liberated in Christ), of the incarnation (not only of the Son but also as the Spirit becomes, temporarily, the dove), and of pneumatology (the Spirit as pigeon). The vision induced and conveyed by the biblical story is profoundly ecological. Humans exist in an animate, dynamic matrix of which they are never independent. All of creation is suffused and enlivened by *ruach*, the breath or wind or atmosphere of God. Humans breathe and ingest the more-the-human creation; they are part of it and it is part of them. In the Christian

---

8. Wallace, *When God Was a Bird*, 27.
9. Wallace, *When God Was a Bird*, 31.

story, creation is triply sanctified. First, creation is made good and delightful. Second, Jesus' incarnation blesses all creation and not just humans. Third, his victorious resurrection liberates all of creation. As the Eastern Orthodox theologian Paulos Mar Gregorios succinctly puts it,

> Christ the Incarnate One assumed flesh—organic, human flesh; he was nurtured by air and water, vegetables and meat, like the rest of us. He took matter into himself, so matter is not alien to him now. His body is a *material* body—transformed, of course, but transformed *matter*. Thus he shares his being with the whole created order: animals and birds, snakes and worms, flowers and seeds. All parts of creation are now reconciled to Christ. And the created order is set free to share in the glorious freedom of the children of God.[10]

A Christian Animism

We are now well poised to say what may properly be meant by a Christian animism. First, as Wallace is careful to say, Christian animism is

> not pantheism—nor is it unadulterated animism per se. On the contrary, the model of animism in a biblical register . . . alternately sounds two different but complementary notes: the enfleshment of God in the world vis-á-vis Jesus' humanity and the Spirit's animality, on the one hand, and the alterity of God in God's self as heterogeneous to the world, on the other. Christian animism does not elide the differences between God and the world—as can happen in some pantheistic and animistic formulations of the God-world relationship—insofar as God and world are not collapsed into the same reality without remainder. Instead, it sets forth both the continuity and discontinuity between the divine life and earthly existence.[11]

Thus Christian animism is open and sensitive to God's immanence, but does not neglect or in any way deny God's transcendence. God and creation are not identical or coterminous.[12] God is indeed wholly other than God's cre-

---

10. Cited in Linzey and Regan, eds., *Animals and Christianity*, 27.
11. Wallace, *When God Was a Bird*, 15.
12. Though Wallace at places clearly affirms the radical difference of God and creation, he can at times seem to perilously elide this difference. So at one point he suggests that if humanity somehow destroys the earth, God may be killed in the process (*When God Was a Bird*, 162–69). I demur here.

ation. The Trinitarian God is not lonely, lacking, or in need. Instead, creation is an act of God's graciousness and abundant, overflowing love.

For Christian animism, too, there can be no true or robust understanding of how the more-than-human creation is alive and sentient apart from God's dealings with Israel and in Christ. In other words, a very human and linguistic mediation is necessary and prior. It is the biblical story that enables us to construe the God-world relation lucidly and rightly. And the Bible is the church's book. So a Christian animism has no place for replacing or substituting (human) ecclesiological involvement with nature as the "church."[13]

With these essential qualifiers in hand, we may affirm the sense in which the biblical cultures were animistic. We must not forget that these cultures were predominantly oral and indigenous. That is, most people did not read and write, or depart far from their places of origin. They were grounded in and intimately connected to the more-than-human creation. And as the phenomenologist David Abram notes, for indigenous, oral cultures, "nature itself is articulate; it *speaks*. The human voice in an oral culture is always to some extent participant with the voices of wolves, wind, and wave—participant, that is, with the encompassing discourse of an animate earth. There is no element of the landscape that is definitively void of expressive resonance and power: any movement may be a gesture, any sound may be a voice, a meaningful utterance."[14]

As Abram elsewhere puts it, "While persons brought up within literate culture often speak *about* the natural world, indigenous, oral peoples sometimes speak directly *to* that world, acknowledging certain animals, plants, and even landforms as expressive subjects with whom they might find themselves in conversation."[15] As we will see shortly, the expressiveness of nature and the possibility of directly addressing and conversing with it are represented in the biblical text. Abram stresses that the animism of oral peoples is participatory. Rather than seeing themselves entirely separate from and independent of nature, the ancient Israelites and Jews of Jesus' day vividly encountered and engaged the natural world, and felt

---

13. Here again I may be departing from Wallace. His chapter on John Muir is rich and edifying, but troubling. He is illuminating on how the young Muir was immersed in Scripture and argues forcefully that Muir's animism was informed, even formed, by ecclesial mediation. But he seems to imply that it was fine for the adult Muir to leave behind the (human) church and replace it with the church as nature. Wallace can even write, with emphasis and apparently approvingly, "*For Muir, then, nature is baptism. Nature is church. Nature is redemption. Nature is God*" (*When God Was a Bird*, 125). I strongly disavow all four of these affirmations.

14. Abram, *The Spell of the Sensuous*, 116–17.

15. Abram, *Becoming Animal*, 10.

themselves encountered and engaged by the natural world. As Abram says, "Careful attention to the evidence suggests that ancient Hebraic religiosity was far more corporeal, and far more responsive to the sensuous earth, than we commonly assume."[16]

But ours is a predominately literate, not an oral, culture. Does this mean we must be out of reach of a Christian animist sensibility? Immersed in alphabetic writing, we do have, in comparison to oral peoples, an extra layer between our experience of the world, and of more-than-human creation in particular. We are insulated in a way the oral peoples are not. Yet Abram argues that we are not entirely shut up, or hermetically sealed, in written language. We still encounter weather, nurture plants, touch and are touched by animals. Some of our science, such as that of Barbara McClintock's, demonstrates that we can still learn from and listen to more-than-human creation in a kind of conversation. We can still be inspired, challenged, transformed, renewed by our engagements with creation in its many forms. Thus Abram seems right in suggesting that the human organism has "a spontaneous propensity" for sensitive participation with the more-than-human world. This is a participation that is "radically transformed, *yet not eradicated,* by alphabetic writing."[17] Consider the following meditation by the twentieth-century monk Thomas Merton:

> The rain surrounded the cabin . . . with a whole world of meaning, of secrecy, of rumor. Think of it: all that speech pouring down, selling nothing, judging nobody, drenching the thick mulch of dead leaves, soaking the trees, filling the gullies and crannies of the wood with water, washing out places where men have stripped the hillsides . . . Nobody started it, nobody is going to stop it. It will talk as long as it wants, the rain. As long as it talks I am going to listen.[18]

Immersed and insulated in literacy, and enamored of a highly technological world that literally screens us off from the rest of creation, we can easily forget that we are finely participant in and with nature. So our reconnection to the more-than-human world will not come without intention and effort.[19] But as Merton shows, we need not necessarily remain oblivious—and with climate change the natural world is more and more intensely and insistently demanding our attention. With that said, let us listen afresh to the biblical text.

16. Abram, *The Spell of the Sensuous*, 240.
17. Abram, *The Spell of the Sensuous*, 176, emphasis added.
18. Quoted in Abram, *The Spell of the Sensuous*, 73.
19. For some counsel to that end, see Abram, *Becoming Animal*, 288–92.

Animistic Biblical Texts

At Genesis 4, in the primeval murder, Cain kills his brother Abel. The ground on which the crime occurs responds actively. It swallows Abel's blood and issues a curse, refusing thereafter to "yield its strength" when Cain tills it (vv. 11–12). Similarly, at Leviticus 18:28, the people are warned against committing abominations, lest "the land vomit you out for defiling it." In other texts, too, because of human sin the earth mourns, dries up, withers (Jer 4:28; 14:1–6; Hos 4:3). It is not much of a stretch to read such texts and imagine the earth's response to global warming. The human defilement of creation results in the atmosphere's rejoinder of vomiting out (or burning out) its human inhabitants. Creation's suffering at human obduracy and obscurity must have been something of what the Apostle Paul had in mind when he wrote of creation "groaning" for its release from futility (Rom 8:10–23).

We have already noted Hosea 2:18, where God promises a covenant with the more-than-human creation. Here we may add Joshua 24:27, where Joshua sets up a stone "as a witness against us; for it has heard all the words of the LORD that he spoke to us; therefore it shall be a witness against you, if you deal falsely with your God." In the biblical animistic vision, creation is addressable and responsible. In this vein, the prophet Ezekiel is commanded to "prophesy to the mountains of Israel. . . . [T]herefore, O mountains of Israel, hear the word of the Lord GOD . . ." (36:1, 4). And the more-than-human creation—in contrast to humans—is portrayed as always faithful to its calling to covenant, witness, and answer prophecy. "Faithfulness will spring up from the ground, and righteousness will look down from the sky. The LORD will give what is good, and our land will yield its increase" (Ps 85:11–12). In this mentality, Jesus responds to the Pharisees who want the acclamatory crowd to shut up: "I tell you, if these were silent, the stones would shout out" (Luke 19:34–40).

In like manner, Job commissions conversation with creation:

> But ask the animals, and they will teach you;
> the birds of the air, and they will tell you.
> Ask the plants of the earth, and they will teach you;
> and the fish of the sea will declare to you. (12:7–8)

Out of its inherent wisdom and faithfulness, the addressable creation is ready to praise God, and exultant with praise.

> Let the sea roar, and all that fills it;
>   the world and those who live in it.
> Let the floods clap their hands;
>   let the hills sing together for joy

> at the presence of the LORD, for he is coming
> > to judge the earth.
> He will judge the world with righteousness,
> > and the peoples with equity. (Ps 98:7–8)
>
> Praise the LORD from the earth,
> > you sea monsters and all deeps,
> Fire and hail, snow and frost,
> > stormy wind fulfilling his command!
> Mountains and all hills,
> > fruit trees and all cedars!
> Wild animals and all cattle,
> > creeping things and flying birds! (Ps 148:7–10)
>
> For you shall go out in joy
> > and be led back in peace;
> the mountains and hills before you
> > shall burst into song,
> > and all the trees of the field shall clap their hands. (Isa 55:12)

Withal, like all orally oriented people, the biblical cultures are vigorously participant in the creation that embeds and surrounds them. They experience creation as conversant and responsive, addressable by God and by themselves. Their catalog of responsive creation bursts in comprehensiveness, including all manner of created entities: the ground, the skies, stones, trees, clouds, mountains and hills, plants and trees, creeping things, domesticated and wild animals, birds, seas and floods, water-dwelling creatures, fire, hail, snow, frost, wind, and atmospheric storms. Creation is agential and can only be described with an abundance of verbs. It variously witnesses, groans, tells, teaches, declares, yields, praises, hears, waits, swallows, vomits, curses, mourns, sings, claps, roars, and looks. Accordingly, it is a participant in the covenant. And, let us note again, it is constant in its faithfulness and ever eager to praise.

Indeed, "This is not a world of objects that sit mutely waiting for the human subject to master them. Rather, this is a world of created fellow subjects, all called into being by the same Creator, all born of the Creator's love, all included in the Creator's covenant of creational restoration, and all responsive agents in the kingdom of the beloved Son. . . . A creation called into being by the Word of God, created in, through and for Christ in whom all creation coheres, is not a mechanistic system but a dynamic, personal, living creation that has a voice."[20] If we will but again learn to

---

20. Keesmaat and Walsh, *Colossians Remixed*, 123.

listen to that voice, the mountains of Israel will shoot out their branches and yield their fruit. As Brian Walsh would be the first to affirm, they, and we, "shall soon come home" (Ezek 36:8–9).

Bibliography

Abram, David. *Becoming Animal: An Earthly Cosmology.* New York: Vintage, 2010.
———. *The Spell of the Sensuous: Perception and Language in a More-Than-Human World.* New York: Vintage, 2017.
Bauckham, Richard. *Living with Other Creatures: Green Exegesis and Theology.* Waco: Baylor University Press, 2011.
Clapp, Rodney. *New Creation: A Primer on Living in the Time between the Times.* Eugene, OR: Cascade Books, 2018.
Garvey, Jon. *God's Good Earth: The Case for an Unfallen Creation.* Eugene, OR: Cascade Books, 2019.
Keesmaat, Sylvia C., and Brian J. Walsh. *Colossians Remixed: Subverting the Empire.* Downers Grove, IL: InterVarsity, 2004.
Linzey, Andrew, and Tom Regan, eds. *Animals and Christianity: A Book of Readings.* 1990. Reprint, Eugene, OR: Wipf & Stock, 2007.
Middleton, J. Richard. *A New Heaven and a New Earth: Reclaiming Biblical Eschatology.* Grand Rapids: Baker Academic, 2014.
Powers, Richard. *The Overstory: A Novel.* New York: Norton, 2018.
Wallace, Mark I. *When God Was a Bird: Christianity, Animism, and the Re-Enchantment of the World.* New York: Fordham University Press, 2019.
Walsh, Brian J., et al. "Trees, Forestry, and the Responsiveness of Creation." *Cross Currents* 44 (Summer 1994) 149–62. http://www.crosscurents.org/trees.htm. Also published in *This Sacred Earth: Religion, Nature, Environment,* edited by Roger S. Gottlieb, 423–35. New York: Routledge, 1995.
Wright, N. T. *Surprised by Hope: Rethinking Heaven, the Resurrection, and the Mission of the Church.* New York: HarperOne, 2008.

20

Home Is Where the Wild Rice Is[1]

Sylvia C. Keesmaat

Creation

In the stories of old we are bound to the land,
Creator's hand shaping us
to be *'adam* from *'adamah*,
earth-creature from the earth.
We image the earth
as much as we image our God,
a union of earth and Spirit,
the very breath of God,
filling shaped earth until it becomes earth creature.[2]

In the stories of old the land is given as gift,
given in abundance for our hunger
and the hunger of other creatures.

In the stories of old the land is our teacher,
the forest and its creatures the ones we serve
with gratitude for all that they offer us:
food, medicines, shelter, clothing.

The land is our teacher:
in observing the creatures, the plants,

---

1. My thanks to Aileen Verdun, Melodie Ng, Jason Chong and Tim Verdun, who carried some of the workload on our farm so that I could work on this chapter. I am grateful that Aileen and Melodie also provided feedback that improved this chapter considerably. This chapter is also very much indebted to the deeply profound work on home found in Bouma-Prediger and Walsh, *Beyond Homelessness*.

2. This paragraph and the following are dependent on Gen 2:4–17; Job 38–9; Pss 19:1–6; 104; 145; Matt 6:25–34.

> the relationships between them,
> and the gifts they offer each other and us,
> we learn patience, love, faithfulness, joy,
> gratitude, self-control and compassion.
> We learn that all of creation is sustained
> by the breath of Creator,
> as we are ourselves.
> All of it a gift
> from a loving, extravagant hand.
> All of it a home
> for joy, and abundance, and love.

In the stories of old, the people of the Michi Saagiig (Mississauga) Nishnaabeg[3] were guided to this land where I now live. Their prophecy had told them to continue west until they reached the place where the food grew on the water. Just to be clear, this is not my story, nor is this my place. I am an immigrant to Turtle Island, born to parents who were taken out of their homeland and their stories by their parents fleeing the trauma of war and the devastation of a destroyed land. I live here with my husband, Brian, a settler whose family has lived on Turtle Island for generations and to whom this book is dedicated.[4] Fourteen years ago we moved together to this place, now called the Kawartha Lakes. We left the geographies that had shaped us as children, and we entered the story of this land and the story of the Michi Saagiig Nishnaabeg whose traditional lands these are and whose stories are deeply rooted in this place.[5]

I talk about the story of the Michi Saagiig Nishnaabeg in an attempt to understand how it is that our stories have participated in the destruction of the people who were first in relationship with this land. I explore these stories in hope that reparations can be made. I tell this story in the hope that perhaps we can make home together. It is a tall order, and perhaps it will not be possible. But I believe that the story that has shaped me more than any other, the story that has given me home—the biblical story—has

---

3. I am following the spelling here of Leanne Betasamosake Simpson in her various works. The Nishnaabeg are also referred to as the Anishnaabek and the Anishnaabeg. In the past they were called the Ojibway by white colonizers. This chapter is a very brief description of the story of the Michi Saagiig Nishnaabeg. There is much more to say about manoomin, the land, home and decolonization in Indigenous thought and practice than it is possible to include here. The footnotes provides helpful further reading.

4. Turtle Island is the Indigenous name for the land we now call North America.

5. By "this place" I am referring to what is now called The City of Kawartha Lakes (a large region) and the City of Peterborough (an actual city) nearby. The latter is called Nogojiwanong by the Michi Saagiig Nishnaabeg. The two largest communities of Michi Saagiig Nishnaabeg in this area are Curve Lake First Nation and Alderville First Nation.

called me to this place. And so, with hesitant steps, in this chapter I will reflect on small sections of two stories. One is the biblical story, which has shaped the home that Brian and I have been given. The other is the story of the Michi Saagiig Nishnaabeg. How do these stories illuminate one another? Is it possible that in harmony they provide a vision for how home can be made together in this place?

In the stories of old, the Michi Saagiig Nishnaabeg were led to this place, where the food grows upon the water. The Nishnaabeg call that food *manoomin;* settlers call it "wild rice." Manoomin is the basis of Michi Saagiig Nishnaabeg life. Its health is important for all of the relations that share the waters: the many fish who live there; the muskrat and the beaver who use the fibres and eat the shoots; the redwing blackbirds, rails, pigeons, quails, herons, cedar birds, woodpeckers and ducks that eat the grain;[6] the frogs, turtles and insects that live in and amongst the rice stalks and provide food for the herons; the deer and moose that graze the foliage. According to James Whetung, who is working to restore manoomin in his traditional lands, "in this region the lake without wild rice is a desert; once the wild rice is established, everything just multiplies, from the bugs to the birds, muskrats, beavers, otters and fish. The whole environment benefits because wild rice provides safety and security to the swimmer, the flyers, the four-legged and to us the two legged."[7]

For the Michi Saagiig Nishnaabeg, as for all Indigenous peoples in general, the land is the place that gave them birth. The land is their teacher, the land and its creatures are part of a web of relationships that uphold and sustain them in the face of change and challenge. In addition, "the land records memories. There are sacred places in such lands—places of covenant with Creator, places of healings and miracles, places where ceremonies and traditions take place."[8]

Such memories and knowledge are deeply rooted in the ceremonies, rituals and practices that surround the manoomin harvest. From the thanksgiving that is offered to Creator before the harvest begins, to the medicine rituals that are connected to it, to the deep traditional ecological knowledge that is necessary for building a canoe, shaping a paddle, finding an appropriate stick to knock the grain off the stalks, knowing when the rice is ready, building just the right fire for parching the rice, sewing the moccasins for hulling and dancing, making the baskets used for the winnowing, making the birch and cedar bark containers for storage, knowing how far down to dig and

6. Jenks, *Wild Rice*, 1027.
7. Anderson and Whetung, *Black Duck*, 23.
8. Woodley, *Shalom*, 120.

how well to wrap to keep moisture from the rice when buried in storage—for all of this the stock of knowledge of plants, trees, weather, soil, and animals is extensive. For instance, there is no point in making a birch bark container if you don't seal it well with pitch, and there is no point in burying your cache of manoomin if a fox is going to be able to dig it up.[9]

But more than the deep and broad knowledge of this place and its plants and animals that are necessary for harvesting and storing the manoomin, the harvest of the rice is crucial for creating the bonds of kinship and community, for teaching patience, humility, cooperation, and respect, and for providing a basis for governance and community organization.[10] As Michi Saagiig Nishnaabeg knowledge-keeper, artist, and activist Leanne Betasamosake Simpson says: "while each individual must have the skills and knowledge to ensure their own safety, survival, and prosperity in both the physical and spiritual realm, their existence is ultimately dependent upon intimate relationships of reciprocity, humility, honesty, and respect with all elements of creation, including plants and animals."[11] In the end, the wild rice harvest occurs in a context of love—for the land, for Creator, for all of the human and animal relations that are enmeshed in the life of manoomin.[12] And being rooted in such love enables the Michi Saagiig Nishnaabeg to know who they are and how they are to live in the world. They are a people who live on and with the land where plants grow on the water. And those plants, this manoomin, sustains them and gives them life.

Colonization and Resistance

> They tell it briefly,
> in the measured calm tones
> that bureaucrats use to hide
> policies of death and genocide.
> These young Israelites are of royal and noble blood:
> wise, strong, attractive,
> self-confident and smart—
> a little too smart, in fact,

---

9. On the thanksgiving and medicine rituals see Vennum, *Wild Rice*, 71–19; on processing and storing see Vennum, *Wild Rice*, 138–146. On knowledge rooted in land see Grey and Patel, "Food Sovereignty as Decolonization," 436–437; Simpson, "Land as Pedagogy," 155–166.

10. Krotz, "The Affective Geography," paragraphs 8 & 22; Grey and Patel, "Food Sovereignty," 436–37.

11. Simpson, "Land as Pedagogy," 154.

12. Simpson, "Land as Pedagogy," 154.

a little too strong and self-confident
in their identity as Israelites.[13]

Just a few small changes to ensure their obedience
to the empire that has captured them,
just a few strategies to discourage resistance:
they were to be taught the literature
and language
of the Chaldeans.
No longer are they to tell the stories of their homeland.
No longer are they to speak the language of their mothers,
the words that grew out of their homes,
out of their land.
The stories that bound them to their place
that wove deep tapestries of memory
about the hills they grew up in
and the wadis of their valleys,
now to be replaced with new words,
new stories,
designed to dis-place them.

No longer were they permitted
to eat the food of their homeland.
Instead they were given the rich food of the empire,
royal rations of meat and wine,
imperial food,
seized from the labour of the poor.
The bread of injustice,
intended to dull their senses,
satiate their longing,
and complete their disconnection from the land.

All their lives, their food
had been given by the land.
The lamb had tasted of their hillsides,
the apricots and olives were from their trees,
the cheese from their own goats,
the spices gathered from their hedgerows
and dried in the rafters of their homes.

No longer were they permitted
to be called by the names that connected

---

13. The following paragraphs are based on Daniel 1.

them to their God:
Daniel, Hananiah, Mishael and Azariah,
worshippers of *El* and *Jah*.
New names, strange names
that echoed strange gods
were used to summon and shape them.

No stories to connect them to the memories of home,
no language to connect them to the rhythms of their home,
no food to connect them to the seasons of their home,
no names to connect them to the God of their home.

But Babylon hadn't anticipated a counter-move.
Just a small resistance:
a refusal of imperial food.
A refusal of food disconnected from their land,
a refusal of food disconnected from their God,
a refusal of food that continued to sever them
from home.
Daniel (who, in this story, also retains
the name given him in his own language),
knows that eating is about connection,
eating is about building connections with home.
Our food feeds us with a story
and creates who we are.
And Daniel does not want to be shaped
into the image of the empire.

What do we do when the life that one people is living is in the way of *our* goals, *our* dreams, *our* comfort, *our* profits? The building of the Trent-Severn waterway had the goals and profits of colonizers at its heart. What did it matter if the locks and dams prevented the salmon and eels from migrating up to the lakes where the Nishnaabeg could eat them?[14] What did it matter that dredging the canal system destroyed the manoomin in its path? What did it matter that the deepening of the lakes drowned most of the shallow-rooted manoomin, and that invasive carp destroyed that which still survived in wetlands? What did it matter that the lakes were soon so polluted that the rice seed which remained could not grow, could not breathe in the death-giving waters under settler control?

How could the Michi Saagiig Nishnaabeg teach their children the rhythms of the wild rice moon when there was no manoomin to harvest?

---

14. Simpson, *Dancing*, 87.

How could they learn to judge the ripeness of the grains, the exact moment when the parching was enough? Why would they learn to make the birch bark baskets and the dancing moccasins? How could the manoomin teach them? And how could they learn from the otters and the muskrat, the rails and the quail? Without manoomin, what would ground their ceremonies? How could they thank the Creator for a gift that had been taken away? About what would they sing? Over what would they dance? The manoomin grounded the Michi Saagiig Nishnaabeg in their place. Without it they were cast adrift.

The destruction of a foodway was, however, as in the days of old, just one way that the colonizers attempted to destroy this people that was so inconveniently in their way. If the Michi Saagiig Nishnaabeg children are removed from the land, forbidden to speak in their own language, given new names, and taught the stories and ways of the colonizers, they will never learn the ways of their mothers. They will never be able to remember the lessons taught to their people by the wild rice, by the salmon, by the maple syrup, by the strawberries.[15] "Unlike Daniel, Hananiah, Mishael and Azariah, the children in the residential schools were unable to refuse the imperial food systems, and were instead subjected to systems of cultural genocide enforced by the very people who were, theoretically, speaking in the name of the God of Daniel."[16]

And if the people who remain are forbidden from hunting, forbidden from fishing, and denied access to their lands, then their identity as a people will gradually disappear.[17] They will be gone, just like the manoomin.

Unless, of course, the manoomin begins to return. And some of the knowledge holders begin to share their memories of the harvest, the ceremonies they remember, the wisdom that had been passed on to them, the stories of manoomin. As the manoomin has begun to return to the less polluted lakes, the lifeways of the Michi Saagiig Nishnaabeg have begun to come to life once more. Just like Daniel in the face of Babylon, some in the Michi Saagiig Nishnaabeg community are saying "no" to the imperial food the colonizers have offered them, "no" to the genocidal attempt to erase them from the land that they have lived in relationship with for thousands of years, "no" to the attempt to sever them from the land that has given them life.[18]

15. Daigle, "Tracing the Terrain," 302; Grey and Patel, "Food Sovereignty," 438; Simpson, "Land as Pedagogy," 153.

16. Verdun, *Imperial Food Systems*, 44.

17. On the suffering and starvation that resulted from the denial of access to hunting and fishing grounds, see Simpson, "Land as Pedagogy," 167–68.

18. See particularly the story of James Whetung in Anderson and Whetung, *Black Duck Wild Rice*; Jackson, "Canada's Wild Rice Wars"; and "Nourishing Communities."

It is not surprising that the empire is striking back. At the heart of imperial control is always the desire of those with privilege, those with power, those with wealth, to ensure that their way of life, their comfort, their own flourishing be given priority over the flourishing of others. For the Michi Saagiig Nishnaabeg this is clearly evident in the insistence of those settlers who have purchased land on the shores of lakes that *their* leisure, *their* entertainment, and *their* interests are threatened by the presence of manoomin on the lakes. The conversation has many ironic twists. Cottagers complain that James Whetung, who currently holds the rights to harvest manoomin on many of the local lakes in Michi Saagiig Nishnaabeg land surrounding the Curve Lake Reserve, has created a "farm" on the lake that they want to enjoy. The irony is that the Williams Treaty of 1923 made legal the seizing of communal Michi Saagiig Nishnaabeg land so that settlers could establish *farms* on it. Cottagers profess a love for the creatures and plants on the lake, even the small wild rice patches that they allow near the shore, yet they do not have lifeways that promote the flourishing of those creatures and plants.[19] Cottagers also profess respect for Indigenous rights to harvest traditionally, yet every year large swathes of manoomin are sabotaged by motorboats with chains strung between them.

In spite of the fact that colonization continues to suppress the access of the Michi Saagiig Nishnaabeg to manoomin, there are those who continue to resist. James Whetung, and his company, Black Duck Wild Rice, not only harvest and plant wild rice, they also lead groups of school children, Indigenous peoples, and allies out into the manoomin every year to learn traditional harvesting and processing techniques. Other Michi Saagiig Nishnaabeg people also spend time harvesting manoomin, in spite of the fact that they often face threats and verbal abuse from settlers in the area.[20] They do so because manoomin is central to their identity as Michi Saagiig Nishnaabeg. They do so because this is who they are. As Leanne Betasamosake Simpson puts it, "They want a beach. We want rice beds. You can't have both. They want to win. We *need* to win. They'll still be white people if they don't have the kind of beach they want. Our kids won't be Mississauga if we can't ever do a single Mississauga thing."[21]

For other strategies of resistance and resurgence see Daigle, "Tracing the Terrain," 303–311; Simpson, *Accident*.

19. While this may seem like a blanket statement, all the evidence is that biodiversity declines and habitat for wildlife is deeply compromised as shorelines become occupied by settlers. Daigle, "Tracing the Terrain," 302, refers to this recent twist in the story as "cottager colonization."

20. For an account of such an event see Simpson, *Accident*, 75–78.

21. Simpson, *Accident*, 78.

Reparation

Some call it a pipe dream.
Others, not historical.
But the vision is unexpectedly clear
and detailed.

There are dates:
seven weeks of years,
seven times seven years,
on the tenth day of the seventh month,
the day of atonement,
the trumpet shall be sounded,
you shall hallow the fiftieth year.[22]

There are laws about the land:
return to your land;
charge only for the harvests on the land;
the land shall not be sold in perpetuity;
provide for redemption of the land;
the land shall be released in the jubilee,
and the property shall be returned.

There are laws about the poor:
you shall support your relatives who fall into difficulty;
do not take interest in advance;
let them live with you;
those who sell themselves to you
are to be freed in the jubilee
to return to their ancestral property.

There are laws that link God with this land:
I will order my blessing,
so that the land will yield for three years;
the land shall not be sold in perpetuity,
for the land is mine.

It only seems like a pipe dream
to those with tight fists,
those who wish to keep what they have amassed,
who wish to pass the land that they have bought
(as if it were a commodity),
on to their children

---

22. This and the following sections are based on Leviticus 25.

(that the father's sin of hoarding
might be passed on to their children
and their children's children).

But the vision
is simple.
After a generation
the land returns into the care and affection
of the first servants.

The vision is simple.
Too simple
for a country with genocide
in its history,
and invasion in its past.

And yet,
that didn't stop Zacchaeus
from practicing jubilee.[23]
Zacchaeus, visited by Jesus,
having heard the stories of Jesus' words
to followers, disciples, rich men and teachers:
"Go, sell all that you have and give it to the poor."

Zacchaeus knew that his salvation
meant righting wrongs,
making reparations,
restoring what he had taken;
in short, returning the land.
Land he had foreclosed on,
land he had taken in payment of debt,
land he had casually amassed
to pass on to his children.

Zacchaeus knew that when Jesus said,
"Sell all that you have and give it to the poor,"
that meant,
"Return the land that you have taken
that made men and women, children and grandchildren poor.
Restore them to their places,
their lifeways,
their homes."
Zacchaeus knew that jubilee was not a pipe dream.

---

23. The Zacchaeus story is found in Luke 19:1–17.

> He knew that reparations were not a pipe dream.
> He knew that only with reparations
> was reconciliation possible with his neighbours,
> with his God,
> and with the land,
> returned once more into the care and affection
> of those who served it,
> not as commodity
> but as gift.[24]

Sometimes an aha moment can turn everything on its head. Like the moment when it becomes clear that the jubilee legislation in Leviticus 25 is not directed to the poor, or to those who have lost their land, but to the wealthy, to those with privilege. They are the ones who are reminded that "in order to create a shalom system of social harmony, no person could be oppressed for too long without hope of ease and eventual release; no family could remain in poverty for generations; no land could be worked until it was depleted and useless; no animals could go hungry for too long. Any of these violations of shalom that were left unmitigated for too long would upset the natural order of reciprocity fixed in all creation."[25]

Those who have benefited from past injustices are the ones called to restore relationships and provide release for the oppressed. Those who have profited from the poverty of others are to give up their wealth so that poverty ends with their generation; those who have gained control over the land are the ones who are to relinquish it into the care of those whose lifeways were rooted in it for many more generations; those who have gained from the destruction of animal habitats are the ones called to self-sacrificially restore such habitats for the flourishing of all of creation.

At its heart this call is rooted in a biblical understanding of land as *gift*, an understanding that the Michi Saagiig Nishnaabeg understand well. And this call is rooted in a certain understanding of power: the power of a God whose authority is seen in self-sacrificial, self-giving love.

Jubilee is at the heart of reparations: making it right, levelling the playing field. Such a re-balancing should be at the heart of reconciliation.[26] "Perhaps this is where we need to consider reparations. If one of the harms done

---

24. I recognize that I have simplified a complicated story that itself included genocide and invasion in its narratives. However, I accept Norman Gottwald's depiction of ancient Israel as an alliance of Indigenous and Hebrew peasants who resisted larger imperial control. See Gottwald, "Early Israel as Anti-Imperial," 5–22.

25. Woodley, *Shalom*, 30.

26. Simpson, *Dancing*, 22.

to Indigenous peoples consisted of stripping them of control over their own foodways, perhaps one way of enacting redistribution is to engage in reparations which restore those foodways. In some cases, this may look like the restoration of land. It may also look like restoring foraging rights in public lands and lakes, or like private landowners granting hunting and gathering rights to Indigenous communities."[27]

In the place where I live, at the very least this would mean honoring the rights of the Michi Saagiig Nishnaabeg to harvest manoomin. However, having the right to harvest isn't enough, for such rights are meaningless if the manoomin has been destroyed, or if access to the manoomin beds are restricted, or if there are so few places to harvest that there is insufficient manoomin for the community, or if harvesting occurs in a context not of ritual and ceremony but is surrounded by abuse, suspicion and distrust.[28] A context needs to be created where manoomin can flourish in such a way that the foodways of the Michi Saagiig Nishnaabeg can be sustained once more in all of their richness. And once the manoomin can flourish, the people will be able to flourish as well.

For Zacchaeus to imagine reparations, he needed to enter into a different story. Zacchaeus had to recognize that the story of the empire, where land was a commodity to be accumulated, was hollow and did not lead to flourishing and to life. He needed to recognize that the land was a gift that he had wrongly grasped, and that he needed to treat it as gift by giving it away. By entering into a different story, Zacchaeus, ironically, was able to come home. It is clear from the story that the other villagers viewed him with distrust and suspicion. Is it possible that, like the other tax collectors in the Gospels, once he had made reparations he was invited to share food with those whom he had formerly oppressed? Was it possible that they were now able to be at home together?[29]

Reparations for the Michi Saagiig Nishnaabeg will require the same relinquishment by settlers of the dominant narrative. The narrative that says that land is "mine" if my family bought it (even if it was only half a century ago). It will require relinquishing the narrative that privileges the needs of settler society, settler leisure, and settler comfort over the flourishing of the Michi Saagiig Nishnaabeg.[30] It will require an attempt to enter into the story of the land, the long story, the story that this land has told for millennia, and

---

27. Verdun, *Imperial Food Systems*, 53.
28. Whyte, "Food Sovereignty," 348–50, 358.
29. I owe this insight to Aileen Verdun, in private conversation.
30. Whyte, "Food Sovereignty," 358, describes how settler society seeks to strengthen its own collective continuance at the expense of the collective continuance of Indigenous peoples.

explore how that story and the story of the Michi Saagiig Nishnaabeg are entwined. What is more, it will require the attempt to envision a new future, where the story continues with the flourishing of settler and Michi Saagiig Nishnaabeg people together where the plants grow on the water. For if all cannot flourish, none can be at home.

Hope

When the stories of old
dreamed of the future,
they dreamed of water
flowing through the center of the community.
A river of life.[31]
For how can a community have life
if it is not connected to the water?

They dreamed
of a tree on both banks of the river.
A tree nourished by the river.
A tree that gives life.
For how can a community have life,
without the
maple and birch,
cedar and pine,
basswood and oak?

They dreamed of fruit on the tree,
produced each moon,
according to the season.
For how can a community have life
without fruit, each according to its moon:
the maple sugar moon,
the strawberry moon,
the wild rice moon?

They dreamed of leaves
for the healing of the nations.
For how can a community recover,
how can a community become whole,
unless they allow the trees to provide their medicines?
And not just for physical ills,

---

31. This section is based on Rev 22:1–2.

but also for the trauma,
the abuses of the spirit,
the genocide.
Only if the settler-colonizers allow the trees
to teach them,
will they be healed of the greed,
the privilege,
the pride
that has bound them.
Only if the trees
are allowed to speak
will the nations,
the Michi Saagiig Nishnaabeg
who have been here from time immemorial,
the settlers who have been here for a lifetime or two,
the immigrants who have been here for the blink of an eye,
be able to learn the lifeways of this place.
Only if the water is allowed
to bear the fruit of manoomin in its moon,
will the nations be able to learn to live together
in health and in peace.

"In Nishnaabeg thought," writes Leanne Betasamosake Simpson, "resurgence is dancing on our turtle's back; it is visioning and dancing new realities and worlds into existence."[32] Part of that visioning is telling the stories of old, and dreaming them into the future. I would suggest that such visioning, such entering into the story and daring to dream a new vision is also the call that is extended to those of us who are settlers, those of us who are immigrants, those of us who follow Creator.

What could such a vision look like? What would it look like for the place where the plants grow on the water to become home for the Michi Saagiig Nishnaabeg and the settler alike? Could it possibly look like a homecoming?

Coming Home

I pray that it will come with a song,
rising over the lake at dawn,
calling the Michi Saagiig Nishnaabeg
from the far corners of their territories,
calling settlers and immigrants

---

32. Simpson, *Dancing*, 70.

from the same places,
calling us all to the manoomin harvest
at the time of the manoomin moon.

I pray that it will come with thanksgiving,
with prayers in Nishnaabewomin and English,
in Tibetan and Arabic.

I pray that we will be willing to learn from the elders
how to tell if the grains are ready,
how to bend the stalks,
how to tell if the parching is complete
and how to dance the husks away.

I pray that the sound of the grains
hitting the bottom of the canoe
will be joined by the laughter of healthy children,
the learning of old ricing songs,
and the creation of new ones,
the stories of elders,
and the song of the birds.

I pray that after the harvest
all will be fed at the feast,
sharing together the good gifts
that have been given from the land that we all cherish.

I pray that all will depart with enough:
enough laughter, enough companionship,
enough love for the journey,
enough manoomin for the winter.

I pray that not only will the manoomin flourish, .
but that we will all flourish,
as we make home together,
in the land of the Michi Saagiig Nishnaabeg,
where the manoomin grows
and calls us home.

Bibliography

Anderson, Paula, and James Whetung. *Black Duck Wild Rice: A Case Study*. Centre for Sustainable Food Systems. Waterloo, ON: Wilfred Laurier University, 2018.

Bouma-Prediger, Steven, and Brian J. Walsh. *Beyond Homelessness: Christian Faith in a Culture of Displacement*. Grand Rapids: Eerdmans, 2008.

Daigle, Michelle. "Tracing the Terrain of Indigenous food sovereignties." *The Journal of Peasant Studies* 46.2 (2019) 297–315.

Gottwald, Norman K. "Early Israel as Anti-Imperial Community." In *Liberating Bible Study: Scholarship, Art and Action in Honor of the Center for the Bible and Social Justice*, edited by Laurel Dykstra and Ched Meyers, 5–22. The Center for the Bible and Social Justice Series 1. Eugene, OR: Cascade Books, 2011.

Grey, Sam, and Raj Patel. "Food Sovereignty as Decolonization: Some Contributions from Indigenous Movements to Food System and Development Politics." *Agriculture and Human Values* 32.3 (2014) 431–44.

Jackson, Lisa. "Canada's Wild Rice Wars." *Al Jazeera*, February 20, 2016. https://www.aljazeera.com/indepth/features/2016/02/canada-wild-rice-wars-160217083126970.html.

Jenks, Albert Ernest. *The Wild Rice Gatherers of the Upper Lakes: A Study In American Primitive Economics*. Washington, DC: Government Print Office, 1901.

Krotz, Sarah Wylie. "The Affective Geography of Wild Rice: A Literary Study." *Studies in Canadian Literature/Études en littérature canadienne* 42.1 (2017) 13–30.

"Nourishing Communities: Sustainable Local Food Systems Research Group." http://nourishingontario.ca/blog/tag/black-duck-wild-rice/

Simpson, Leanne. *Dancing on Our Turtle's Back: Stories of Nishnaabeg Re-Creation, Resurgence and a New Emergence*. Winnipeg: ARP, 2011.

Simpson, Leanne Betasamosake. *This Accident of Being Lost: Songs and Stories*. Toronto: House of Anansi, 2017.

———. "Land as Pedagogy." In *As We Have Always Done: Indigenous Freedom through Radical Resistance*, 145–74. Minneapolis: University of Minnesota Press, 2017.

Vennum, Thomas, Jr. *Wild Rice and the Ojibway People*. St. Paul, MN: Minnesota Historical Press Society, 1988.

Verdun, K. Aileen. "Imperial Food Systems Then and Now: Jesus and Indigenous Food Sovereignty." MTS thesis, Wycliffe College, University of Toronto, 2019.

Whyte, Kyle Powys. "Food Sovereignty, Justice and Indigenous Peoples: An Essay On Settler Colonialism and Collective Continuance." In *Oxford Handbook of Food Ethics*, edited by Anne Barnhill, et al., 345–66. Oxford: Oxford University Press, 2018.

Woodley, Randy S. *Shalom and the Community of Creation: An Indigenous Vision*. Grand Rapids: Eerdmans, 2012.

Afterword

Martyn Joseph

Sometimes we move into the center of an idea or movement and feel at home. It gives us the reassurance of belonging to something that feels genuine and real. We find ourselves more than happy to commit. But then, all too often, life happens. The plan we committed to doesn't always fit with our experiences. In that moment we either decide it wasn't the truth in the first place, or we realize the need to re-evaluate our expectations.

An old friend once told me that you cannot be disillusioned unless you're suffering from an illusion. Those words led me to re-evaluate my faith. Over time, it became quite a different proposition from what my awkward teenager frame had first embraced. One beautiful day, thousands of miles from home as I sat amongst a suffering people and the poorest of souls, it all changed. It was there that I discovered faith was going to be more about asking questions rather than having a hat full of answers. I've been running with that ever since.

The difficulty of this, perhaps, is that it can be something of a lonely journey. Out on the perimeter, you're either a little too much of a God-botherer to fit fully into the mainstream, or you're not carrying the fundamental torch to keep that lot happy. And, nope, ain't gonna do that. And so it goes.

You work it out as best you can, and it's ok. It really is. It helps to have some decent revelatory moments or glimpses of the divine along the way . . . occasional moments when you feel his or her pleasure in what you're trying to do. For me, this is often revealed more in the sorrow and setbacks rather than any victories . . . and you need a little glue.

For me, Brian Walsh is a big part of that glue. Here is a guy you can sit down with and have a beer (he knows far more about that stuff than I do!)

and just say it as it is. By return he will challenge and encourage, taking on the roles of both friend and elder.

You see, I'm a big fan of the one who is responsible to the same people week after week, year after year. Life is different for me. I get to ride into town, gather a crowd, kick up the dust for an hour or two, and hope I make a difference. But then, I get up and leave those folks behind. I head out of town to do the same thing somewhere else. Those, like Brian, who choose the pulpit usually have to dream it all up every week and be responsible to the same tribe that gather again, and again, and again.

I've always admired the commitment and consistency of those in ministry. There is not much room to hide there (at least for the good guys). Brian knows a huge amount more than I do about service and scripture, about discipleship, and about nurturing others. I have a feeling we both wrestle with angels and pace the cage. But I'll just run off and write a song, whereas he stands before the book and finds the real sense hidden there, and then plays his gig. That's what he does for me.

It's what I always sense and walk away with after time in his company. Time with Brian brings a reconnection to what I hold dear in my heart. He reminds me that somehow this is all worth it: the joy, the loss, the heartbreak, the thirst for justice, and a level playing field. He reminds me of all that's missing, of all that we know, and all that we cannot.

I'm grateful for Brian's passionate soul. There are not many professors of theology who do it for me these days. Prof. Walsh is amongst the few who do. There are thousands of sojourners who walk a good path and who want to thank him for his steadfast work. They have been helped by his dedicated scholarship, and that's more than good reason to rejoice. But there are some like me, folks who have become unsure of where we find ourselves in relationship to faith, but just can't leave the building. We want to thank him for always keeping that door open and for reminding us of the possibility of connection with a light we saw and embraced a long time ago.

Diolch Yn Fawr Iawn my friend xo

Martyn Joseph

www.ingramcontent.com/pod-product-compliance
Lightning Source LLC
Chambersburg PA
CBHW070239230426

43664CB00014B/2354